ECONOMICS AND SOCIETY No. 9

Labour Market Economics

ECONOMICS AND SOCIETY SERIES

General Editor: Professor Colin Harbury

ECONOMICS AND SOCIETY SERIES

Labour Market Economics

DAVID SAPSFORD B.Sc.(Econ.), M.Phil., Ph.D.
Lecturer in Economics, University of East Anglia

London
GEORGE ALLEN & UNWIN
Boston   Sydney

First published in 1981

GEORGE ALLEN & UNWIN LTD
40 Museum Street, London WC1A 1LU

© George Allen & Unwin (Publishers) Ltd, 1981

British Library Cataloguing in Publication Data

Sapsford, David
   Labour market economics. – (Economics and Society; no. 9).
   1.   Labour supply – Great Britain
   I.   Title   II.   Series
   331.12'0941   HD 5765.A6   80-41342

ISBN 0-04-331082-6
ISBN 0-04-331083-4 Pbk

Set in 10 on 11 point Press Roman by Alden Press,
Oxford, London and Northampton
and printed in Great Britain
by Biddles Ltd, Guildford, Surrey

Contents

Preface

This book arose out of the author's experience in teaching labour economics to undergraduate students. It is designed for second and third-year undergraduates taking courses in labour economics or economics, business studies, social sciences or related degree programmes in universities, polytechnics and colleges. In addition, it is envisaged that *Labour Market Economics* will provide a useful introduction to labour economics for those coming to the subject for the first time at graduate level, as part of a programme in either economics or in such areas as industrial relations. This book assumes that the reader has a knowledge of basic economic theory to the level of a standard first-year introductory course.

The book begins with an introductory chapter, in which the student is introduced to the structure of the UK labour market and to the sorts of problems to be examined in the book. The remainder of the book is divided into three parts. In the first part the economists' theory of wages is introduced and the determination of wages and employment examined. In the second part the analysis is extended to unionised labour markets, and a variety of economic aspects of union behaviour is considered. In the final part the analysis developed in the previous chapters is used to examine three selected topics of current interest: wage inflation, unemployment and the structure of wage differentials. Throughout the book emphasis is placed on the economic theory of the labour market and the role of empirical work in testing its predictions. Wherever available, evidence from studies of the UK labour market is cited, but in some instances relevant evidence from studies of other countries, principally the USA, is also introduced. At the end of each chapter there are notes giving guidance to further reading for students who wish to pursue in more detail the material introduced in the text. Throughout the book the author–date system is used for references, and in cases where only specific parts of the cited reference are of relevance, page numbers are also cited.

Labour economics may be broadly defined as the study of the pricing and allocation of the factor of production, labour. The structure of *Labour Market Economics* reflects the author's view that an understanding of the economic theory of the labour market is an essential prerequisite for a proper understanding of the actual workings of labour markets. In consequence, Part 1 sets out at some length the basic theoretical tools of labour market analysis, which are then used in the subsequent chapters to analyse a variety of aspects of labour market behaviour. A labour market is composed of individuals and households as sellers of labour services and of firms as purchasers or employers of labour services, and the determinants of their supplies of, and demands for, labour are examined in Chapters 2 and 3 respectively. In Chapter 4 the demand and supply sides are brought together in an analysis of the determination of the equilibrium levels of wages and employment. An important feature of the UK labour market and that of other industrialised countries is the existence of trade unions as organisations of sellers of labour, and in Part 2 the analysis is extended to cover unionised labour markets. In Chapter 5 the history and determinants of union growth are examined, along with the various economic theories of union behaviour. In Chapter 6 the determination of the wage rate under collective bargaining, and the effects of trade unions on the allocation of resources and relative wages, are considered.

In Part 3 three further topics are considered. In Chapter 7 the determinants of the rate of wage inflation are examined. Wage inflation is a topic that gives rise to considerable controversy among economists, and in this chapter the various competing theories are presented and the relevant empirical evidence discussed. The theory and evidence surrounding the roles of trade unions and inflationary expectations in the inflationary process are considered in this chapter, and in its final section the effects of incomes policies on the rate of wage inflation are examined. In Chapter 8 unemployment and unfilled vacancies are considered. In this chapter the structure of unemployment in the UK and the inadequacies of the official unemployment statistics are discussed, along with recent developments in the analysis of job search and the influence of state benefits on the level of unemployment. In the final chapter the determinants of the structure of relative wages are considered and the human capital approach discussed.

In view of space constraints, it was necessary to be selective as to the material covered in this book. The topics included were chosen in light of both topicality and their potential in illustrating the ways in which the basic theoretical tools of the labour economist (as set out in Part 1) can be applied to the analysis of observed labour-market behaviour.

I am indebted to the series editor, Professor Colin Harbury (City University) for his detailed comments and suggestions on each chapter and to David Greenaway (University College at Buckingham) for his valuable comments on the draft text. Any remaining errors or omissions are, however, the author's responsibility alone. In addition, I owe much to my teacher of labour economics, Professor J. R. Crossley (University of Leeds). Thanks are due to Brid Quinn, Regina Cosgrove, Mary Cleary and Min Swords for their skill and efficiency in typing the manuscript. Last, but by no means least, I am indebted to Mary, Ben and Nicola for their untiring patience.

DAVID SAPSFORD
The Economic and Social Research Institute, Dublin
February 1980

ECONOMICS AND SOCIETY No. 9

Labour Market Economics

Chapter 1

Introduction: The Economic Analysis of Labour

In 1976–7 the middle 20 per cent of income-earners in Britain received 78 per cent of their total income as earnings from employment. This book is concerned with the forces that determine the incomes that people earn from employment.

Individuals receive income from various different sources (from employment or self-employment, from the state in the form of transfer income or as investment income arising from the ownership of assets of capital or land) and although the proportion of total income received from each of these sources varies according to income level, Figure 1.1 shows that, for the population as a whole, the single largest component of total income is earnings from employment.

Labour is one of the factors of production, and the subject matter of labour economics is, broadly speaking, its pricing and allocation. The purpose of this opening chapter is to introduce the reader to the sorts of problems that are considered in this book and to provide a brief sketch of the structure of the UK labour market.

SOME BASIC QUESTIONS IN LABOUR ECONOMICS

The problems and issues analysed by labour economists are many and varied and span both the macro and microeconomic areas. The questions considered in this book include:

(1) What determines the numbers of people in paid employment, their hours of work and their rates of pay?
(2) Why do people join trade unions? What is collective bargaining, and how do unions and employers arrive at an agreed wage by negotiation? Do unions succeed in raising their members' wages and conditions of work above the levels that they would otherwise be?

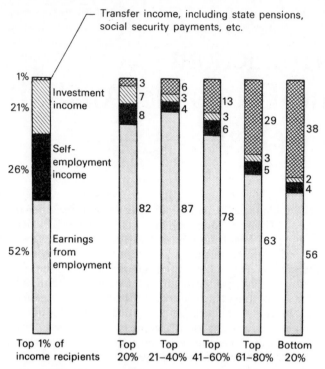

Figure 1.1   Earnings and other forms of income in Britain, 1976–7.
Source: Based on data contained in *An A to Z of Income and Wealth* (London: HMSO, 1980), p. 10

(3) What determines the changes in wages that occur between one year and the next, and what roles, if any, are played by trade unions and/or price expectations?

(4) What is unemployment, and what are its causes and cures? Why is it that some people remain unemployed for only short periods of time, while others remain unemployed for many months or sometimes even years? Does the payment by the state of unemployment benefit have any influence on the level of unemployment?

(5) Why do wages differ between different occupations and different industries? Why do skilled workers typically earn more than their unskilled colleagues, and why do earnings rise with a worker's level of education and training?

(6) What are the factors determining the observed movements in wage differentials over time? More specifically, why is it that in Britain

the differential between the craftsman builder's wage and that of the building labourer remained virtually unchanged over the five centuries up to 1914, and why is it that the average earnings of professional workers such as doctors, dentists and solicitors in Britain fell between the First World War and the late 1970s from over five times those of the unskilled manual worker to only about two and a half times?

THE ECONOMIST'S APPROACH

In his approach to the analysis of pay determination and related matters, the economist sees wages as the price of labour, and he sees these as being determined, in analogous fashion to the prices of goods and services, by the interaction of supply and demand forces in the market for labour (Harbury, 1980, pp. 80–94). Although there are other approaches to questions of pay determination (see Phelps-Brown, 1977, pp. 10–21), emphasis is placed throughout this book on the economist's approach, utilising the tools of supply and demand analysis and examining the ways in which these forces operate and interact in the market for labour as a factor of production.

LABOUR IN THE UK ECONOMY

The market for labour has two sides: on the one hand there is the *demand side*, made up of producers of goods and services as employers or purchasers of labour services, while on the other there is the *supply side*, composed of individuals and households as sellers or suppliers of labour services.

The Demand for Labour

The demand for labour (like the demand for the other factors of production) is said to be a *derived demand*, because producers demand labour not directly for itself but for the contribution that it makes, when used in conjunction with other factors of production, to the production of goods and services.

In the UK economy purchasers of labour come in many different 'shapes and sizes', ranging from the small firm employing only a few workers to the large national and multinational companies and public corporations employing, in some cases, many thousands of workers. The largest single purchaser of labour services in the UK economy is the state. In 1978 employment in central government, local authorities and the public corporations accounted for almost 30 per cent of total employment.

As we shall see below, the amount of labour that a rational employer or employers will seek to hire at any given wage will depend on labour's contribution to the firm's revenue in relation to its effects on the firm's costs. Labour's contribution to a firm's revenue has two dimensions: first, its contribution to the firm's *physical output* (or labour's physical productivity) and secondly, the contribution that each additional physical unit of output makes to the firm's *revenue*. When analysing the forces lying behind the demand side of the labour market, it is therefore necessary to consider two things: first, the way in which firms combine the factors of production and secondly, the conditions prevailing in the firm's product market, since these will influence the contribution that each additional unit of physical output makes to its revenue.

In considering the first of these dimensions, economists distinguish between short and long-run periods. In the short run the firm has a fixed amount of some input or inputs (say capital goods) and it is concerned with the consequences of adding additional amounts of a variable factor (say labour) to its fixed stock of capital. In the long run the firm is by definition free to vary its inputs of all factors of production, so that, when considering such periods, it is necessary to take account of the fact that producers may vary the input mix of their production method, within the limits imposed by what is technically feasible, in response to changes in the relative costs of the different factors of production.

The other dimension to be considered in the analysis of labour demand is concerned with the contribution that additional units of output make to the firm's revenue, and to examine this it is necessary to consider the employer firm's product market. The simplest case is the one where the firm sells its output in a perfectly competitive product market. Under such circumstances each unit of output is sold at the prevailing market price and adds a constant amount, equal to the market price, to the firm's revenue. However, in the UK, as elsewhere, many employers operate in product markets that are non-perfect and therefore, after initially considering the perfectly competitive product-market case, we proceed to extend the analysis to allow for product market imperfections.

The Supply of Labour
On the sellers' side of the labour market, there are men and women of different ages, with different skills, abilities, motivations and family circumstances, who offer their labour services for hire. In the UK, as in other societies, most individuals live in a household unit of some form, and in the analysis of labour supply economists see decisions

about who is to supply how much labour as being made in the house-hold context, as part of its decision regarding the optimum allocation of its members' available time between alternative uses.

In mid 1978 the total population of the UK was 55.9 million, and there were almost 26.4 million men and women (equal to about 47 per cent of the total population) recorded as either being in or seeking paid employment (which together are referred to as the *labour force*). How-ever, of the total UK population of almost 56 million in 1978, some 13.2 million could be expected to remain outside the labour force, as they were under the school-leaving age of 16, while a further 9.5 million were over the official retirement age (60 for women and 65 for men). The exclusion of these people leaves a total population of 'working age' of about 33.2 million, and expressing the recorded labour force as a percentage of this amount we obtain a figure of almost 80 per cent.

COMPETITION IN THE LABOUR MARKET

Factor markets, like the markets for goods and services, exhibit varying degrees of competition. In the analysis of labour markets, economists frequently take the *perfectly competitive model* as their analytical starting point. In practice, some labour markets are highly competitive and approximate (in some cases quite closely) to the perfectly competitive model, while others display imperfections on either the demand side, the supply side or both sides. In the following chapters we begin by examining the interaction of demand and supply side forces in competitive markets and then proceed to extend the analysis to imperfectly competitive labour markets.

On the buyers' side there are some labour markets in which there is only a small number of purchasers of a particular sort of labour (in a particular geographical locality perhaps). The limiting case, where there is only a single purchaser of labour in the market in question, is known as *monopsony*, and this situation sometimes arises when purchasers of labour combine to form an employers' association that acts as a single purchaser in a particular labour market.

TRADE UNIONS IN THE UK

An important characteristic of the sellers' side of many labour markets is the existence of trade unions as organisations of sellers of labour. Unionisation is not a new phenomenon. By the end of 1920 there were almost 1,400 unions in the UK, with a total membership of over 8.3 million men and women, equivalent to about 40 per cent of the labour force. However, mainly as a result of union amalgamations the number of unions in the UK has fallen over the last sixty or so years to somewhat less than 500 by 1970, while their membership has risen to around 13 million.

The extent of unionisation, however, varies markedly between different labour markets, and estimates of the degree of unionisation by industry suggest that in Britain in 1971 actual union membership as a percentage of potential membership varied from as little as 11.6 per cent in distribution to 96.4 per cent in entertainment, with national government coming a close second with 94 per cent (Bain and Elsheikh, 1979, p. 138).

The existence of trade unions raises a number of questions that are of interest. For example, why do workers join unions, and what determines the observed fluctuations in union membership? What are the objectives of trade unions, and what methods do they use in their efforts to achieve these? Of particular importance is the question of whether the existence of unions causes either the wages and employment conditions of their members, or the allocation of resources in the economy, to be any different from what they would be in their absence.

COLLECTIVE BARGAINING

As we shall see below, the individual purchaser or seller of labour is a wage-taker in a perfectly competitive labour market, deciding how much labour to sell or hire at the prevailing market wage rate. In cases where labour markets are organised on both sides (say the single union and single employer case), both buyers and sellers cease to be wage-takers. In such circumstances each side will have its own objectives and desired outcome, and the actual wage that is eventually agreed will be determined not by the interaction of supply and demand forces in a competitive market but as the outcome of a process of negotiation or collective bargaining that takes place between the two parties, within certain limits determined by economic forces.

Collective bargaining is a complex process. It generally commences with each side putting forward its case, proceeds through a series of offers, concessions, compromises, counteroffers, threats and counter-threats, and continues until some mutually acceptable settlement, which generally lies somewhere between the parties' respective opening demands, is eventually achieved. Collective bargaining does not in practice occur over wages alone. Various other issues, including hours of work and other conditions of employment, are often determined by collective bargaining, although it should be noted that bargaining over some of these issues (such as a demand for a reduction in hours of

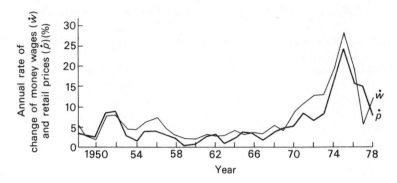

Figure 1.2. UK inflation, 1948–78
Source: Compiled using data from *Economic Trends: Annual Supplement* (London: HMSO, 1980)

work, with weekly wages remaining unchanged) can be interpreted as being equivalent to bargaining for an increased wage rate. In the UK, as in some other countries, governments sometimes intervene in the collective-bargaining process. In cases where negotiations break down or a dispute occurs, the state in the UK offers, when requested, the services of conciliation and arbitration, through the auspices of the Advisory Conciliation and Arbitration Service (ACAS). Under *concili-ation* (often called mediation) an impartial third party is appointed to help the parties to clarify their positions and resume negotiations. Alternatively, a neutral third party or *arbitrator* may be appointed to investigate the issues involved and award, on the basis of his findings, a settlement that both parties generally agree in advance to accept.

Given that about one out of every two members of the UK labour force currently belongs to a trade union (and that some non-union members also receive the union wage rate through 'spillover' effects), it is obviously of importance to understand how wages are determined in unionised labour markets, and this question is examined in Chapter 6.

INFLATION AND THE LABOUR MARKET

The causes of, and cures for, inflation have for many years been important economic and political issues. As can be seen from Figure 1.2, the rates of increase of prices and wages in the UK (as indeed else-where) have been closely related, and the question arises as to whether it is wages that influence prices, or prices that influence wages, or both?

Inflation is a topic that persistently gives rise to controversy among economists in respect of both its causes and cures, and particular controversy surrounds such issues as the precise roles of trade unions and price expectations in the inflationary process. From the policy viewpoint successive UK governments have placed heavy reliance on incomes and prices policies in their attempts to control inflation, and an important question examined below is whether such policies have actually succeeded in holding the rates of increase of wages and prices at lower levels than they would otherwise have been.

UNEMPLOYMENT

In mid 1979 there were just under 1.5 million people in the UK (equal to about 6 per cent of the labour force) who were registered at either local employment or careers offices as unemployed. When we look at less aggregated data, we see that the incidence of unemployment does not fall equally on all sections of the population or on all sectors of the economy. For example, there are marked divergences in the incidence of unemployment between different regions, industries and occupations and between different age groups and the sexes. There are also very wide discrepancies in the duration of the spells of unemployment experienced by different groups of individuals. For example, in Britain in 1978 the median duration of current unemployment spells for men under the age of 18 was four weeks, while for men aged 60–65 it was forty-eight weeks.

Alongside these registered unemployed there existed in mid 1979 almost 195,000 recorded unfilled vacancies, and one question that arises is how and why do unemployed workers and unfilled vacancies exist simultaneously?

THE INEQUALITY OF PAY

There are very marked differences between the wages and salaries (or 'earnings') of different individuals. For example, the results of the New Earnings Survey of April 1978 showed that in Britain the gross weekly earnings of a man 1 per cent from the top of the earnings league were almost three times those of a man exactly in the middle of the league.

The distribution of earnings between individuals can be illustrated by the *size* or *personal distribution* of earnings, which is a graph with earnings on the horizontal axis and the percentage of workers receiving each level of earnings on the vertical axis. Figure 1.3 shows the size distribution of the gross weekly earnings of full-time male adult

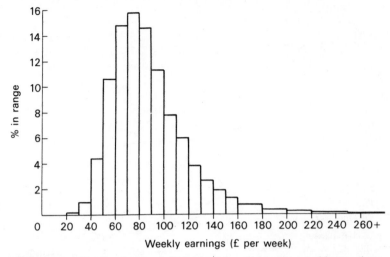

Figure 1.3. The distribution of earnings by size: gross weekly earnings of full-time male adult employees aged 21 and over in Britain, April 1978
Source: Compiled using data from the New Earnings Survey, 1978, as given in the *Department of Employment Gazette* (1978), p. 1160

employees in Britain in April 1978 and illustrates the typical shape of such distributions. Size distributions of earnings have been compiled for many different countries and time periods, and one notable feature is that, in all countries and at all times, the earnings distribution of full-time male employees has the characteristic shape shown in Figure 1.3: having a single peak and a long right-hand tail, the presence of which indicates the existence of a very small number of extremely high income-earners. The meaning of the observed shape of distributions of earnings according to size was forcefully illustrated by Pen (1974, pp. 48–59), who described a parade in which every income-earner takes part and has height proportional to his earnings. If this parade of individuals is arranged in ascending order of income, Pen pointed out that it becomes a spectacle of a large number of dwarfs followed by a few very large giants.

In Britain data on the distribution of the gross weekly earnings of full-time male manual workers go back as far as 1886, and these figures show a remarkable degree of stability in the relationship between different earnings levels. For example, if we consider the earnings of the man who is 10 per cent from the top of the distribution (the highest decile) and express these as a proportion of those of the

Occupational group

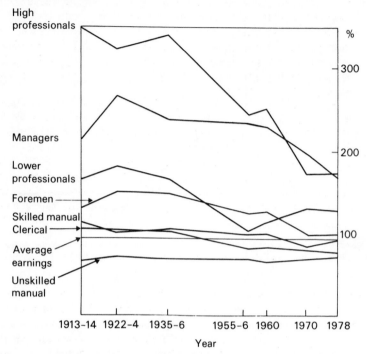

Figure 1.4.   Changes in occupational differentials in Britain, 1913–78
Source: *An A to Z of Income and Wealth* (London: HMSO, 1980), p. 11

man who is exactly in the middle of the distribution (the median), we see that the ratio of these two amounts was 1.431 in 1886, 1.452 in 1960 and 1.441 in 1974 and that between 1960 and 1974 it was always within the range 1.452–1.478 (Diamond, 1975, p. 57).

Since individuals differ in various respects, it is possible to examine a number of different types of *wage differentials*. For example, one may consider differences in the wages of individuals employed in different occupations, different industries or different firms. Alternatively, one may distinguish between individuals according to various personal characteristics and examine differentials in wages between people of different sexes, ages, races and levels of education. The structure of differentials between different occupations has attracted considerable attention from labour economists, who have sought to provide answers to such questions as why dustmen in Britain in 1978 earned on average about 16 per cent more than road-sweepers and why coal-miners, computer-programmers and secondary school-teachers each earned on average about 80 per cent more than road-sweepers. Figure 1.4 shows the earnings of males in Britain in several occupational groups as a percentage of average earnings at various times between 1913 and 1978. This diagram gives some indication of the changes that have occurred in the occupational pay structure in Britain, most notably the marked narrowing of the higher professional workers' lead.

Other aspects of the structure of wage differentials that have attracted the attention of economists include the determinants of variations in average wages between different industries. Economists have sought to answer such questions as why the average earnings of male manual workers in mining and quarrying in Britain in 1979 were almost twice as high as those in agriculture, forestry and fishing. Over recent years the differentials that accrue to different levels of education have attracted particular attention from economists, who have sought to explain the observed tendency for an individual's earnings to rise with his or her level of education and training.

PLAN OF THIS BOOK

The economist's approach to the study of the sorts of problems outlined in this chapter emphasises the forces of labour demand and supply and their interaction in the market for labour. The first part of this book sets out and develops in some depth the basic theoretical tools of the labour economist, and in the remaining chapters of the book these are used in the analysis of a wide variety of labour market issues. Throughout the book emphasis is placed on the economic analysis of the UK labour market and wherever available, relevant evidence from studies of the UK labour market is presented.

Part One
WAGE THEORY

Chapter 2

Labour Supply

The *supply of labour* is defined as the amount of labour, measured in person-hours, offered for hire during a given time period. Taking population as given, the quantity of labour supplied depends on two main factors. First, there are the numbers engaged in, or seeking, paid employment, which together make up the *labour force* or the *supply of workers*. This amount can conveniently be expressed as a fraction or percentage of the total population, to give an *activity* or *labour-force participation rate*. Secondly, there is the number of hours that each person is willing to supply once he is in the labour force – the *supply of hours*. The determinants of these two dimensions of labour supply are discussed in this chapter. First, we consider the supply of workers.

WHO SUPPLIES LABOUR?

In UK official statistics the *working population* is defined as the sum of the numbers of employees in employment,[1] employers and self-employed and HM forces (which together comprise the *employed labour force*) plus the number of *registered unemployed,* excluding adult students. Table 2.1 gives a breakdown of its estimated size and composition in mid 1978.

Table 2.1   *UK working population, mid 1978 (thousands)*

Employees in employment	Self-employed persons (with or without employees)	HM forces	Employed labour force	Registered unemployed (excluding adult students)	Working population
22,724	1,886	318	24,928	1,446	26,374

Note: Since 1971, estimates of employees in employment have been obtained from the annual census of employment taken in June each year. Prior to this date estimates were obtained from a count of National Insurance cards exchanged.
Source: Department of Employment Gazette (1979), p. 1166.

While the official definition of the employed labour force corresponds closely to the first component of the supply of workers (i.e. the numbers engaged in paid employment), there are some important doubts about the adequacy of the official unemployed statistics as a measure of its second component (i.e. the numbers seeking paid employment). There are two reasons for this. First, because the official statistics refer to those registered for employment at local employment or careers offices, and since registration is, in general, a necessary condition for receipt of unemployment and supplementary benefits, not all those officially classed as unemployed are actually seeking paid work; some are instead voluntarily unemployed. Secondly, the official statistics do not include all those actually searching for paid employment, since a number of people (such as some married women and pensioners) do not register as unemployed, presumably because of their non-entitlement to, or ignorance of, their eligibility for benefits or perhaps because they prefer to conduct their own job search through such channels as newspaper advertisements, contacts with friends and relatives, or private employment agencies.[2]

In the UK the estimated population in mid 1978 was 55.9 million giving an estimated activity rate of 47.2 per cent. Population is important in the analysis of labour supply, because its size in the period in question sets an upper limit to the supply of workers. Since each member of the population is either in or out of the labour force, the membership criterion being the actual or desired performance of paid or market work, we can usefully begin our discussion of the supply of workers by asking why, in 1978, over half of the UK population remained outside the labour force.

Not all of this population was eligible to enter the labour force, since all those under the age of 16 were required to attend school on a full-time basis, while the majority of men over the age of 65, and women over 60, were retired. Others were prevented from joining the labour force for such reasons as physical or mental disability. In order to allow for the influence of the population's age structure, it is useful to consider the activity rate for those of working age, which in the UK can be estimated by calculating the percentage of those aged 16 and over but under retirement age who are in the working population; in mid 1978 this activity rate was approximately 79.4 per cent. Most of the 20.6 per cent of the population in this age group who remained outside the labour force were either full-time students in schools and colleges or married women with homes to run and families to care for. While both these activities involve considerable work, neither receives payment, and therefore neither qualifies its performers for membership of the labour force.

THE LABOUR-FORCE PARTICIPATION DECISION

Table 2.2 gives a breakdown of activity rates in Britain in 1978 according to sex, age and marital status and shows the existence of considerable variability between different age and personal characteristics categories, with activity rates varying from 8.9 per cent for non-married women of 60 and over to 97.7 per cent for males aged between 25 and 44. In order to explain such variations in activity rates, it is necessary to explore the forces that influence the individual's decision on whether to enter or remain outside the labour force.

Table 2.2 *Activity rates in Britain by age and sex, 1975 (%).*

Age	Males	Married females	Non-married females
16–19	65.8	51.9	60.2
20–24	88.9	54.3	77.0
25–44	97.7	55.1	79.2
45–59	96.7	59.6	73.1
60–64	85.1		
65 and over	15.3		
60 and over		13.3	8.9
All ages	80.6	47.9	41.8

Source: Social Trends 10 (London: HMSO, 1979), p. 122.

As we have seen, the concepts of the supply of labour and the labour force separate paid or *market work* from all other non-market uses of time. The traditional analysis of labour supply, which is reviewed later in this chapter in connection with the supply of hours, views the individual as a decision-maker who divides his time between two mutually exclusive uses: market work and time not paid for, with the latter often being referred to as *leisure*. However, as Hunter (1970, p. 42) pointed out, this analysis is essentially one of marginal changes in the hours of work of those who are not only already in the labour force but also in employment, and as such it is not readily applicable to the discrete in/out labour-force participation decision, which generally involves non-marginal changes in the allocation of one's time, because hours of work are typically demanded in the form of blocks of time to be supplied on a regular basis at or within certain specified times.

Households and participation decisions

Recent studies have sought to improve on the traditional analysis by explicitly recognising (1) that decisions about who enters the labour force, and the allied question of how many hours to work, are made in the context of the family or household as part of its decision about the optimum allocation of its members' time between alternative uses (Ashenfelter and Heckman, 1974; Gronau, 1973), and (2) that non-market activity is composed not only of leisure in the everyday sense but also of household work, which is one input in the production of a variety of home-produced goods and services, such as home cooking, child care and a tidy house (Mincer, 1962).

Taking the household as their unit of analysis, Bowen and Finegan (1969) argued that the allocation of members' time between work in the market and all other non-market uses of time – such as working in the household, eating, sleeping, pursuing education and leisure – is determined by four classes of variables: its tastes, expected market earnings rates,[3] productivities in non-market activities[4] and its total resource constraint. A household's allocation of time is held to reflect its *tastes* for market goods relative to leisure and to home goods (e.g. its valuation of the services of a paid childminder relative to a mother's care) and its preferences about the performance of particular tasks by particular family members (e.g. its attitude to the wife's performing heavy manual work during night shifts in a factory and to the customary social role in the UK of the male as a breadwinner). The household's time allocation decision will also reflect the *expected market earnings* of its members (net of tax, other stoppages and travelling expenses), as well as their *productivities* – or, more precisely, their *comparative advantages* – in various non-market activities. Last, the allocation decision will also reflect the household's *total available resources,* which are made up of the total time at its disposal (i.e. 24 hours per member per day), its income from sources other than market work and the monetary value of its assets.

Effect of Changes in Non-labour Income
In order to see how these forces interact to determine the labour force status of each family member, consider the case of a household that experiences a large increase in its resources, such as the inheritance of a large annuity, unaccompanied by any other change. This situation represents the familiar case of an *income effect* and on the usual assumption that for at least some family members leisure or some other non-market activity is a normal good (i.e. one having a positive income elasticity of demand), we can expect the labour supplied by the household to decrease. This is because the increase in non-labour income enables family members to 'purchase' more of their preferred activity, and consequently we may see a decrease in its members' labour force participation, as either an elderly member takes early retirement,

or a working wife becomes a full-time housewife or resumes her education, or children stay on longer in, or return to, full-time education.

Effect of Changes in Market Earnings

To illustrate the effect of a change in market earnings open to a household member, let us suppose that the wage rate of (say) short-hand-typists increases, other things remaining equal. In households that already include a working shorthand-typist, this increase results, assuming that her hours of work remain unchanged, in an income increase for the family, which may result in decreased participation by other family members for reasons discussed in the previous paragraph, or alternatively it may lead to other members working shorter hours in their market activity. In households where wives have left work to raise their families, some may be tempted to return to work as shorthand-typists by the prospect of the increased earnings. The price of non-market activity to the worker is its *opportunity cost* (i.e. the earnings foregone by using hours in non-market rather than market activity); and as we shall see below, the total effect of a change in market earnings (i.e. in the price of non-market activities) can be subdivided into an income and a substitution effect. In this case the increase in market earnings results in an increase in the price of non-market activities, since each hour spent in non-market activities now involves a greater opportunity cost in the form of foregone earnings. A *substitution effect* arises from the changed price of non-market relative to market activity, and this encourages the wife to substitute market activity for the now more expensive non-market activities. If she actually resumes employment, the household experiences an income effect from which the possibility of decreased labour-force participation by other family members now arises.

The wife's resumption of employment can be expected to bring about various changes to the household's non-market production and consumption activities. In its production of home goods, we can expect there to be some reallocation of housework to husbands and children, together with some adjustments in the household's production methods. For example, there may be increased use of hired labour and the employment of more capital-intensive production methods, with the increased use of various labour-saving devices. In its consumption activities the household may also decide to substitute market for home goods, with convenience meals replacing home cooking, or it may simply decide to consume less goods (e.g. by tolerating a less tidy house).

PARTICIPATION AND THE DEMAND FOR LABOUR

The influence of demand conditions in the labour market on labour force participation has attracted considerable interest since the 1930s, with attention centring on two conflicting hypotheses concerning the influence of variations in employment opportunities on labour-force participation rates. On the one hand there is the *added worker hypothesis,* according to which additional household members, principally wives and older children, enter the labour force in order to supplement family income when this suffers a transitory decline because the husband has become unemployed or is experiencing a reduction in the hours of work available to him. According to this hypothesis, labour-force participation rates rise as unemployment increases.

On the other hand, the *discouraged worker hypothesis* holds that, during periods of high unemployment, some of the unemployed become so dispirited in their job search that they withdraw from the labour force altogether, while others who would otherwise enter the labour force do not bother to do so. These workers leave or fail to enter the labour force because, during periods of high unemployment, the potential wages facing them are lower or because the probability of finding a satisfactory job after a reasonable period of search is reduced. This hypothesis therefore suggests that labour-force participation rates are negatively related to unemployment. In addition, the discouraged worker hypothesis carries the implication that a more adequate indication of the extent of unemployment is obtained if we add to those actually seeking employment under prevailing conditions those, the *hidden unemployed,* who would be in the labour force seeking employment if they did not feel job search to be hopeless.

Both added and discouraged worker effects can exist simultaneously in different households as unemployment changes, and the question of which, if either, effect is the stronger arises. As we shall see in the following section, this question of the direction of the net effect of these two opposing forces has been the subject of considerable empirical investigation.

SOME EMPIRICAL EVIDENCE

In the analysis of labour supply it is usual to subdivide the total potential supply of workers into two groups according to their degree of attachment to the labour force. Those who have a high degree of attachment, principally married men as the main breadwinners of the family, are likely to be permanently attached to the labour force until they reach retirement age and are referred to as *primary workers.*

Others – such as married women who move into and out of the labour force in response to various family and other circumstances, and students who join the labour force at various times while completing their education – have a lower degree of labour force attachment and are termed *secondary workers*. This classification of workers as primary or secondary corresponds to a partition of the total labour force into its permanent and transitory components.

There is in existence a large number of empirical studies of the labour-force participation behaviour of various sex, age and race groups, and in this section we briefly review some of the major findings of this research.

Primary workers
It is clear that the labour-force participation rates of primary workers are higher than those of secondary workers (look again at Table 2.2, and compare the rates of men and single females with those of married women) and as we might expect, their variability is generally more easily explained. To illustrate the determinants of the labour-force participation rates of primary workers, consider the case of men in the prime of their working lives or *prime age males,* defined as those between 25 and 54 years of age (Bowen and Finegan, 1969, p. 39). In a detailed study of US experience, these authors pointed out that in 1967 the participation rate of this group as a whole was to the order of 97 per cent, and they divided the factors that determine the labour force status of prime age males into personal characteristics and variables reflecting market conditions.

From their detailed analysis of 1960 US census data, Bowen and Finegan concluded that the most important factor in determining the labour force status of prime age males is marital status. In the census week of 1960, the participation rate of married prime-age males (living with their wives) was 97.6 per cent, compared to 79.1 per cent for the separated, 81.3 per cent for those who had never married, 83.1 per cent for widowers and 84.3 per cent for the divorced. However, Bowen and Finegan rightly pointed out that this result requires a cautious interpretation, since it is not clear exactly what marital status is proxying. On the one hand, marital status may be proxying tastes for money income brought about by the increased financial responsibilities that accompany marriage. Alternatively, it may be proxying tastes for market work, in that those who prefer regular market work may also prefer to marry and stay married, and indeed may find it easier to do so. In addition, the accepted social role of the married man as bread-winner may mean that there are psychic costs of non-participation, which are higher for married than unmarried men. On the other hand, labour force participation may be related to marital status via market earnings, in that a male's marital status may serve as a proxy for various personal, mental and physical characteristics that influence his prospective market earnings and thus his labour force status. According to this latter interpretation, it is higher market earnings, and therefore a higher (opportunity) cost of non-market activity, that is responsible for the higher participation rates of married men.

Other personal characteristics that were found to exert a significant influence on the labour force participation of prime age males include race, number of years of schooling and the size of non-labour income. Rates were found to be higher for whites than for similar blacks and to rise with the number of years of education. Bowen and Finegan argued that both these effects correspond to differences in market earnings (i.e. the opportunity costs of non-participation), since these are typically higher for whites than for non-whites and (as we discuss in Chapter 9) tend to rise in all race groups with years of education. Participation rates were also found to be negatively related to the size of non-labour income – a result consistent with the positive income elasticity of demand for non-market activity discussed above.

Turning now to the influence of labour market conditions, the basic hypothesis that Bowen and Finegan sought to test, by means of regression analysis, was that the participation rates of prime age males are positively related to their expected market earnings. Since a worker's expected market earnings are influenced not only by the wages that he can earn in employment but also by the likelihood of his actually finding a job, independent variables were specified to represent both these dimensions of expected earnings. In a cross-section analysis by standard metropolitan statistical areas, Bowen and Finegan used the unemployment rate in the locality and a job mix variable (i.e. the proportion of jobs that can be expected, by experience elsewhere in the economy, to be filled by males) to indicate the probability that a worker will find a job after a particular period of search, as well as a measure of average wages in the area. All three independent variables were found to exert significant influences on participation rates and to have signs consistent with the expected-market-earnings hypothesis. Participation rates were found to be negatively related to unemployment and positively related to the 'maleness' of the job mix – results that suggest that unfavourable job opportunities discourage participation by lowering the probability of finding a job and hence the level of expected market earnings. In addition, the wage variable was found to exert the expected positive influence on participation rates.

Secondary workers

Married women are the most important group of secondary workers, and their labour supply has attracted considerable research interest. Studies of US cross-section data by cities (e.g. Mincer, 1962; Cain, 1966; Bowen and Finegan, 1969) have shown that participation rates of married women are inversely related to their husbands' incomes and positively related to female earnings. Similar findings have emerged from recent studies by Greenhalgh (1977) and McNabb (1977) of British data derived from the Population Census of 1971. As Rees (1973, p. 10) pointed out, a husband's income affects his wife's labour force participation in much the same way as non-labour income does, and the observed relationship corresponds to the negative (non-labour) income effect discussed above. The observed positive influence of female earnings indicates that improvements in prospective market earnings, which increase the opportunity costs of non-participation, increase married women's participation rates by encouraging some wives to begin and others to resume market work.

Other factors that have been shown to exert a significant influence on the participation rates of married women include the number and age of their children, their level of educational attainment and their colour. Not surprisingly, the presence of children, particularly those of preschool age, has been found to inhibit married women's participation, and rates have been found to rise with educational attainment and to be higher among non-whites. To the extent that potential earnings rise with the level of educational attainment, the observed positive relation between participation and education reflects, as in the case of prime age males, the influence of market earnings. Because education increases a married woman's potential market earnings, it increases the value of her time in market activity relative to that in non-market activity and therefore, as we have seen, it increases, *ceteris paribus*, the probability of her being in the labour force. In addition, it is probably also true that education influences participation via tastes, in that education increases a married woman's preference for the challenges and social interactions offered by the sorts of market work now open to her.

Regarding differences in participation by ethnic group, Bowen and Finegan (1969, pp. 89-96) showed that in the USA the participation rates of black married women are higher than those of otherwise similar white women. Likewise, Greenhalgh's (1977) results suggest that in Britain participation rates are higher among foreign-born married women than among those born in the UK. While cultural differences in attitudes towards wives' roles are important in explaining this finding, various further explanations were put forward by Cain (1966). In particular, he suggested that in the USA the lower degree of job discrimination faced by black women than by men is one factor that results in a tendency for black households to substitute wives' market work for that of husbands.

Finally, it is useful to recognise the apparent conflict that exists between the labour-force participation behaviour of married women in time series and cross-section data. While cross-section analyses have shown that wives' participation rates are negatively related to their husbands' incomes, the evidence from time series studies shows that married women's participation rates have risen dramatically over time (e.g. from 21.7 per cent in Britain in 1951 to 47.9 per cent in 1975) despite the increasing real incomes of their husbands. This apparent contradiction attracted considerable attention in the early literature and was eventually resolved by Mincer (1962). Explicitly recognising the distinction between permanent and transitory income (Friedman, 1957, p. 21), Mincer in effect showed that over time the upward influence of rising female earnings on wives' participation rates was of such a magnitude that it outweighed the downward influence of rising husbands' (permanent) income on their wives' participation rates and hence gave rise to the observed upward trend.[5]

Added or Discouraged Workers?

As already noted, the strengths of the opposing added and discouraged worker effects have been the subject of much empirical investigation, and indeed the question of the direction of their net effect is one of importance from a policy viewpoint. If the discouraged worker effect dominates, measured unemployment will underestimate the extent of actual unemployment, and consequently government policies designed to increase employment will, if based on the measured unemployment data, fail to provide enough jobs for all who will be looking for them once employment opportunities improve. On the other hand, if the added worker effect is the stronger, employment expansion policies based on measured unemployment data will provide too many jobs, because the added workers will drop out of the labour force as employment begins to increase.

The balance of evidence from empirical studies of both time series and cross-section data suggests that the discouraged worker effect predominates, thereby giving rise to an observed negative relationship between labour-force participation rates and unemployment (Bowen and Finegan, 1969; Corry and Roberts, 1970; Dernburg and Strand, 1966; McNabb, 1977; Tella, 1964). As can be seen from the following example, this result is a reasonable one. Suppose that the rate of unemployment doubles from 4 per cent to 8 per cent, then the added worker effect will tend to operate in the 4 per cent of households with a newly unemployed member, whereas the discouraged worker effect may well apply in a large proportion of the remaining 96 per cent of households.

Analysis of the participation rates of various age–sex subgroups reveals that females as a whole, and in particular married ones, are more sensitive to changes in employment opportunities than men are and that in both sexes sensitivity is higher among extreme age groups than among middle ones (Bowen and Finegan, 1969). In other words, the evidence suggests that responsiveness of participation to employment opportunities is greater among secondary than among primary workers (Mincer, 1966).

Hidden Unemployment

Given the observed dominance of the discouraged worker effect, many studies of the determinants of labour force participation have gone on to estimate the extent of hidden (or disguised) unemployment (e.g. Bowen and Finegan, 1969; Dernburg and Strand, 1966; Tella, 1965). As already noted, the hidden unemployed are those who, at the time in question, are not in the labour force but who would be if the prospects of finding a job were more favourable. Estimation of the amount of hidden unemployment is of particular importance from the viewpoint of providing a more adequate index of the extent to which labour is *underutilised* than is given by the official data of the numbers registered as unemployed.

The usual procedure for measuring hidden unemployment is to estimate a regression equation relating participation rates to rates of registered unemployment, or some similar variable, as an index of job opportunities. Given the estimated coefficients of this equation, one merely substitutes in some assumed full-employment rate of unemployment[6] and uses the estimated equation to predict what the participation rate would have been had the economy achieved 'full employment'. Multiplying the predicted full employment and the observed participation rates by the population of the group in question, we obtain respectively the sizes of estimated full employment (or potential) labour force and of the recorded one. Hidden unemployment is then simply estimated as the excess of the estimated over the recorded labour force.[7]

Using this sort of method, Corry and Roberts (1970, 1974) derived estimates of the extent of hidden unemployment in the UK. However, in a more recent study Berg and Dalton (1977) reconsidered the Corry–Roberts model and argued that their estimating equation is mis-specified because of their omission of wage and price variables, with the consequence that their parameter estimates, and hence also their estimates of hidden unemployment, are biased (Johnston, 1972, pp. 168–9). Using a participation equation derived from Wachter (1972, 1974), which basically differs from that used by Corry and Roberts by the inclusion of the real wage as an additional explanatory variable, Berg and Dalton derived alternative estimates of UK hidden unemployment. Re-estimating the Corry–Roberts model, Berg and Dalton calculated that in 1972 108,000 men and 115,000 women remained out of the labour force who would have joined had the average 1947–73 rate of unemployment prevailed, whereas their own model gave hidden unemployment estimates of 10,000 men and 516,000 women.

The remainder of this chapter is concerned with the supply of hours i.e. the number of hours that workers are willing to supply once they are in the labour force. In the next section the theory of the individual worker's work/leisure choice is considered, and in the following one analysis is used to derive his labour supply function. In subsequent sections the implications of the analysis for overtime payment arrangements are considered, and some aspects of the relationship between actual hours of work and the supply of hours are discussed.

THE INDIVIDUAL'S WORK/LEISURE CHOICE

The traditional analysis of the supply of hours is concerned with the individual worker's allocation of his time between work in the market and all other non-market activities.[8] Following the usual convention, we refer for convenience, in the remainder of this chapter, to all uses of time other than market (i.e. paid) activity as *leisure*.

The individual worker's *utility* is assumed to be an increasing function of the number of hours of leisure 'consumed' and the income obtained, where the latter, on the assumption of constant prices, serves as a proxy for purchases of consumer goods and services. The worker is assumed to allocate his time between the two mutually exclusive uses, market work and leisure, in such a way that his utility is maximised. However, the worker faces a constraint, which is imposed by the maximum time that is available to him (i.e. 24 hours per day) and by the prevailing, assumed exogenously given, wage rate. The worker's problem is thus the familiar one of constrained utility maximisation, and it can therefore be analysed diagrammatically with the use of indifference curves.

Fig. 2.1 depicts the individual's choice between work and leisure.

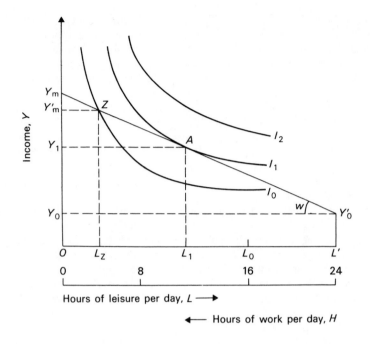

Figure 2.1　The individual's work/leisure choice

The abscissa in this diagram denotes the numbers of hours of leisure that are consumed (L) and the ordinate denotes income (Y). The maximum number of hours available for leisure in any one day is 24, and the number of hours devoted to market work (H) is given by 24 minus the number of hours of leisure consumed. Therefore, in Figure 2.1 the horizontal axis denotes leisure hours when measuring to the right from the origin and hours of market work when measuring to the left from L'. For example, level L_0 represents 8 hours of market work and, therefore, 16 hours of leisure per day.

Indifference curves
Curve I_0 is an *indifference curve*, showing the various combinations of leisure (L) and income (Y) that yield a given level of utility. Its negative slope indicates that, if leisure time is sacrificed, additional income is required to maintain the individual's utility at the level in question. The *marginal rate of substitution* of leisure for income is defined as the amount of income that must be sacrificed if the worker, after con-

suming an additional unit of leisure, is to maintain a given level of utility. For sufficiently small changes in leisure consumption, the marginal rate of substitution is measured by the absolute value of the slope of the indifference curve at the point in question, and the convexity to the origin of the indifference curves in Figure 2.1 represents the usual assumption of a diminishing marginal rate of substitution between the arguments of the utility function. (See, for example, Ferguson and Gould, 1975, pp. 25–6; Mansfield, 1975, p. 30). Since more of both income and leisure is assumed to be preferable to less, the further an indifference curve lies to the northeast on the indifference map, the higher is the level of total utility that it represents.

The budget constraint
Turning now to the constraint faced by the worker, it is clear that, given the prevailing hourly wage rate (w), which is assumed at this stage to remain constant irrespective of the number of hours worked, the worker's wage income is equal to w multiplied by the number of hours worked and that the upper limit to this sum is $24w$ (i.e. the amount of wage income that is earned if all available time is devoted to market activity). Each hour of leisure that is consumed involves a sacrifice of income (or opportunity cost) equal to w, and therefore the individual worker faces a choice between market work and hence income (or goods) on the one hand and leisure on the other. For example, at a given wage rate the worker may choose to enjoy more leisure, in which case he will experience a lower income (with a consequent reduction in his consumption of market goods and services), or alternatively he may choose to work longer hours to obtain increased income at the expense of his consumption of leisure.

Two additional points are to be stressed. First, in practice, the number of hours that any individual can spend in market activity is less than 24 per day, because some minimum amount of leisure time must be devoted to such activities as eating and sleeping. Secondly, even when hours of market work are zero, income may not be zero because of the receipt of unearned (or non-labour) income accruing from the ownership of assets and from state payments such as Child Benefit in the UK in the early 1980s, which is payable regardless of hours worked and income received.

The budget line $L'Y'_0ZY'_m$ in Figure 2.1 illustrates the constraint faced by the worker. When zero hours are worked, income is given by the amount of non-labour income Y_0. Income in excess of this amount can only be earned by substituting work for leisure, and the budget constraint to the left of L' is linear of slope $-w$,[9] indicating that each additional hour of leisure that is foregone increases income by a constant amount equal to the hourly wage rate (w), which therefore represents the rate at which money income is exchanged for leisure time. In Figure 2.1 the budget constraint is continued until it intersects the ordinate at Y_m, which indicates the level of income that is obtained if all available time is devoted to market activity. At this point total income (Y_m) is given by $24w$ plus the amount of non-labour income. However, as already noted, there is in practice some upper limit of less than 24 hours on the total amount of time that the individual can devote to market activity, and accordingly we can terminate the budget line at some cut-off point Z, which shows the required minimum amount of leisure L_Z and the corresponding effective maximum income of Y'_m.

Utility maximisation

Given the worker's indifference-mapping and his budget constraint, we are now able to derive his optimum income–leisure combination. The solution to the worker's constrained utility-maximisation problem lies at point A in Figure 2.1, where the budget line is tangential to indifference curve I_1. Assuming that the worker is free to select his own hours of work, he therefore maximises his utility by choosing the combination L_1 hours of leisure – i.e. he works for $(24 - L_1)$ hours per day – and $(Y_1 - Y_0)$ units of wage income. At A we obtain, in the usual way, the first-order condition for constrained utility maximisation, namely, that the slope of the budget line, the wage rate in this case, is equal to the marginal rate of substitution of leisure for income.[10,11]

THE INDIVIDUAL'S LABOUR SUPPLY CURVE

In order to derive the individual's supply of hours as a function of their price (i.e. the hourly wage rate), it is necessary to examine the way in which the optimum leisure–income combination alters as the wage rate changes. This is considered in Figure 2.2, where point A illustrates the worker's utility-maximising combination, given an initial hourly wage rate of w. Suppose now that the hourly wage rate is increased from its initial level w to some higher level w_1. This gives rise to a new, more steeply sloping, budget line $Y'_0 Y'_m$ and a new utility-maximising combination on the higher indifference curve I_2, as shown by point B. In this case the increase in the worker's hourly wage rate from w to w_1 results in an increase in his utility-maximising supply of hours from $(L' - L_1)$ to $(L' - L_2)$, accompanied by an increase in his income from Y_1 to Y_2. The locus of utility-maximising combinations that is traced out when the wage rate is continually varied is known as the *wage–*

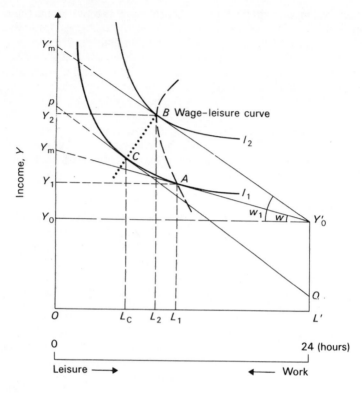

Figure 2.2 The effect of a change in the wage rate

leisure curve and is shown in Figure 2.2 by the broken line passing through *A* and *B*. The wage–leisure curve corresponds to the price-consumption curve of consumer demand theory.

To obtain the worker's labour supply curve – the relation-ship between his supply of hours and their price (i.e. the hourly wage rate) – it is necessary to transpose the utility-maximising positions shown by the wage–leisure curve on to the wage rate versus supply of hours plane. Considering wage rates in the range w to w_1 and plotting the wage, as shown by the slope of the budget line, against the supply of hours indicated by the wage–leisure curve, we obtain the supply curve shown by the solid line L_s in Figure 2.3. This curve has a positive slope in the range w to w_1, indicating that, as the wage rate increases from w to w_1, the number of hours of labour offered for sale by this worker increases from $(L' - L_1)$ to $(L' - L_2)$.

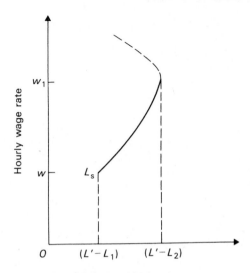

Figure 2.3 The individual's labour supply curve

INCOME AND SUBSTITUTION EFFECTS

The effect of a change in the wage rate on the worker's supply of hours can be subdivided into an income effect and a substitution effect. In Figure 2.2 *PQ* is a hypothetical budget line, which is drawn parallel to the new budget line $Y'_0 Y'_m$ and tangential to indifference curve I_1 at *C*. If the worker's non-labour income were reduced by an amount or *compensating variation* equal to $Y'_m P (= Y'_0 Q)$, he would, given the new wage rate w_1, be neither better nor worse off in terms of his utility than he was before the wage rate rose.

The movement around the original indifference curve I_1 from *A* to *C* shows the substitution effect, which arises because of the changed price of leisure relative to market work, with utility held constant. In the current example the wage rate, and therefore the price or opportunity cost of leisure relative to market work, has risen, and the substitution effect encourages the worker to decrease his consumption of the now relatively more expensive good (i.e. leisure) by the amount $(L_1 - L_C)$ hours per day. In cases where indifference curves are convex to the origin, the substitution effect must always be *negative*; that is, it must encourage reduced consumption of the good whose price has risen. (See, for example, Laidler, 1974, p. 24.) This is easily seen from Figure 2.2 by noting that, because *A* and *C* are tangency points, the slope of I_1 at these points is given by w and w_1 respectively. Since I_1 is convex to the origin, the absolute value of its gradient increases as we move around it from right to left; and consequently, since w_1 exceeds w, C must lie to the left of A, which means that the substitution effect of a wage increase must induce the worker to substitute market work for leisure.

The movement from C to B denotes the income effect, and it illustrates the worker's response to an increase in real income – or, more precisely, in utility – with relative prices held constant. If leisure is a *normal good* (i.e. one having a positive income elasticity of demand), the *income–consumption* curve (CB) will have a *positive* slope, showing that, as income rises, consumption of leisure increases, in this case by the amount $(L_2 - L_C)$ hours per day.

Provided that leisure is a normal good, the income and substitution effects of a wage change work in opposite directions, with the negative substitution effect encouraging the worker to substitute work for leisure, while the positive income effect encourages him to substitute leisure for work. In the current example the net effect of the increase in the wage rate from w to w_1 is to decrease leisure consumption (i.e. increase market work) by $(L_1 - L_2)$ hours per day. This occurs because the positive income effect is of insufficient magnitude to outweigh the negative substitution effect, with the consequence that the supply curve of hours shown in Figure 2.3 is positively sloping between wage rates w and w_1. If leisure were an *inferior good*, both income and substitution effects would pull in the same direction.

The backward-bending labour-supply curve

It is reasonable to expect that for the vast majority of people leisure is a normal good, because, as their income rises, they have more to spend on the goods and services that enable them to enjoy their leisure. However, there is no particular reason to suppose that the relative magnitudes of the income and substitution effects are as shown in Figure 2.2, although it is perhaps reasonable to expect the income effect to be of relatively greater importance at higher levels of income than at low ones. An important possibility, which has been widely discussed in the literature, is the one where the income effect of a wage increase is positive and of sufficient strength to outweigh the negative substitution effect, so that the net effect of the wage increase is an increase in the worker's consumption of leisure. In this case the worker's labour supply curve is negatively sloped, indicating that an increase in the wage rate results in a decrease in his supply of hours.

The possibility that the individual's labour supply curve may be backward sloping over some range of wage rates has a long genealogy in economics,[12] and the case where the income effect dominates the substitution effect at high wage levels is illustrated in Figure 2.2. At wage levels in excess of w_1, the wage-leisure curve becomes positively sloped, indicating that, when wages are above w_1, any increase in the wage rate gives rise to increased consumption of leisure and thus calls forth a decreased supply of hours. When this section of the wage–leisure curve is mapped on to the labour supply curve of Figure 2.3, we obtain the backward-sloping section for wage rates above w_1, which is shown by the broken line.

Considered from the viewpoint of the amount of work demanded rather than leisure consumed, we see that the backward-bending labour-supply curve of the individual results from work being a *Giffen good*. If leisure is a normal good, work must be an inferior one, because it will have a negative income elasticity of demand. If we consider an increase in the wage rate as representing a decrease in the price of market work relative to leisure, it follows that, if the negative income effect of the wage increase (which discourages the demand for work) is strong enough to outweigh the negative substitution effect (which encourages the substitution of work for leisure), work is by definition a Giffen good. If this is the case, the individual's supply curve of hours will be backward sloping, because the substitution effect of a wage increase on the worker's demand for work will be more than offset by the negative income effect.

The above analysis refers to the individual worker's supply of hours, and it should be noted that whether the supply function relating aggregate hours of labour supply to the wage rate becomes backward bending or not depends on the precise shapes of the individual labour-supply curves being aggregated. The secular decline in average hours worked that has accompanied increased real wages, as well as the inverse relation between wage rates and hours worked that is present in cross-section data, are frequently put forward as evidence to suggest the dominance of income over substitution effects, with the consequence that the individual's labour supply curve will be negatively sloping at current wage levels (Douglas, 1939; Finegan, 1962). However, such evidence, which is derived from the analysis of hours actually worked, must be interpreted with caution, since actual hours are determined by, and their behaviour reflects, not only supply side forces but also, as we see in Chapter 4, demand side ones.[13] We return to some aspects of the relation between actual hours worked and the supply of hours in the final section of this chapter.

OVERTIME WORKING

The analysis so far has been confined to the case where the wage rate facing the worker remains constant, regardless of the number of hours worked. In Britain, as elsewhere, it is usual for hours worked in excess of some minimum number, often 8 hours in any one day or at weekends, to be paid at a higher than standard rate. The Department of Employment estimated that, in the week ending 10 June 1978, some 34.3 per cent of all operatives in British manufacturing industry worked overtime, which amounted on average to $8\frac{1}{2}$ hours per week each.[14] In Britain payments for overtime working are generally in the range one and a quarter to twice the rate paid for standard hours.

The analysis of the individual's choice between work and leisure is easily extended to take account of the existence of premium payments for overtime working. Suppose that, in the absence of overtime payments, our representative worker is in equilibrium at point A in Figure 2.4, supplying 8 hours of labour per day. If overtime payments are introduced for hours worked in excess of 8 per day, the budget line becomes kinked at A. The slope of section $Y'_0 A$ of the budget line denotes the wage rate for standard hours (w) and the slope of the section AE represents that paid for overtime hours (say time and a half).[15] In this example a new equilibrium is established at point B, and we see that the introduction of overtime payments results, assuming that the worker is free to select the number of hours of overtime that he actually works, in an increase in his hours of work from 8 to 10 per day, accompanied by an increase in income and the level of total utility attained.[16]

Overtime payments are a form of price discrimination, because they involve a payment of a different price for different units of the same commodity. In the case where a constant wage rate is paid regardless of the number of hours worked, we have seen that an increase in the wage rate does not necessarily lead to an increase in hours of labour supplied but that the direction of the net effect of such an increase depends on the relative strengths of the income and substitution effects. However, it can be shown that the introduction of overtime payments prevents the individual's supply curve of labour hours from becoming backward sloping.

In our discussions of income and substitution effects, we have so far considered the individual's real income in terms of his ability to purchase goods yielding a certain level of utility. This constant utility notion of *real income* is referred to as Hicks real income, and on the basis of this definition we have considered the income effect that arises when the worker moves from one indifference curve (i.e. level of real income) to another, relative prices remaining constant. Alternatively, we may define real income in the Slutsky manner as the ability to buy a particular bundle of goods (Laidler, 1974, pp. 34–5). In Figure 2.4 the steeper section of the budget line (*AE*) passes through

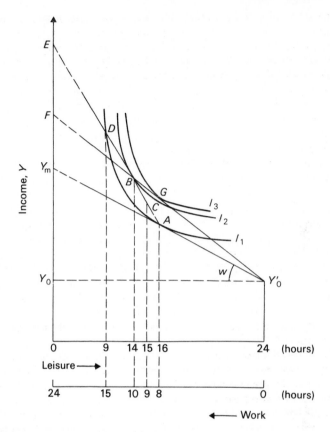

Figure 2.4 Overtime payments

the original income–leisure bundle at *A* and therefore represents a constant level of (Slutsky) real income. The movement from *A* to *B* brought about by the introduction of overtime payments is a pure Slutsky substitution effect, because it arises from a change in relative prices, with Slutsky real income held constant.

It can be seen from Figure 2.4 that, provided that the worker's indifference curves are convex to the origin, the introduction of over-time payment cannot lead to a reduction in his supply of hours. By moving to the right of *A*, the worker reverts to the flatter section of the budget line (AY'_0), because overtime payments are only made for hours worked in excess of 8 per day, and he can clearly only move to indifference curves that are below I_1. Therefore, the worker moves to left of A, by decreasing his consumption of the more expensive good (i.e. leisure), and thereby reaches successively higher indifference curves, until utility is maximised at the tangency point B. The introduction of overtime payments involves only a (Slutsky) substitution effect, which, as we have seen, cannot induce an increase in leisure consumption and therefore prevents the individual's labour supply curve from becoming backward sloping. Note also that payment of the straight hourly wage rate that would give the worker the same income at B as the overtime payment system, as illustrated by the slope of the budget line $Y_0' BF$, results in a new equilibrium at point G, at which point the worker supplies less labour but achieves a higher level of utility than under the overtime payment system.

SUPPLY OF HOURS AND HOURS ACTUALLY WORKED

Our analysis of the work/leisure choice has so far been based on the assumption that the representative worker is free to choose his own hours of work. On this assumption the hours that the individual actually works will, at any particular wage rate, always equal his supply of hours. In reality, however, individual workers are rarely totally free to choose their own hours of work; rather, they must typically decide whether or not to work some fixed number of hours at or within certain specified times. In such circumstances the preceding analysis of the work/leisure choice can best be thought of as one of desired rather than actual hours of work.[17]

At the opposite extreme to the supply-dominated case, where the worker is free to choose his own precise hours of work, is the demand-dominated one, where the employer sets the length of the working day and where the worker must decide whether to work these hours or to work none at all. This case is illustrated in Figure 2.5. If the employer were to fix the length of the working day at $(L' - H)$ hours, then, as Figure 2.5 is drawn, the worker in question would be indifferent between (1) not working and having an income of Y_0 (his non-labour income) and (2) working $(L' - H)$ hours and achieving income Y_1. If the length of the working day were set at some level below $(L' - H)$, such as $(L' - H_1)$, the worker would choose to work, because by so doing he would reach an indifference curve higher than the one he could achieve by not working. But note that, if the worker were free to choose his own hours, he would elect to work a shorter day of $(L' - H^*)$ hours and thereby maximise his utility. Such a situation arises in practice when a worker who desires to work only part time takes a full-time job in preference to the alternative of not working.

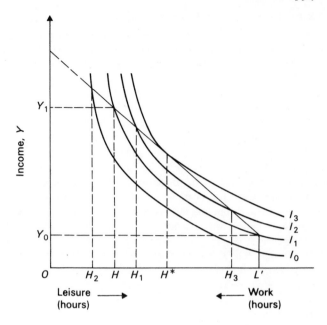

Figure 2.5 Employer-determined working day

In addition, the worker in such circumstances may decrease the effective length of his actual working week by taking extra leisure in the form of absenteeism, provided that the amount of such absenteeism is consistent with his retaining his job. Conversely, if the employer were to set the length of the working day in excess of $(L' - H)$ hours, at say $(L' - H_2)$ hours, the worker would choose not to work, because by so doing he would achieve the higher indifference curve I_1.

An interesting case is the one where the employer sets the length of the working day below that at which the worker's utility is maximised. If the working day were of, say, $(L' - H_3)$ hours, the individual in question would choose work in preference to non-participation and thereby reach indifference curve I_2. In this situation the worker, particularly if the opportunity of working overtime hours is not available, may take a second or even a third job in order to get nearer to his desired hours of work. Multiple job-holders are known as *moonlighters*, and it has been estimated that in Britain in 1972 some 3.5 per cent of working males and 2.6 per cent of working females were multiple job-holders.[18]

NOTES ON FURTHER READING

A useful survey of empirical work on labour supply is given in Byers
(1976), a detailed survey of British work in Bowers (1975), and a
concise survey of recent trends in labour supply in Britain in Thatcher
(1979).

Of particular importance in the theory of labour supply is Becker's
(1965) model, which explicitly recognises the household as both a production and a consumption unit that combines inputs of time and
market goods, according to its production function, to produce utility-
yielding *commodities,* some of which are time intensive (e.g. digging the
garden by spade), while others are goods intensive (e.g. eating caviar).
On the assumption of utility maximisation, Becker explored the implications of this approach for a variety of questions, including the effects
of changes in incomes and market earnings on hours of work and on
the household's consumption and production of commodities of
differing time intensities. In particular, Becker showed that an increase
in market earnings that is accompanied by a compensating downward
variation in income, increases the relative price of those commodities
involving relatively large foregone earnings and therefore induces households to shift away from earnings-intensive commodities towards
goods-intensive ones. At a more advanced level the contributions of
Fisher (1971), Gronau (1973) and Ashenfelter and Heckman (1974)
should be consulted.

The conventional indifference-curve analysis of the work/leisure
choice has been extended by various writers in a number of directions.
For example, the effect of income taxation on married men's labour
supply was considered within this type of framework by Brown *et al.*
(1976), while McClements (1978) and Perlman (1969) introduced
into the analysis social security payments and benefits, and commuting
time, respectively. For a modification of indifference curve analysis
to take account of moonlighting, see Perlman (1969, pp. 39–48) and
for a discussion of the extent of the phenomenon in Britain, see Alden
(1977). A comprehensive survey of theoretical and empirical work on
the effects of taxation on labour supply is given in Godfrey (1975).

Chapter 3

Labour Demand

Labour demand is defined as the amount of labour that employers seek to employ during a given time period at a particular wage rate. The demand for labour as a factor of production is a *derived demand*, in that labour is demanded not for its own sake but for its contribution to the production of goods and services. In this chapter we examine the theory of labour demand, which is an application of the marginal productivity theory to the particular factor of production labour,[1] and in the following one we consider the interaction of demand and supply forces in the determination of the price of labour (i.e. the *wage rate*).

Throughout this chapter we make the following two simplifying assumptions: first, that there are no costs other than the hourly wage associated with the employment of labour, and second, that firms purchase their labour in perfectly competitive *labour markets*.[2] The second of these assumptions means that the individual firm faces a perfectly elastic supply curve for its labour input, illustrating that it is a price-taker in the market for its labour, because labour's supply price (i.e. the wage rate) does not vary with the quantity purchased. The case of an imperfectly competitive labour market is considered in the following chapter.

This chapter begins by considering the individual firm's demand for labour in the short run under various *product-market* conditions, and in subsequent sections labour demand in the long run and at the industry level is considered.

THE INDIVIDUAL FIRM'S DEMAND FOR LABOUR IN THE SHORT RUN

Perfectly Competitive Product Markets
In this section the short-run labour-demand function of the firm is derived in the case where it sells its output in a perfectly competitive product market. Suppose that the firm combines inputs of two factors of production, capital and labour services, according to its production function in order to produce a single product. In the short run capital will be a fixed factor of production, whereas labour will be a variable one. This situation is depicted in Figure 3.1, where curves Q_1,

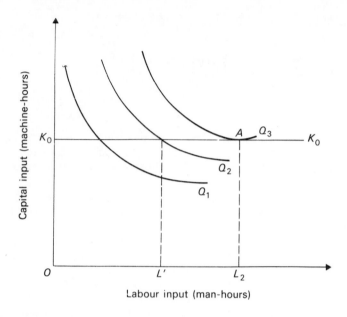

Figure 3.1 The firm's isoquant map

Q_2 and Q_3 are *isoquants,* each of which is the locus of all combinations of capital and labour inputs (measured in machine-hours and man-hours respectively) that yield a specified level of output.[3] In the long-run it is possible for the firm to vary its inputs of both labour and capital, but in the short run labour is its only variable factor of production.

Denoting the level of the firm's capital inputs by K_0 and its labour input by L, we see from Figure 3.1 that it is constrained, when altering output in the short run, with capital fully utilised, to move horizontally along the line $K_0 K_0$. The further an isoquant lies to the northeast, the higher is the level of output to which it refers and consequently, by moving along $K_0 K_0$ from left to right, the firm can increase its output in the short run. The curve that is obtained by plotting the firm's output level against its level of labour input as it moves horizontally along $K_0 K_0$ is known as the *total physical product* (*TPP*) curve of labour and is shown in Figure 3.2(a). For example, if the firm's labour input were L' man-hours, its level of output would be given by that represented by isoquant Q_2 (say q_2 units of output), and this is shown as the ordinate in Figure 3.2(a) corresponding to this level of labour input. It should be stressed that this curve illustrates the relationship between the firm's

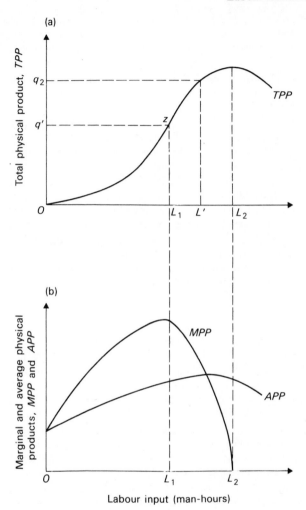

Figure 3.2   The firm's short-run production function

physical output and its labour input in the short run when its capital input is fixed (at the level K_0 in the current example). By varying the level
at which the firm's capital input is fixed, a family of *TPP* curves is
obtained, with a different curve corresponding to each level of capital
input. The curve illustrated in Figure 3.2(a) shows total product as a
cubic function of labour input, since this is a specific functional form
that exhibits properties that are often assumed by economists

The *average physical product* (*APP*) of labour is defined as total physical product per unit of labour input (i.e. *TPP/L*), and the *marginal physical product* (*MPP*) of labour is defined as the rate of change of total physical product with respect to the level of labour inputs (i.e. $\Delta TPP/\Delta L$). The *APP* and *MPP* curves that correspond to the *TPP* curve in Figure 3.2(a) are shown in Figure 3.2(b).[4] Note that each of the *MPP* and *APP* curves displays a single maximum and that marginal physical product reaches its maximum value at the level of labour input (L_1) that corresponds to the *TPP* curve's point of inflection (Z). Note also that the *MPP* curve cuts the *APP* curve at the latter's maximum value and that marginal physical product equals zero at the *TPP* curve's maximum.[5] The *MPP* curve in Figure 3.2(b) shows, for each level of labour input, the addition of total physical product that results when an additional unit of labour input is employed in the production process, with the capital input held constant at K_0. Its negative slope to the right of L_1 illustrates the *law of diminishing marginal returns* (or variable proportions), according to which the marginal physical product of any variable factor of production eventually begins to decline as increasing amounts of it are employed with a fixed quantity of some other factor. For further discussion, see Sapsford and Ladd (1978, pp. 58–62).

The Firm's Short-Run Labour-Demand Curve. If we assume that the firm's objective is the maximisation of its profits, we are now in a position to derive its short-run labour-demand function. Since it is a profit-maximiser, the firm is interested not only in the physical product of its labour input but also in the contribution that this makes to revenue. More specifically, in deciding whether or not to employ an additional unit of labour, the firm must weigh the increase in revenue that would result from the employment of this unit against the resulting increase in its costs. Since the firm, by assumption, sells its output in a perfectly competitive product market, its product price is given, as say P, regardless of its sales level. Therefore, to evaluate the contribution that the employment of an additional unit of labour would make to the firm's revenue, it is necessary to multiply the unit's contribution to total physical product (i.e. its marginal physical product) by the contribution that each unit of output makes to revenue, which in this case is simply the given product price (P). The quantity $MPP \cdot P$ thus obtained is referred to as the *marginal revenue product* (*MRP*) of labour. Under perfect competition the firm's product price (P) is equal to its *marginal revenue* (*MR*), which means that the marginal revenue product of its labour (defined as $MPP \cdot MR$) equals the *value of marginal product* (*VMP*) of labour (defined as $MPP \cdot P$). Figure 3.3 illustrates the *MRP*

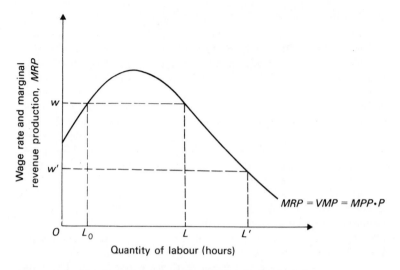

Figure 3.3 The firm's marginal-revenue-product schedule

curve of labour, which is obtained by multiplying the marginal physical product at each level of labour input, as given in Figure 3.2(b), by the constant output price (P).

The *MRP* curve shown in Figure 3.3 is in fact the firm's short-run demand curve for labour. Since the firm is a profit-maximiser, it will increase its employment of labour whenever the contribution of an additional unit of labour to its revenue (i.e. its marginal revenue product) exceeds the increase in costs resulting from the unit's employment, because under such circumstances an increase in employment and output will result in a net addition to profits. The increase in cost associated with the employment of an additional labour unit is the amount that its employment adds to the firm's wage bill and is referred to as *marginal labour cost* (*MLC*). By assumption, the firm purchases its labour inputs in a perfectly competitive labour market, with the consequence that it is confronted with a fixed wage, and therefore marginal labour cost, of say, w. In order to maximise profits, the firm therefore expands its employment of labour, and hence its output, whenever the marginal revenue product exceeds the wage w, and it continues to do so until the point is reached where the marginal revenue product falls into equality with w. Beyond this level of employment, the use of another unit of labour would increase the firm's wage bill by more than it would increase its revenue and would therefore reduce its profits.

By plotting both the wage rate and marginal revenue product on the vertical axis in Figure 3.3, it is easy to see that the *MRP* schedule is the firm's short-run labour-demand curve. If the wage rate were w, the profit-maximising firm would set its employment of labour at L hours – the level at which the wage equals labour's marginal revenue product. If, however, the wage rate were to fall to w', the firm would find that, at the existing employment level of L hours, labour's marginal revenue product would exceed the prevailing wage, and it would accordingly expand its demand for labour to the new profit-maximising level of L' hours, at which level marginal revenue product equals the new lower wage w'. Because the *MRP* curve shows the amount of labour that the firm will seek to employ, in the short run at different wage rates, it is the firm's short-run labour-demand curve.

It should be noted that only the downward-sloping section of the *MRP* curve is the firm's short-run labour-demand curve, because the second-order conditions for profit maximisation require the *MRP* curve to be downward sloping at the point where the wage equals marginal revenue product. To illustrate this, consider the wage w in Figure 3.3. The first-order condition that wage equals marginal revenue product is satisfied at employment levels L_0 and L. However, L_0 cannot represent a profit-maximising position, because it is possible to increase profits further by expanding employment past L_0, since for additional labour hours marginal revenue product exceeds w. The firm therefore maximises its profits by employing L units of labour, because any expansion of its employment past this point would lead to a reduction in profits, as the wage paid to hire each additional man-hour of labour would exceed the value of its addition to total revenue.

The area under the *MRP* curve up to a given level of employment measures the value of the total output produced, and this can be divided into payments to labour services and payments to capital services. For example, if the wage rate is w', the profit-maximising firm employs L' hours of labour services, and the area of the rectangle below w' measures the wage bill or the payments to labour, while the area above the wage line and below the *MRP* curve measures payments to capital services.[6]

An Alternative Derivation. The equivalence of labour's *MRP* curve and the individual firm's short-run labour-demand curve can alternatively be derived by straightforward application of elementary calculus.

Letting q denote the firm's output and L and K its inputs of labour and capital respectively, its production function can be written as

$$q = q(L, K)$$

In the short run the firm's input of capital is fixed, at level K_0 in our example, and accordingly its short-run production function can be written as

$$q = f(L)$$

where dq/dL is the marginal physical product of labour, which is assumed to be non-negative. According to our assumptions, the firm buys its labour inputs and sells its output on perfectly competitive markets, and it therefore faces a given wage rate (w) and product price (P). Letting F denote the firm's fixed costs, its profits (π) can be written as the difference between its total revenue and its total cost, that is,

$$\pi = P{\cdot}f(L) - wL - F$$

The firm's problem is therefore to select that level of labour usage at which profits are maximised. Differentiating the profit function with respect to L and equating to zero, we obtain

$$\frac{d\pi}{dL} = P \cdot \frac{dq}{dL} - w = 0$$

Since $dq/dL = MPP$, this can be rearranged to give the first-order condition $MPP{\cdot}P = w$, which requires labour to be utilised up to the point where its marginal revenue product (which in this case equals its value of marginal product) equals the wage rate (w).

The second-order condition for profit maximisation requires that

$$\frac{d^2\pi}{dL^2} = P \cdot \frac{d^2q}{dL^2} = P \cdot \frac{d}{dL}(MPP) < 0$$

Since $P > 0$, this requires d^2q/dL^2 (i.e. the slope of the MPP curve) to be negative at the point where $w = MRP$.

A Note on Profit Maximisation. Our analysis of the profit-maximising firm's behaviour has been in terms of its optimal usage of labour inputs. Implicit in the firm's decisions about input usage are decisions about its level of output, and it is important to recognise that the profit maximisation condition that labour be utilised up to the point where $w = MRP$ is equivalent to the condition that profits are maximised when output is such that the *marginal cost* (MC) of production equals the marginal revenue (MR) from the sale of output.

To demonstrate this equivalence in terms of our example, we have the first-order condition for profit maximisation, viewed from the firm's factor market, as

$$w = MPP \cdot P$$

from which we obtain

$$\frac{w}{MPP} = P$$

Now, given that the firm's product market is perfectly competitive, its product price (P) equals its marginal revenue (MR), and the above condition can be written as

$$\frac{w}{MPP} = MR$$

Since labour inputs are purchased in a perfectly competitive market, the employment of an additional unit of labour adds the amount w to total costs and the amount MPP to total physical output. The ratio w/MPP is therefore the additional cost that is incurred in the production of one additional unit of output (i.e. the marginal cost of output). Substituting, we obtain

$$MC = MR$$

which is the familiar condition for profit maximisation in terms of the firm's output, according to which the firm maximises profits by setting its output at the level where the marginal cost of output equals the marginal revenue from its sale.

Non-competitive Product Markets

So far we have considered the individual firm's short-run demand for labour in the case where it is a perfect competitor in both the market for its labour inputs and the market for its output. Under these conditions, as we have seen, the profit-maximising firm's labour demand curve is the marginal revenue product (MRP) of labour curve which, given the perfect product-market assumption, is also labour's value of marginal product (VMP) curve. (See Figure 3.4(c).) In this section we retain the assumption that the firm is a perfect competitor in the market for its labour (the case of the imperfectly competitive labour market is considered in Chapter 4), but we relax the perfectly competitive product-market assumption and consider the case where the firm possesses some degree of monopoly power in its product market.[7] In this case the firm faces a downward-sloping demand curve for its product, indicating that in order to sell additional units of output it must, in the absence of price discrimination, decrease the price that it

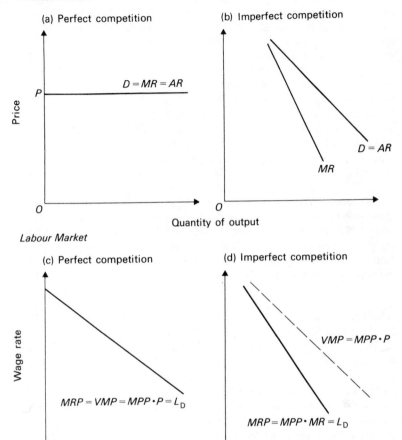

Figure 3.4 The firm's short-run labour-demand curve and competitive conditions in the product market

charges for each unit of its output. Consequently, its marginal revenue (*MR*) is less than its product price (*P*) at each level of sales, and its marginal revenue curve is more steeply sloping than its *average revenue* (*AR*) or demand curve (*D*). (See Figure 3.4(b).)

Like the perfect competitor, the imperfect competitor will maximise profits by expanding his employment of labour up to the point where the cost of an additional unit of labour services equals the addition to total revenue generated by its employment. In the case of a perfect competitor, as we saw in a previous section, each additional unit of output sold increases total revenue by a constant amount equal to the product price, and accordingly marginal revenue product of labour is calculated by multiplying marginal physical product by the product price. In contrast to the perfect competitor, the (non-price-discriminating) imperfect competitor employing an additional unit of labour must, if he is to sell the additional output thus produced, decrease the price of each and every unit of his product. In this case the contribution that an additional unit of labour input makes to the firm's revenue (i.e. its marginal revenue product) is equal to marginal physical product multiplied not by the product price but the producer's marginal revenue (MR) at the sales level in question. (See Figure 3.4(d).)

In order to maximise profits, the imperfect competitor who purchases his labour inputs in a perfectly competitive labour market will employ labour up to the point where the wage rate equals labour's marginal revenue product. Therefore, this firm's short-run labour-demand curve is, like that of the perfect competitor, its MRP schedule for labour. As we have noted, the firm's MRP schedule is equivalent to its VMP schedule in cases where product markets are perfectly competitive. However, in cases where the product market is imperfectly competitive, the value of marginal product (defined as $MPP \cdot P$) exceeds marginal revenue product $(= MPP \cdot MR)$ at each level of employment, because at each level of sales the firm's product price exceeds its marginal revenue. In addition, since the imperfect competitor's MR curve slopes downwards more steeply than its AR curve, it follows that such a firm's short-run labour-demand curve is more steeply sloped than its VMP curve. This can be seen from Figures 3.4(b), (c) and (d).

Perfect versus Imperfect Competition

Consider now the case where a given firm moves from a perfectly competitive product-market situation (A) to an imperfectly competitive one (B), while all other things, including its MPP curve, remain unchanged. Suppose that its demand and revenue curves before and after this change are as shown in Figure 3.5(a), and note that its marginal cost curve will remain unchanged, because by assumption both the wage at which it purchases its labour and labour's MPP curve remain unaltered. The firm's short-run labour-demand curve for each product-market structure is shown in Figure 3.5(b) by L_D^A and L_D^B. In both cases the firm's short-run labour-demand curve is its MRP curve. In the perfectly competitive product-market case, this curve is obtained by multiplying marginal physical product at each level of labour input by

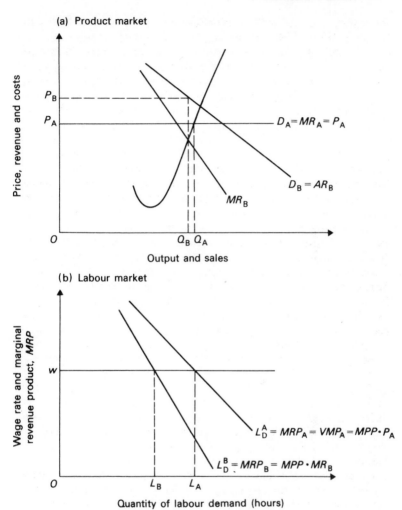

(a) Product market

(b) Labour market

Figure 3.5 Perfect versus imperfect competition

the constant market price P_A and as we have seen, the resulting labour-demand curve (L_D^A) is negatively sloped, because marginal physical product declines as the level of labour input is increased. In the imperfectly competitive case the *MPP* curve is unchanged, and marginal revenue product is obtained by multiplying marginal physical product by marginal revenue (MR_B) and as can be seen from Figure 3.5(b), the resulting MRP or labour demand curve (L_D^B) slopes downwards more steeply than its perfectly competitive counterpart (L_D^A). The steeper slope of L_D^B, for the given MPP curve, reflects the fact that, in the imperfectly competitive case, marginal revenue (MR_B), as well as marginal physical product declines as employment, and hence output, is increased.

As can be seen from Figure 3.5(b), the profit-maximising firm's equilibrium level of employment is lower, at each wage level, in the imperfectly competitive market situation. For example, at the wage rate w, on the basis of which the MC curve shown in Figure 3.5(a) is constructed, we see that imperfect competition results in a level of employment ($L_A - L_B$) man-hours below the perfectly competitive level. This restriction of employment is merely the reflection in the labour market of the imperfect competitor's tendency to restrict his output below the level of an otherwise identical perfect competitor. This can be seen in Figure 3.5(a). The profit-maximising perfect competitor's equilibrium output is Q_A (where $MC = MR_A = P_A$) whereas the imperfect competitor's is only Q_B (where $MC = MR_B$). Note also that, although the wage w received by labour in the imperfectly competitive case equals its marginal revenue product ($= MPP \cdot MR_B$), it is below the value of its marginal product in this market situation ($= MPP \cdot P_B$).[8]

THE FIRM'S DEMAND FOR LABOUR IN THE LONG RUN

In the long run the firm is, by definition, able to alter its inputs of capital services as well labour, and in this section we examine its demand for labour when all factors may be varied. Although our analysis is confined to the case of a firm that has one fixed and one variable factor of production, it is important to recognise that the following analysis of the long-run case, in which both factors become variable, is no different from the short-run case of a firm that has two variable factors, labour and raw materials perhaps.

In terms of Figure 3.1, the firm in the long run is no longer constrained to move along the horizontal line $K_0 K_0$ when varying its output. To maximise its profits in the long run, the firm must – assuming that capital, like labour, is purchased in a perfectly competitive markets, its isocost lines will be linear of slope equal to minus one times marginal revenue product of each factor is equated to its price. The argument here is simply an extension of that considered in the short-run case. If the marginal revenue product of either factor of production were greater than its price, the firm could increase its profit by expanding employment of the factor in question, because the increased employment (and output) would add more to revenue than to costs. Only when the marginal revenue product of each factor had fallen into equality with its price would it no longer be possible to increase profits further by employing additional units of inputs.[9]

If the firm were a cost-minimiser rather than a profit-maximiser, it would produce its output with the input combination represented by the point on its isoquant-mapping at which an *isocost* line (which is the locus of all input combinations that can be purchased for a particular total cost) is tangential to the isoquant in question. Since the firm purchases both capital and labour inputs in perfectly competitive markets, its isocost lines will be linear of slope equal to minus one times the input price ratio.[10] The negative of the slope of an isoquant at any point is defined as the *marginal rate of technical substitution,* which is the increase in one input per unit decrease in the other that is just sufficient to maintain a constant level of output, and this can be shown to equal the ratio of the marginal physical product of labour to that of capital at the point.[11] The first-order condition for the cost of producing a given level of output to be minimised is therefore that the ratio of the price of labour to that of capital equal the ratio of the marginal physical product of labour to that of capital,

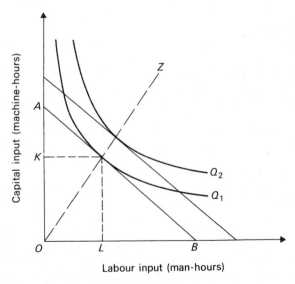

Figure 3.6 A long-run expansion path

In Figure 3.6 *AB* is an isocost line, and the firm minimises the cost of producing the level of output represented by isoquant Q_1 by using the input combination K units of capital and L units of labour. The locus of such tangency points (*OZ* in Figure 3.6) shows the firm's cost-minimising input combinations, given prevailing input prices, for each output level and is known as its (long-run) *expansion path* (which for simplicity is drawn as a straight line).[12] At each point along the expansion path, the input price ratio equals the ratio of the inputs' marginal physical products. However, for long-run profit maximisation each input must be utilised up to the point where its marginal revenue product equals its price and the firm's long-run profit-maximising input combination must therefore lie at some point on its expansion path.[13]

The Firm's Long-Run Labour-Demand Curve with Perfectly Competitive Product Markets. To derive the firm's long-run demand curve for labour, let us suppose that it is a perfect competitor in its product market and that it is initially in long-run equilibrium at point A in Figure 3.7(a). Thus, at A the marginal revenue products of labour and capital equal their respective prices, say w and r. If the wage rate fell from its prevailing level w to w_1, the firm would, as we have seen, maximise its profits in the short run by expanding its employment of labour, with its capital inputs fixed, along K_0K_0 to, say, L' man-hours at point B, where the new lower wage equals labour's marginal revenue product. The expansion of employment that would result in the short run from this fall in the wage rate is shown by the firm's short-run labour-demand curve, which is illustrated in Figure 3.7(b) by L_D. On the usual assumption about the properties of production functions,[14] the employment of additional units of labour results in an increase in the marginal physical product of capital and hence also in its marginal revenue product. With the given price of capital inputs (r), the firm now finds itself in the position where the marginal revenue product of capital exceeds its price, and therefore in the long run it will seek to increase its employment of capital inputs in order to reach its new long-run equilibrium position.

This increase in the firm's employment of capital inputs results in an increase in labour's marginal physical product, with the consequence that its *MRP* curve shifts outwards, so that at each wage rate the firm will tend to expand its employment of labour. However, an increase in the employment of labour in turn raises the marginal revenue product of capital inputs, which results in a further increase in employment of capital and a further outward shift in labour's *MRP* curve, and so on. Once all these effects have occurred, labour's *MRP* curve will have shifted to, say, *MRP'* in Figure 3.7(b), and long-run equilibrium

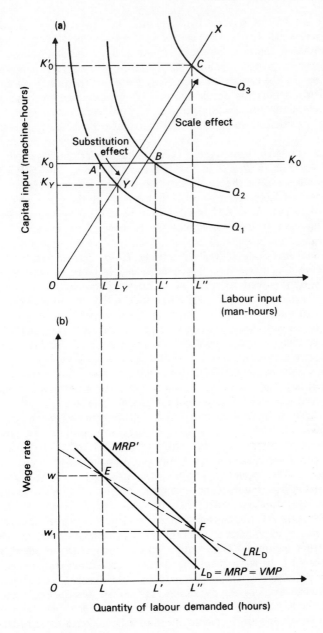

Figure 3.7 The firm's long-run labour demand curve

will be re-established at point C in Figure 3.7(a),[15] where the marginal revenue products of labour and capital once again equal their respective prices. Points E and F in Figure 3.7(b) are both on the firm's long-run demand curve for labour, and other points can be derived in a similar manner to give the complete curve LRL_D. Note that the firm's long-run labour-demand curve is not labour's MRP curve but an amalgam of movements along, and shifts in, this curve. However, at each point on the long-run curve the wage rate does equal labour's marginal revenue product.

As can be seen from Figure 3.7(b), the firm's long-run labour-demand curve is more elastic than its short-run one. The short-run effect of a decrease in the wage rate from w to w_1 is an increase in the employment of labour from L to L'. In the long run the firm is able to increase its inputs of capital services to their new optimum level K_0', and its employment of labour increases by a further $(L'' - L')$ units.

Substitution and Scale Effects of a Wage Change. It is possible to examine the long run effect of a wage change in more detail by sub-dividing the movement from the initial long-run equilibrium A to the new one C into a substitution and a scale effect, the analysis here being analogous to the subdivision in consumer theory of the effect of a price change into substitution and income effects. In Figure 3.7(a) OX is the firm's expansion path corresponding to the input prices w_1 and r; and if the firm were a cost-minimiser, it would, as a result of the decrease in the price of its labour inputs, move around isoquant Q_1 to the new cost-minimising position at point Y, where the relevant expansion path and isoquant intersect. This movement around isoquant Q_1 between A and Y arises because the given level of output can now be produced at minimum cost with the use of a higher proportion of the now relatively cheaper input, labour. This movement is referred to as a *substitution effect* because it represents the substitution of labour for capital that would occur as a result of a reduction in the price of labour relative to capital, if the firm were constrained to maintain its original output level. Provided that the isoquants are convex to the origin (see note 3), the substitution effect of a wage decrease must always result in an increase in the firm's employment of labour. As can be seen from Figure 3.7(a), the substitution effect of the decrease in the wage from w to w_1 results in an increase in the firm's employment of labour from L to L_Y units.

The movement along the expansion path OX between points Y and C is termed the *scale effect* of the wage change. This represents the extent to which the firm's employment of labour increases, with the relative input price held constant at its new level, as a result of the increase in the firm's long-run equilibrium level of output that arises from the fall in the wage rate. As can be seen, the scale effect of the fall in the wage rate from w to w_1 results in an increase in the employment of labour inputs from L_Y to L'' units.[16]

INDUSTRY DEMAND FOR LABOUR

So far we have considered the individual firm's demand for labour under various conditions. When considering the industry's demand for labour, it is not, however, possible merely to sum horizontally the labour demand curves of the individual firms that comprise the industry without allowing for price changes. In an industry where there is a perfectly competitive product market, the individual firm is so small in relation to the size of the market that changes in its own output have no perceptible effect on the price of the product that it sells. However, when we consider the whole industry, we must recognise that a decrease in the wage rate will result in each firm's increasing its labour input, and hence its output, with the consequence that, for a given demand curve for the industry's product, the market price of output will fall.

Figure 3.8(a) depicts a representative firm from a perfectly competitive industry, and for the initial output price its short-run demand curve for labour is given by its marginal revenue product curve MRP_1. Our representative firm employs e_1 units of labour at the ruling wage w, and aggregating across all firms in the industry we see from Figure 3.8(b) that a total of E_1 units of labour are employed at this wage. In the analysis of the individual firm's labour demand, it was assumed that the output of all other firms in the industry, and hence the product price, remains unchanged. However, at the industry level we would expect the employment and output of each firm, and hence the product price, to vary when the price of labour varies. To the representative firm the decrease in output price that occurs as industry output expands in response to a fall in the wage rate results in a leftward shift in its MRP curve to, say, MRP_2. If the product price were held constant, the representative firm confronted with a fall in its wage rate from w to w' would expand its employment of labour, along MRP_1, from e_1 to e'. Summing horizontally across firms, we see that the industry demand for labour would expand in this constant output-price case from E_1 to E'. However, when each firm in the industry expands its output the market price falls, and at the lower wage rate our representative firm expands its employment to only e_2. Aggregating, we obtain the industry demand for labour in this case as E_2.

Points a and b lie on the representative firm's short-run labour-demand curve in the case where market price varies, and repeating this

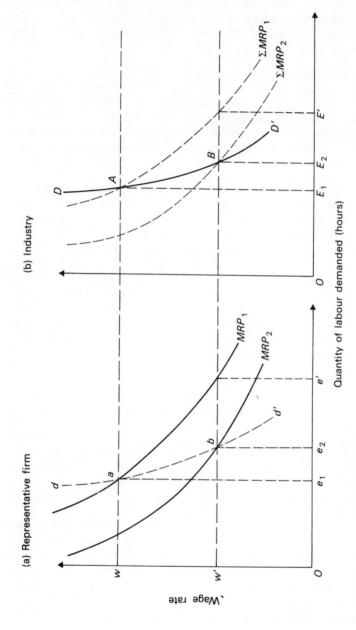

(a) Representative firm

(b) Industry

Figure 3.8 Industry demand for labour

procedure for each possible wage rate we obtain the firm's demand curve *dd'*. Points *A* and *B* lie on the industry labour-demand curve, and summing horizontally each firm's demand curve *dd'* we obtain the industry's labour demand curve *DD'*. Note that in this case the individual firm's labour–demand curve is steeper than the fixed product-price one and that the industry's short-run labour-demand curve is more steeply sloped than the various horizontally summed (constant-price) *MRP* curves. The industry's short-run labour-demand curve is more steeply sloped than the summed *MRP* curves because the latter slope downwards solely because of labour's diminishing marginal physical product, while the former slopes down, in addition, because the product price falls as industry output expands. How much steeper this demand curve is depends on how quickly the product price falls as industry output expands (i.e. on the elasticity of market demand for the product).

If the industry in question is the sole employer of this particular sort of homogeneous labour, the industry labour-demand curve *DD'* will also be the market demand curve for this input. If, however, firms in several industries employ labour of this sort in the production of their respective outputs, the market demand curve is obtained by horizontal summation of the non-constant price labour-demand curves, such as *dd'*, across all firms that use this particular input.

THE ELASTICITY OF DERIVED DEMAND

The demand for labour is a derived demand, and the determinants of its own price elasticity were identified by Marshall (1890, pp. 384–6, 852–3) and summarised in his four rules of derived demand, one of which was subsequently corrected by Hicks (1963, pp. 241–6). Marshall's rules can be stated in the two-factor case, where the price of the other factor remains constant, as follows. The elasticity of demand for labour will be greater (1) the greater the elasticity of substitution in production[17] (2) the greater the elasticity of demand for the final product (3) the greater the share of labour in total cost[18] and (4) the greater the elasticity of supply of the other factor of production.

According to rule (1), the elasticity of demand for labour is higher, *ceteris paribus*, the greater are the opportunities to substitute capital for labour in the production process. This is because the greater the firm's ability to substitute capital for labour when the price of labour increases, the larger will be the contraction in its demand for labour that results from a given wage increase. Rule (2) states that the more elastic the demand for the final product, the more elastic, *ceteris paribus,* is the firm's demand for labour. Thus, a given wage increase will, *ceteris paribus,* lead to a greater decrease in product demand, and hence also in the derived demand for labour, the more elastic is the demand for the final output produced. According to rule (3) (assuming Hicks' condition is satisfied), the demand for labour is more elastic the greater is the proportion of total costs accounted for by labour. Thus, in two firms that differ only in the ratio of their labour costs to total costs, a given wage increase will, *ceteris paribus,* lead to a greater rise in product price, and hence a greater fall in product demand and in the derived demand for labour, in the firm with the higher labour cost ratio than in the one with the lower ratio. Finally, rule (4) states that the greater the firm's ability to attract supplies of the other factor of production, to substitute in place of labour when the wage rises, without pushing up its price, the greater, *ceteris paribus,* will be the elasticity of its demand for labour.

A CAUTIONARY NOTE

In this chapter we have considered marginal productivity theory as applied to labour as a factor of production. It is important to recognise that this does not provide a theory of wages but only a theory of the demand for labour. As Rees pointed out, 'to speak of the marginal productivity theory of wages is exactly analogous to speaking of the demand theory of prices' (1973, pp. 58–9). In order to construct a theory of wage and employment determination, it is necessary to bring together the contents of Chapters 2 and 3 (i.e. to consider the interaction of demand and supply side forces), and this is the subject of the following chapter.

NOTES ON FURTHER READING

The marginal productivity analysis implicitly assumes that the position of labour's *MPP* schedule is independent of the wage level. The case where higher wages lead to higher marginal productivities at given levels of employment, through offering improved worker nutrition and health, is referred to in the literature as the *economy of high wages.* For further discussion of this situation, which is more likely to occur in developing than in developed economies, and for the derivation of the labour demand schedule in such circumstances, see Perlman (1969, pp. 50–6) or Rees (1973, pp. 80–3).

For an interesting criticism of the marginal productivity theory as applied to labour demand, see Lester (1946) and for a well-known reply in defence of the marginal analysis, see Machlup (1946).

For a useful survey of the major issues involved, see Cartter (1959, pp. 33–44).

An alternative approach to the demand for labour, which has attracted considerable theoretical and empirical interest in the recent literature, is the *employment function* approach. In simple terms, this approach consists of the inversion, with appropriate assumptions, of the cost-minimising firm's production function to obtain its short-run demand for labour services as a function of its output, other inputs and the state of technology, and on to this function there is typically grafted a short-term employment-adjustment mechanism describing the adjustment of actual to desired employment. This approach, which was initially associated with Brechling (1965) and Ball and St Cyr (1966), is usefully surveyed in Fair (1969) and was recently used to analyse UK experience by Hart and Sharot (1978). For further discussion, see Hazledine (1978) and Peel and Walker (1978).

Chapter 4

Wage and Employment Determination

In this chapter we examine the interaction of the demand and supply side forces considered in the preceding two chapters in the determination of the levels of wages and employment. We begin by considering the simplest case, that of a firm operating in a perfectly competitive labour market, and the analysis is then modified to take account of the existence of monopsony in the labour market. In the final sections of the chapter some implications of the existence of fixed employment costs are discussed.

WAGES AND EMPLOYMENT AT THE LEVEL OF THE FIRM IN A PERFECTLY COMPETITIVE LABOUR MARKET

The individual firm's demand for labour under various product market conditions was considered in Chapter 3, where it was shown that the profit-maximising firm's short-run demand curve for labour is the schedule of its marginal revenue product. In Chapter 2 we considered the forces that determine the amount of labour supplied by individuals and households, and in order to analyse the firm's wage and employment decisions it is necessary to consider how the labour supply behaviour of individual workers and households manifests itself to the individual firm as an employer of labour.

Reference was made in Chapter 3 to the perfectly competitive labour market. Under this labour market structure there are a large number of individual, perfectly informed, buyers and sellers of homogeneous labour, and workers are assumed to be perfectly mobile. Under these conditions the individual firm as a purchaser of labour is able to hire as much labour as it wishes at the prevailing market wage, which itself is determined in the broader market for the type of labour in question of which this particular firm makes up a small part. Thus, in a perfectly competitive labour market the individual firm, like all others in the market, faces a perfectly elastic supply curve for its labour input, indicating that it is unable to exert any influence on the prevailing wage rate by varying its purchases of labour.

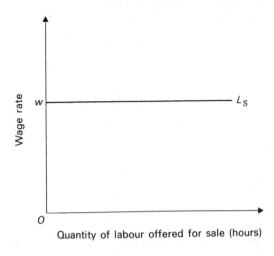

Figure 4.1 Perfectly elastic labour-supply curve

This situation is illustrated in Figure 4.1. The perfectly elastic labour supply curve (L_S) at the going wage rate (w) indicates that the individual firm is a price-taker in the market for its labour input. If it offers a wage of less than w, the firm will be unable to attract any labour, because workers will supply their labour to other firms and obtain the going wage (w). It has no incentive to offer a wage in excess of w, because it can recruit any amount of labour that it requires at wage w. The case of a single employer of a particular sort of labour (such as shorthand-typists of a particular speed) in a large metropolitan area is often cited as an example of a situation where an employer faces a perfectly elastic labour-supply curve.

In a perfectly competitive labour market the individual firm faces a given wage rate, and its problem is to select its level of employment, and hence output, in such a way as to maximise its profits. This situation was considered in Chapter 3, where it was shown that the firm maximises its profits in the short run by employing labour up to the point where the money wage equals labour's marginal revenue product (*MRP*). Graphically, the firm's profit-maximising wage–employment combination is found at the point of intersection of its labour demand curve and its perfectly elastic labour-supply curve.

In Figure 4.2 L_D is the firm's short-run labour-demand curve and L_S its labour supply curve, and from their intersection at point A we see that the firm's equilibrium level of employment is e labour hours. The fact that a firm is a perfect competitor in the market for its labour

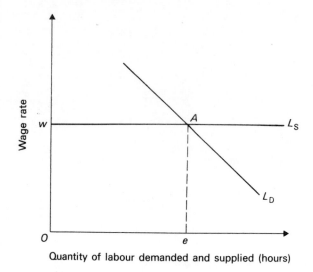

Figure 4.2 Wage and employment determination under perfect competition

input need not imply anything about the competitive conditions that it faces in its product market. As we have seen, the firm's short-run labour-demand function (L_D) is its *MRP* curve. If it is a perfect competitor in its product market it follows that it is in equilibrium at the point where the wage rate equals the value of the marginal product. On the other hand, if the firm is an imperfect competitor in its product market, its *MRP* curve is more steeply sloping than its value of marginal product (*VMP*) curve (look again at Figures 3.4(d) and 3.5), and it follows that the firm's equilibrium in this case is at the point where the money wage equals labour's marginal physical product (*MPP*) multiplied by marginal revenue (*MR*). Because the wage rate is given to the firm that hires its labour in a perfectly competitive labour market, it should be noted that in this case the marginal productivity theory of labour demand becomes in effect a theory of employment at the level of the individual firm (Cartter, 1959, p. 45).

MONOPSONY IN THE LABOUR MARKET

A case of some importance arises if we drop the assumption of perfect competition on the buyers' side of the labour market (while retaining the assumption of perfect competition among the sellers of labour) in favour of the assumption that the firm is the sole purchaser of the type of labour in question – the case of *monopsony.* In the case where there is perfect competition on the buyers' side of the labour market, the individual firm faces a perfectly elastic labour-supply curve at the prevailing wage (w), and its marginal labour cost (MLC) (i.e. the amount that the employment of an additional unit of labour adds to its wage bill) is therefore equal to w. If the firm is a large enough employer of labour for its decisions about the quantity of labour to employ to affect the wage rate, it is said to possess a degree of monopsony power. In the same way that a product market monopolist faces a downward-sloping demand curve for his product, indicating that the price of his product varies inversely with his sales, so the monopsonistic purchaser of labour faces an upward-sloping labour-supply curve, which indicates that the wage rate that he pays for his labour is an increasing function of the quantity that he hires.[1]

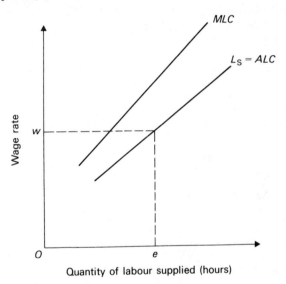

Figure 4.3 Monopsonist's labour supply curve

Figure 4.3 shows the upward-sloping labour-supply curve (L_S) faced by a monopsonist, and this indicates that in order to attract additional units of labour he must offer a higher wage rate. Such a situation arises when the firm is the sole purchaser of a certain type of labour in a particular locality or *local labour market,* and the upward slope of its labour supply curve indicates that to obtain extra units of this type of labour it is necessary for the firm to increase the wage that it offers[2] in order to attract suitable workers from firms in other localities, to attract suitable workers who may have chosen non-participation or work in other occupations within the locality, and to encourage existing workers to increase their supply of hours (although the possibility that the individual's labour supply curve may become backward sloping should be recalled).[3] Alternatively, monopsony may arise in practice when purchasers of labour combine to form an employers' association that acts as a single purchasing entity in the labour market – the case of *collusive monopsony*.

If the firm is a *non-discriminating monopsonist*, it pays each unit of its labour input the same wage rate, which is therefore equal to its average labour cost (*ALC*), and this means that its marginal labour cost is greater than the wage rate at each level of employment. To attract an additional worker the monopsonist must offer a wage in excess of that which he currently pays to those already in his employment, and in the absence of discrimination he must also increase the wage of each existing employee to the new level. The addition to the wage bill that results from the employment of an additional worker (i.e. the marginal labour cost) is the wage that is offered to attract the marginal worker plus the extra amounts that have to be paid to existing workers to bring their wage to the new level. Figure 4.3 illustrates the labour supply curve facing the non-discriminating monopsonist, and the steeper curve indicates the marginal labour cost as a function of the level of employment.

WAGES AND EMPLOYMENT IN IMPERFECT LABOUR MARKETS

If the firm is a profit-maximiser, it will in the short run set its employment so that the cost of an additional unit of labour (i.e. the marginal labour cost) equals the addition to total revenue generated by its employment (i.e. the marginal revenue product). The downward-sloping curve in Figure 4.4 is the firm's *MRP* function, and the monopsonist's equilibrium is given by point *A*, where the *MLC* and *MRP* curves intersect.[4] The monopsonist's profit-maximising level of employment is *e* workers, and the wage rate associated with this employment level is *w*, the ordinate of the supply curve at point *B*.[5]

It should be noted that the monopsonist's *MRP* curve is not his short-run labour-demand curve. In the same way that a monopolistic seller does not possess a supply curve for his product (see, for example, Lipsey, 1975, pp. 266–7), so the monopsonistic purchaser of labour has no labour–demand curve, because there exists for a monopsonist no

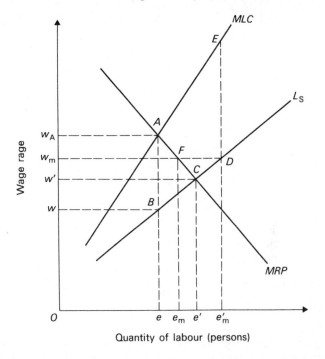

Figure 4.4 Monopsony

unique functional relationship between the quantity of labour demanded and the wage rate. As can be seen from Figure 4.4, the monopsonist's equilibrium employment level is determined as *e* by the intersection of his *MLC* and *MRP* curves, and the equilibrium wage rate is
w, the ordinate of the labour supply curve corresponding to this employment level. However, the wage at which the profit-maximising
monopsonist seeks to hire this quantity of labour is not uniquely
determined by his *MRP* curve and its point of intersection with the
MLC curve; it depends also on the elasticity of the labour supply
curve. The absence of a labour demand curve under monopsony is
illustrated in Figure 4.5, which shows how with a given *MRP* curve the
same quantity of labour (*e*) can be demanded at different wage rates
(*w* and w_0), according to the shape of the labour supply curve. This
situation occurs under monopsony because differently shaped labour-
supply curves can give rise to equal *MLC* values at a given employment
level.

In the same way that the existence of monopoly in the product

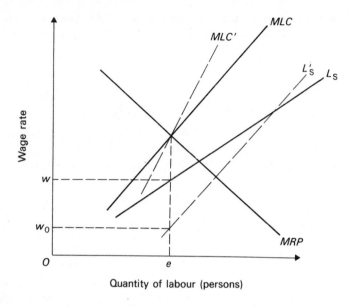

Figure 4.5 Absence of a labour demand curve under monopsony

market results in a lower level of output and a higher price than when
there is perfect competition, the existence of monopsony in the labour
market results in levels of employment and wages that are each lower
than the corresponding perfectly competitive levels. In Figure 4.4 the
monopsonist's equilibrium position is at point A, where employment is
e and the wage rate is w. Since the monopsonist is the sole purchaser of
the type of labour in question in the particular market, the labour
supply curve that he faces is in fact the market labour-supply curve.
If this labour market were perfectly competitive, with a market labour-
demand curve identical to the *MRP* curve facing the monopsonist,
market equilibrium would be established at point C, where the wage
rate equals the marginal revenue product of labour, giving employment
e' and wage w', both of which are greater than the corresponding equilibrium values under monopsony. Because the monopsonist faces an
upward-sloping supply curve for his labour, he realises that by increasing his level of employment he will drive up the wage rate, and he therefore maximises profits by expanding employment only to A, where
marginal labour cost equals marginal revenue product, stopping short
of the perfectly competitive equilibrium point at C. It is important to
remember that the analysis so far has assumed the absence of any
monopoly on the sellers' side of the labour market. This assumption

will, however, be relaxed in the following two chapters, when we consider trade unions as monopoly sellers of their members' labour services.

THE IMPOSITION OF A MINIMUM WAGE

In a perfectly competitive labour market the imposition of a minimum wage, if it is set above the equilibrium level, results in a reduction of employment below its equilibrium value. However, the imposition of such a minimum wage under monopsony can, under certain circumstances, result in an increase in the level of employment.

If the labour market of Figure 4.4 were perfectly competitive, with a market demand schedule equal to the monopsonist's *MRP* curve, the effective imposition (by legislation or by a trade union perhaps) of a minimum wage of w_m will result in a contraction of employment from the competitive equilibrium level e' to e_m. At the same time the quantity of labour supplied will expand from e' to e'_m, giving rise to an excess supply of labour of $\overline{(e'_m - e_m)}$ units at the minimum wage. Note that this excess supply is made up of two components: first, the $(e' - e_m)$ workers who have lost their employment as a result of the rise in the wage rate from w' to w_m and second, the $(e'_m - e')$ workers who are now attracted to offer their labour for hire by the higher wage rate.

In contrast, the imposition of a minimum wage above the equilibrium one can under certain circumstances lead to an increase in the amount of labour employed by a monopsonist. In the absence of the minimum wage, the monopsonist's equilibrium employment in Figure 4.4 is e at wage w. If a minimum wage of w_m is imposed and effectively enforced, the monopsonist's labour supply curve is no longer L_S but becomes $w_m DL_S$. This is because at any wage rate below w_m the firm cannot hire any labour at all, while at the wage rate w_m it can hire any amount of labour up to e'_m units. The monopsonist's marginal labour cost is no longer the *MLC* curve in Figure 4.4 but becomes instead $w_m DEMLC$, which intersects its *MRP* curve at point F, giving rise to an equilibrium level of employment of e_m (equal to the level brought about by the same minimum wage in the perfectly competitive case), which is larger than the previous employment level (e) despite an increase in the wage rate from w to w_m. For this effect to occur, the minimum wage must lie between w and w_A. If it were set above w_A, its effect would be to reduce the level of employment, as in the perfectly competitive case.

DISCRIMINATING MONOPSONY

So far we have considered the case where the monopsonistic employer pays each of the workers whom he employs the same wage rate. In this section we consider the case of a discriminating monopsonist (i.e. one who does not pay all of his employees the same wage rate). At the extreme is the case of the perfectly discriminating monopsonist, who pays each of his employees a different wage rate. However, in the absence of a piecework or other incentive-payment system, the scope for paying different hourly wages to different workers doing the same work is probably, in practice, fairly limited, particularly in the case of manual workers, where there is often a strong tradition of equal pay for equal work plus a general knowledge of wage rates actually being paid. The scope for monopsonistic discrimination is somewhat larger in the case of white collar and professional workers, where information on the earnings of others is often less than perfect and where remuneration is frequently, by tradition, confidential and often determined on an individual basis according to merit and other considerations. As we have seen, overtime payment systems are a form of discrimination in the payment of the labour hours of given workers, and other cases where monopsonistic discrimination may arise are in the payment of workers of different sexes, races and ages. There is, however, a more general topic of labour market discrimination, which is of importance in the analysis of wage differentials (see above, p. 212).

In its most extreme form monopsonistic discrimination involves paying each worker only his supply price. In this case, which is termed *perfect discrimination*, the monopsonist must offer a higher wage to attract an additional worker, but it is not necessary for him to increase the wage of any existing worker to the new level. He pays the higher wage to the marginal worker only and continues to pay those already employed only their supply prices (i.e. the minimum amounts necessary to keep them in his employment). To the non-discriminating monopsonist his labour supply curve (L_S in Figure 4.4) shows the average labour cost as a function of the level of employment, but to the perfect discriminator this curve shows his marginal labour cost at each employment level. Therefore, the perfect discriminator's profit-maximising position is at point C in Figure 4.4, where his marginal labour cost equals his marginal revenue product. Notice that the perfect discriminator's equilibrium position with respect to the numbers employed is the same as that of an otherwise identical perfectly competitive market. However, although these equilibria give rise to the same wage–employment combination, they do differ from the distributional viewpoint. In the perfectly competitive case the area in the rectangle $Ow'Ce'$

represents the wage bill, while the remaining area under the *MRP* curve represents capital's share of total revenue product. In the perfect discrimination case the wage bill comprises only that part of the rectangle $Ow'Ce'$ that lies under the labour supply curve (L_S), while the remainder of total revenue product accrues to capital.

Discrimination of a lower degree can arise when a monopsonist is able to purchase his labour inputs in two different markets. For discrimination of this sort to be feasible, two conditions must be satisfied: (1) the elasticities of labour supply must differ between the two markets and (2) the markets must be separate, in the sense that it is not possible for suppliers of labour in one market to transfer their labour to the other one. This situation is depicted in Figures 4.6(a) to (c). Diagrams (a) and (b) show the labour supply and *MLC* functions in each separate market, and diagram (c) shows the monopsonist's *MRP* function and the curves ΣMLC and ΣL_S, which are obtained by horizontal summation of the *MLC* and L_S curves for each separate market. For example, at wage w the first market supplies e_1 units of labour and the second market e_2 units, so that at this wage the combined market supplies the quantity e of labour ($= e_1 + e_2$), as shown by the curve ΣL_S.

If the monopsonist were unable to discriminate, he would pay the same wage for each worker regardless of the market in which he is hired and as can be seen from Figures 4.6(a) and (b), the payment of the common wage, say w (which is equal to the non-discriminating monopsonist's profit-maximising wage rate), gives rise to a different marginal labour cost in each market (i.e. c_A compared to c_B). If the monopsonist were able to discriminate by paying a different wage in each market, he would clearly be able to reduce the wage costs associated with a given level of employment by decreasing his purchases of labour in the second market and substituting in their place labour units hired in the first market, where the marginal labour cost is lower.

In a similar way to that in which a discriminating monopolist maximises his profits by equating his marginal revenue in each market to the marginal cost of his output as a whole, so the discriminating monopsonist maximises his profits by equating the marginal labour cost in each market to the marginal revenue product of his labour force as a whole. The monopsonist's equilibrium level of employment is determined by the point of intersection of his *MRP* curve and the combined *MLC* curve, and his employment of the amount of labour thus determined is allocated between his two submarkets in such a way that the marginal labour cost in each market is equalised. The discriminating monopsonist's equilibrium level of employment is shown in Figure 4.6(c) as e workers, e_A of whom are hired in his first and e_B in

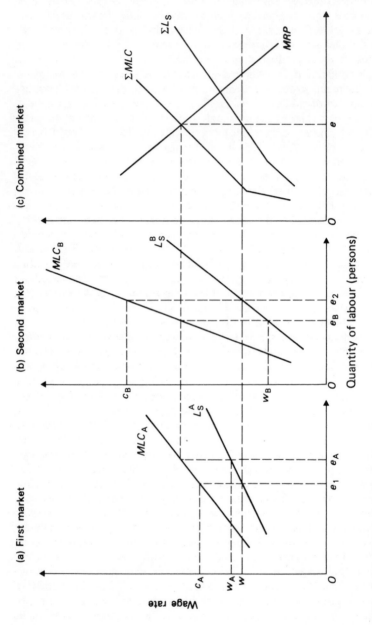

(a) First market

(b) Second market

(c) Combined market

Quantity of labour (persons)

Wage rate

Figure 4.6 Discriminating monopsony

his second market. Although the marginal labour cost is equal in each market (indeed, this is a necessary condition for profit maximisation), the wage paid in each, as indicated by the ordinate of the relevant supply curve at the employment level in question, differs. Labour hired in the first market is paid wage w_A, while labour hired in the second is paid only w_B. It should be noted too that discriminating monopsony results in the paying of a lower wage in the market where the elasticity of labour supply is lower.

FIXED EMPLOYMENT COSTS

In our analysis of the demand for labour we have so far made the usual simplifying assumption that there are no costs, other than the hourly wage, associated with the employment of labour. This assumption has allowed us to measure inputs of labour services in person-hours, without having to subdivide these into the number of workers and number of hours, and it implies that an employer will be indifferent between employing one man to work (say) 16 hours per day or two men to each work 8 hours per day. However, Oi (1962) argued that labour is not a completely variable factor of production, in the sense that total labour costs fluctuate directly with hours worked, but that it is in fact a *quasi-fixed factor*, because the total costs associated with the employment of labour are partially fixed and partially variable.

Fixed employment costs are those which do not vary with hours worked, and these are of two sorts. First, there are *turnover costs,* which consist of the costs associated with hiring and firing. These include employer search costs, initial training costs and severance payments. These costs are generally assumed to be a function of the number of new workers hired and existing ones quitting or laid off, and it is also argued that these costs rise as a proportion of total labour cost with the skill level of the employee. Secondly, there are those costs which are unrelated to the hours worked by an individual employee but which occur throughout the period of his employment. These include the administrative costs associated with a worker's employment, such as the costs of keeping employment and payroll records, of operating the PAYE system for income tax and National Insurance payments and of making wage and other payments. *Per capita* labour taxes, such as Selective Employment Tax in the UK during the late 1960s, and employer contributions, such as UK National Insurance contributions (which are of a fixed amount per employee over a specified income limit) also come into this category, as do employers' superannuation contributions in cases where these are a certain percentage of a salary that is payable regardless of variations in hours actually worked. Indeed, in cases (which are commonly found in white collar and professional occupations) where employees are paid a certain annual salary regardless of any fluctuations in their actual hours of work from standard hours that may occur, the whole of such salary payments can be regarded as fixed costs.

As noted, turnover costs are usually assumed to increase as a proportion of total labour costs with the skill level of the type of labour being considered. Employer search costs are the costs of recruiting and screening new employees, and these are likely to increase with skill level for several reasons. The costs of advertising vacancies are likely to be higher in the case of skilled workers, as advertising may be conducted on a national or international rather than a local basis and recruitment and personnel agency fees may be involved. In addition, interview expenses may be paid, and more expensive management time is likely to be used in interviewing prospective employees. Likewise, initial training costs are likely to increase with skill level, because the period of on-the-job training that is required before a new employee achieves his full productivity may be longer at higher skill levels. While a manual worker may be able to become fully operational in a new job in a matter of days, a managerial worker taking up employment in a different company may require several months to familiarise himself with relevant data and conditions before becoming fully operational.[6] Firing or separation costs may include redundancy payments, and these too are likely to increase with skill level to the extent that their magnitude is determined as some fraction or multiple, generally determined by length of service, of remuneration at the time of separation.

The existence of fixed employment costs means that the costs to the firm of increasing its labour input by hiring more workers, in general, differ from the costs involved in increasing its labour input by increasing the working hours of existing employees. As we shall see in the following section, the costs of varying the number of employees relative to those associated with changing hours worked are important determinants of the structure of an employer's labour demand as between workers and hours. In addition, the existence of fixed employment costs helps to explain observed variations in employment stability and unemployment by skill level.

Hours versus workers

To illustrate the importance of fixed costs in determining the structure of labour demand as between workers and hours, let us consider an employer's reaction to cyclical variations in the demand for his output. During the early stages of a recession, employers may tend to be reluctant to lay off workers, as they are likely to be uncertain about the likely duration of the fall-off in their product demand. Fearing the costs of discharging workers, and the possibility of incurring further search and training costs in the near future should the fall-off in demand prove to be only shortlived, the employer is likely to adjust his employment by reducing hours of work in preference to the number of employees. This adjustment in hours may take the form of either a reduction in overtime, if this is being worked, or the introduction of short-time working.

Once the strength of the recession becomes clear, the employer may then revise downwards his output plans and begin to run down his workforce. However, the incidence of lay-offs among the workforce will be influenced by variations in fixed employment costs between different skill levels. The longer a worker remains with an employer, the longer is the timespan over which the fixed cost expenditure that the employer has invested in him can be spread, and consequently an employer is likely to be more reluctant to lay off skilled than unskilled workers during a recession, for to lay off a skilled worker now in response to a current reduction in product demand may well involve incurring significant new fixed costs in the future when demand revives, as the laid-off worker may well by that time have found suitable employment elsewhere. The situation where an employer retains labour in excess of current requirements is known as *labour-hoarding* (see Taylor, 1974, pp. 26–8). Thus, the presence and nature of fixed employment costs gives an explanation of the observed greater employment stability and lower incidence of lay-offs among skilled than among unskilled workers, and in addition offers an explanation of the frequently observed tendency of changes in hours to precede changes in numbers employed at cyclical turning points.

During the initial stages of an upswing, employers are likely to be reluctant to hire extra workers and thereby incur additional fixed costs. Until they become satisfied that the recovery is likely to be sustained, employers prefer to meet increased product demand by utilising existing employees more intensively – by initially restoring working hours back to standard hours and subsequently by offering overtime-working at premium rates. Once the employer is satisfied that the recovery is likely to be prolonged, he will contemplate increasing his workforce. By so doing, additional fixed employment costs are incurred, but the costs of recruitment and initial training may be reduced if former employees who were previously laid off can be re-employed. As in the case of the downturn, we once again see adjustments in hours preceding adjustments in the same direction in numbers employed over the cycle.

Voluntary Quits

An employer who lays off a worker stands, especially if the skill of the worker in question is of a general type rather than one specific to the particular employer, to lose his previous investment of fixed cost expenditure on the worker. Similar losses arise when a worker voluntarily quits his employment, and in order to minimise such losses employers frequently operate various devices designed to cut down voluntary mobility among experienced workers by establishing seniority as an important characteristic. For example, up to a certain age senior employees are generally guaranteed greater employment stability, because lay-offs are typically arranged on a 'last in, first out' basis. In addition, holiday and pension entitlements are frequently tied to years of service, and seniority is often established as one criterion for promotion.[7]

Demand for Overtime Hours

In Chapter 2 we examined the responses of labour-suppliers to the existence of premium rates of pay for overtime-working, and in this section we consider the effect of overtime payments on the employer's demand for hours relative to workers.

Consider the case of a firm whose employees are already working standard hours, and suppose that it is confronted with an increase in the demand for its product. In order to satisfy this increased demand in the short term, the employer can either increase the hours worked by his existing workforce or recruit additional workers. If the first alternative is chosen, the employer must pay premium rates of pay for the additional hours worked, and there is a possibility of decreased efficiency through increased fatigue and on-the-job leisure, particularly in cases where large amounts of overtime are worked over long periods. Alternatively, the hiring of additional workers involves the employer's incurring fresh fixed employment costs, although, as we have seen, these can to some extent be reduced if the employer is able to rehire previously laid-off workers.

As we have seen, adjustments in hours tend to precede adjustments in numbers employed over the cycle, as employers estimate the likely duration of demand changes. If the increase in demand is expected to be only temporary, the employer will tend to prefer not to hire additional workers, because the overtime payments involved in meeting the increased product demand by increasing working hours will be less than the fixed costs involved in hiring additional workers now and laying them off in the near future. The longer the increase in demand is expected to last, the more likely is the employer to err towards employing additional men in preference to additional hours, as he estimates that the additional fixed costs will be spread over a sufficiently long period to compare favourably with the costs of over-time working.

NOTES ON FURTHER READING

A comprehensive discussion of the wage and employment decisions of the firm is given in Cartter (1959, pp. 52–74) and a useful discussion of the case of monopsony can be found in Laidler (1974, pp. 193–7).

On the subject of fixed employment costs, the reader should consult Oi's (1962) original paper for further discussion, and the mathematically inclined reader can usefully consult Nickell's (1978) analysis of the effects of fixed employment costs on employment and labour demand over the cycle. For an illustration of the way in which fixed employment costs can be incorporated into a profit-maximising framework, see Wickens (1974).

Part Two

ECONOMIC ASPECTS OF
TRADE UNION BEHAVIOUR

Chapter 5

The Economics of Trade Unions

In the previous chapter the determination of the levels of wages and employment was considered in cases where there is perfect competition among sellers of labour. An important characteristic of the UK labour market and that of other industrialised countries is the existence of trade unions as organisations of sellers of labour. Trade unions are complex institutions, which can be analysed from social and political as well as economic viewpoints, but in this chapter we concentrate exclusively on the economic analysis of trade unions. There is a large body of literature in the industrial relations or 'institutional' school, which stresses the role of social, political and psychological forces in its analysis of trade union structure, government and organisation, and this approach is discussed in detail in Palmer (forthcoming in this series).

The present chapter begins with a brief history of trade unions in the UK, which is followed by a discussion of the economic theory of union growth together with a summary of the available empirical evidence relating to the theory. In the next section the questions of union objectives and the specification of a model of union behaviour are considered. In the following chapter we consider the determination of wages under collective bargaining and discuss the relative wage effect of trade unions (i.e. their impact on the wages of their members relative to those of non-members) and their effect on the allocation of resources. In Chapter 7 the role of trade unions in wage inflation is considered.

TRADE UNIONS IN THE UK: A BRIEF HISTORY

A trade union was defined by the Royal Commission on Trade Unions and Employers' Associations as 'any combination of employees the principal activity of which is the regulation of relations between employees and employers' (Donovan, 1968, p. 207), and these unions have existed in various forms in the UK since the early nineteenth century, if not earlier. Table 5.1 shows the number of trade unions that

Table 5.1   *Trade unions in the UK, selected years 1892–1977.*

Year	No. of trade unions at end of year	Membership at end of year (000s)	Union density (%)
1892	1,233	1,576	10.6
1900	1,323	2,022	12.7
1910	1,269	2,565	14.6
1920	1,384	8,348	42.2
1930	1,121	4,842	25.4
1940	1,004	6,613	33.1
1950	732	9,289	44.1
1960	664	9,835	43.1
1970	543	11,187	47.7
1977	480	12.707	52.6

Sources:
(1) Numbers of trade unions and membership: Department of Employment (1971), table 196, and *Department of Employment Gazette* (1979), p. 27.
(2) Union density is defined as

$$\frac{\text{Actual union membership}}{\text{Potential union membership}} \times 100$$

The data series on potential membership for the period 1892–1970 was obtained from Bain and Elsheikh (1976, pp. 134–5), who defined potential union membership as the total number of employees (i.e. employed plus unemployed). Data for subsequent years were defined in the same way and obtained from the *Department of Employment Gazette* (1978), p. 1422.

existed in the UK in various years between 1892 and 1977, together with details of their membership in absolute terms and expressed as a percentage of potential membership to give what is termed *union density*. As can be seen from Table 5.1, the organisation of sellers of labour in the UK into trade unions is by no means a new phenomenon. By 1892 there were some 1,233 unions in existence with a total membership of over 1.5 million workers, constituting 10.6 per cent of potential membership. However, by 1977 the number of unions had fallen to 480, while membership had risen to 12.7 million workers or 52.6 per cent of potential membership.

The development of trade unionism in the UK, as elsewhere, has been a complex process influenced not only by economic forces but also by political and legal factors, and there is a well-developed literature covering these influences. (See, for example, Pelling, 1971, and Clegg, 1972.) Nevertheless, a number of important features do emerge from an inspection of the aggregate data set out in Table 5.1. Throughout the period covered by the table, there was a marked downward trend in the number of unions in existence, and this was accompanied by an upward trend in union membership and union density. Over and above these trends there was a cyclical pattern in membership, and as we see in a following section, the relationship between this and the level of economic activity has attracted considerable research interest.

A more detailed analysis shows the existence of a number of fairly distinct phases in the growth of trade unions in the UK, and international comparisons suggest that similar phases existed in the experiences of other countries (Davis, 1941).

Craft unions
The first trade unions to emerge in the UK were *craft unions* of skilled workers, and throughout most of the nineteenth century unionism was largely confined to skilled workers, with the consequence that unionisation covered only a small proportion of the total labour force, giving a low union-density value.[1] Prior to the industrial revolution the acquisition of a craftman's skills typically provided the passport to self-employment or employer status. However, after the emergence of the industrial society, a significant proportion of craftsmen found themselves confined to remain as employees (rather than employers or self-employed) throughout their working lives, with a consequent lessening in their ability to represent their own interests, and it has been argued that this factor provided an important impetus to the formation of craft unions by skilled workers. Historically, the wages of skilled craftsmen had exceeded those of the unskilled (Phelps-Brown, 1977, pp. 68–81), and the formation of craft unions represented a largely successful attempt by skilled workers to maintain their favourable relative-wage position. A rapid growth in the demand for the services of skilled workers accompanied the process of industrialisation, and it has been argued that, faced with this, craft unions restricted entry into the crafts in order to prevent an influx of new entrants, attracted by craftsmen's wages, from increasing the conditions of labour supply to the craft and thereby depressing their relative wage position. The principal instrument by which the craft unions restricted entry was the apprenticeship system, which, although ostensibly designed to ensure proper standards of training and qualifications, was often used as a barrier to entry against new entrants to the craft.

The determinants of the elasticity of demand for labour (i.e. the Marshall rules) were considered in Chapter 3 (see pp. 57–8), and it is important to notice that according to these rules the demand for craft union labour will be inelastic (Friedman, 1951, pp. 207–15). This is because the possession by craft union members alone of the skill in question limits, particularly in the short-term, the possibilities of substituting non-craft union labour or other factors of production for craft union labour when its wage rate is increased. In addition, the demand for craft union labour will, subject to the Hicksian condition, be inelastic because the fraction of total costs accounted for by craft labour is normally small.[2] Given the inelastic demand for their members' services, the main method by which the craft unions were able to achieve their objective of maintaining their favourable wage position relative to unskilled labour was through the manipulation of the supply of labour. By controlling entry to the craft, these unions were able to shift the supply curve of craft labour to the left and thereby, given the inelastic demand curve for their labour, to achieve a high wage in relation to that of non-craft union labour, with little contraction in employment.

In the longer term, when employers can substitute other factors of production for craft union labour, demand tends to become more elastic, and to counter this craft unions have frequently attempted to restrict the substitution of other, non-union or less skilled, labour and/or capital for their members' services, by employing such devices as manning and demarcation rules or even a straightforward refusal to accept new technologies. The hostility among the craft unions in the UK newspaper-printing industry in 1979 towards the introduction of new production techniques is a clear contemporary example of this point.

Unskilled Labour and the 'New Unionism'

Up until the final decade of the nineteenth century, unionism in the UK was still on a fairly limited scale and largely confined to skilled craftsmen. As can be seen from Table 5.1, only about 10 per cent of potential membership was actually unionised by 1892. During the 1890s unionism in the UK took off into its second phase of growth – a phase characterised by the growth of the so called *new unionism*. The spread of unionism in the London area in 1889 and during the immediately following years is generally regarded as the take-off phase of the new unionism, which, in contrast to the old (craft) unionism, catered mainly for unskilled, poorly paid workers.

This phase of UK union growth lasted until about the outbreak of the First World War and was characterised by the formation of *general unions*, which opened their doors to all comers, regardless of their industry of employment, and charged only low subscriptions. The years immediately preceding the outbreak of the First World War saw a particularly rapid growth in UK union membership. Between 1910 and 1913 total membership rose by 61 per cent, from about 2.5 million to over 4.1 million, and this was due in large part to the integration of unions' benefit functions into the state health and unemployment schemes.

As we have seen, the craft unions were able, given the inelastic demand for their members' labour services, to increase their members' wages relative to those of other workers by manipulating the supply of labour. However, general union labour is non-essential (in the sense that there exist adequate substitutes for union labour in the form of non-union labour with the consequence that there is a high elasticity of substitution between these two types of labour input), and it generally accounts for a fairly high proportion of total costs. In addition, in the late nineteenth and early twentieth centuries there was frequently a highly elastic supply of non-union labour from the sometimes massive pool of available unskilled labour made up of those shifting out of agriculture and the unemployed. Given the combination of these factors, it follows from the Marshall rules that the demand for general union labour is likely to be highly elastic. Consequently, the general unions of the new unionism era had little opportunity to increase their members' wages by restricting the supply of union labour, except in periods when a high level of economic activity increased employment by an amount sufficient to drain the pool of available non-union labour and in cases where substitution by non-union labour could be prevented. Being generally unable to capitalise on the demand and supply situation, general unions therefore sought, as far as possible, to organise all sellers of labour and thereby minimise substitution by non-union labour.

Industrial and White Collar Unionism
The depressed economic conditions of the interwar years had their effect on trade unionism in the UK. Membership reached its interwar peak in 1920 at 8.35 million, but it declined quickly with the rapidly rising level of unemployment, as those losing their jobs tended to stop their union subscriptions and withdraw from membership. Between December 1920 and December 1921 unemployment among insured workers in the UK rose from 7.9 per cent to 18 per cent, and union membership declined by one-fifth to only 6.6 million. This decline continued until membership reached only 4.4 million, or just over half of its 1920 level, in the depths of the depression in 1932, when unemployment rose to 22.1 per cent of insured workers.

The economic climate of the interwar period had two main effects on trade unionism in the UK. First, there was a marked decline in the number of unions in existence (which fell between 1920 and 1940 from 1,384 to 1,004; see Table 5.1), as falling membership forced many smaller unions to merge with the larger ones. Indeed, a number of today's best-known unions had their origins in the amalgamations of this period. For example, in 1921 a merger between the Amalgamated Society of Engineers and six smaller craft unions gave rise to the Amalgamated Engineering Union (AEU), and the Transport and General Workers Union (TGWU) was formed in 1922 from an amalgamation of unions of dockers and transport workers, and this swiftly absorbed a number of other smaller unions. Similarly, the National Union of General and Municipal Workers (NUGMW) arose at this time from an amalgamation of the Gas Workers' Union and other general unions.

Secondly, faced with falling membership, unions sought to increase membership by making inroads into new areas. In an attempt to recruit new members, the AEU, for example, opened membership for the first time to semi- and unskilled workers in 1929, and both the TGWU and the NUGMW sought during the interwar period to recruit new members from among clerical workers and from the new and expanding mass-production sections, such as automobile-manufacturing and the electrical industries.

Industrial unions, which sought to organise all workers in a particular industry (usually defined by reference to its product market) irrespective of their individual skill or status, emerged in the USA in the 1920s in an attempt to organise fully the mass production industries, and although this type of union also became common in mainland Europe, it did not become widespread in the UK, principally because of the existence of well-established craft and general unions by this time. However, a number of industrial unions did arise as a result of mergers between several unions operating in the same industry, the National Union of Mineworkers being a case in point.

During the postwar period there was a marked change in the occupational structure of the UK labour force with a shift in employment away from manufacturing towards the service sector, and this resulted in the UK, as in a number of other industrialised countries, in the latest phase of union growth: the emergence of large-scale and quickly growing *white collar unions*. The process of trade union amalgamation continued during the postwar period, so that by 1977 the number of unions had fallen to under half of its 1940 level, while membership, boosted by white collar unionisation, had almost doubled.

In the UK white collar unions have made significant inroads into both the public and private sectors, and union membership is now a common feature of various white collar employments, with, for example, the Association of Scientific, Technical and Managerial Staffs (ASTMS) organising, among others, some supervisory and managerial grades in industry and commerce and the National Association of Local Government Officers (NALGO) organising most salaried local-government employees. In addition, unionisation is now common in many professional employments, with various unions, the largest of which is the National Union of Teachers, organising school teachers and the Association of University Teachers representing university teaching staff. It is, however, important to recognise that not all trade unions include the term 'union' in their title (ASTMS and NALGO are examples) and as we see in the following section, various professional bodies conform very closely in their behaviour to the craft unions described above.

TRADE UNION STRUCTURE

The above fourfold classification of unions as craft, general, industrial or white collar corresponds broadly to their historical development. However, Turner (1962) argued that in practice it is not easy to find unions that conform closely to this classification, since they frequently possess characteristics and behave in ways that resemble more than one of the above union types, and that in any case a union's characteristics and behaviour vary over its life cycle. Turner therefore proposed an alternative threefold classification of unions as being either closed, open or intermediate unions.

Closed unions are those characterised by the existence of restrictive membership policies and entry controls of the sort employed by the traditional craft unions considered above. Current examples of closed unions can be found in the UK printing industry. In contrast, *open unions* are those which pursue expansionist policies, designed to increase their membership. These unions correspond closely to the general and industrial unions already considered, particularly in cases where the latter's expansionist aspirations spill over to recruitment outside its industrial boundaries, as in the case of the National Union of Railwaymen, which has recruited into its membership some road transport workers. Finally, there are *intermediate unions*, which contain both closed and open compartments. These comprise those closed unions which have expanded to embrace groups of workers previously excluded. While the nineteenth-century craft unions fit well into the closed union model, craft unions can and do become intermediate ones, as we saw in the example of the AEU's recruitment of semi- and unskilled workers, which began in 1929.

In the UK, as elsewhere, various professional bodies, such as those of the legal and medical professions, fit closely the traditional craft or closed union model, restricting supply or entry via their control of the training of prospective entrants. However, it is not entirely clear to what extent these entry restrictions are necessary, as these bodies often claim, to maintain standards and to what extent they represent barriers to entry designed to maintain or increase the wages of existing practitioners (see Friedman and Kuznets, 1945).

A detailed analysis of the structure of the UK trade-union movement would take us into the realms of the industrial relations school and is therefore outside the scope of the present book (but see Palmer, forthcoming, for a survey). It is, however, important to notice that the development of trade unions in the UK along craft, general and white collar rather than industrial lines has resulted in the characterisation of many bargaining units, at both industry and workplace levels, by a situation of *multiunionism*. Throughout the 1970s the UK railways, for example, had three main unions (approximate memberships shown in brackets): the Associated Society of Locomotive Engineers and Firemen (29,000) with membership drawn from drivers and firemen, the Transport Salaried Staffs' Association (75,000) with a membership drawn from clerical workers, and the National Union of Railwaymen (198,000), whose members are porters, ticket-collectors and workers in similar work.

THE THEORY OF UNION GROWTH

A brief description of the trends and fluctuations that occurred in union membership and numbers in the UK was given above, but a more detailed analysis of the data of the UK and other countries shows that the growth of aggregate union membership is characterised by cyclical fluctuations of varying amplitude and duration. Early writers saw fluctuations in aggregate membership as being related to fluctuations in the level of economic activity or the business cycle. (See Bain and Elsheikh, 1976, pp. 5–25, for a literature survey.) More recently, however, researchers have employed econometric techniques to explain observed fluctuations in aggregate trade-union membership in various countries in terms of a vector of explanatory variables that is specified to represent various individual components of the business cycle.

In one such study Bain and Elsheikh (1976) analysed the determinants of union growth in the UK, USA, Australia and Sweden during the twentieth century. The principal significant finding that emerged from their analysis was that the annual proportional rate of change of aggregate trade-union membership is positively related to the rates of change of retail prices and wages and negatively related to union density and the level and rate of change of unemployment.[3]

These authors argued that workers are more likely to become and to remain union members during periods of rapid price inflation (as they attempt to secure money wage increases sufficient to protect their real living standards from being eroded by rising prices) and during periods when money wages are rising quickly (as workers tend during such periods to credit wage increases to unions and hope that by joining or staying with them they will do as well, if not better, in the future).

It is argued that the rate of union growth is negatively related to union density principally because of the existence of a *saturation effect*, in that the higher is union density the greater will be the difficulties of further increasing membership, because there will be fewer workers left to recruit and because those who are left will have a lower propensity and ability to unionise. Finally, it is argued that membership is likely to grow more slowly or to fall when unemployment is high or rising, because the opportunities for extending union membership are less favourable during such periods. This is so because, given the low level of aggregate demand prevailing, employers are more able to resist the spread of unionism, as the opportunity costs, in terms of foregone output, of production disruptions in the cause of extending unionisation tend to be low. In addition, unemployment influences a worker's propensity to become and to remain a union member through its effect on the expected benefits of membership relative to the costs of membership. Those becoming unemployed tend to withdraw from the union, as they feel that membership has little to offer them and as the cost of membership typically rises relative to their incomes. In addition, employed members also tend to leave the union during periods of high and rising unemployment, as they feel that in the prevailing economic climate the expected benefits from membership, in the form of improvements in wages and conditions of work won by the union, are no longer sufficient to outweigh membership costs.

Broadly similar determinants of union growth emerged from an alternative, although closely related, study of UK data by Burkitt and Bowers (1978), who also found evidence to support the hypothesis that workers are more likely to join unions during periods of rising profits, because they judge that the scope for union-won gains is higher during such periods.

TRADE UNIONS: ECONOMIC OR POLITICAL INSTITUTIONS?

The question of whether it is valid to analyse trade unions as economic institutions has excited considerable controversy and gave rise to the so-called Ross–Dunlop debate of the late 1940s and early 1950s.

Conventionally, economists have analysed questions of trade-union wage policy by drawing analogies with the rational firms and households of microeconomic theory, which are typically assumed to maximise (or minimise) some clearly defined objective or utility function.

The classic pronouncement of this viewpoint is due to Dunlop, who argued that an 'economic theory of a trade union requires that the organisation be assumed to maximise (or minimize) something' (1944, p. 4). However, considerable difficulties arise in the specification of precisely what this something is that the union is supposed to be maximising and, as we shall see, a wide variety of union maximands have been suggested.

Over and above the difficulties inherent in the specification of the precise form and arguments of a union objective function, Ross (1948) challenged the economic approach to the analysis of trade union behaviour on the grounds that unions are organisations composed of a heterogeneous set of members with heterogeneous interests and goals. Ross argued that union policies are formulated not on the basis of any simple maximising objective but on the basis of a political decision-making process, whereby the union-leaders, given their own objectives, reconcile the pressures brought to bear on them both internally (by the various factions within the union) and externally (by employers, other unions and governments). Because of their own professional ambitions and their identification with the union, Ross saw the central objective of union-leaders and decision-makers as being organisational survival and viewed economic factors as being of only secondary importance, to the extent that they generate political pressures that have to be dealt with. In short, Ross argued that unions behave in ways that appear irrational by the criterion of orthodox economic analysis but that their behaviour is rational when viewed within a political framework. He therefore concluded that union objectives and behaviour cannot be properly understood by conventional economic analysis and appealed instead for a political approach.

In response to this challenge, Dunlop argued that, while unions do have political dimensions, these are by no means as significant as Ross would lead us to believe and that, on the basis of US evidence, the dominance of political factors is in fact a characteristic of the behaviour of only a small number of new unions. Dunlop went on to argue that, despite the existence of political forces, union leaders are aware of economic, particularly long-run, realities, as is evidenced by the fact that the behaviour of wages can be well explained by market variables.

In broad terms, the divergence of opinion between Ross and Dunlop as to the appropriate method by which to approach the analysis of unions, boils down to a disagreement over the relative weights to be attached to political and economic factors.[4] While it is perhaps true that the policy-making mechanisms internal to the union can only be fully understood within a wider framework than is offered by conventional economic analysis, it is nevertheless true that union policies, once formulated, are generally expressed in terms of economic variables, such as changes in the level of wages and conditions of employment. These policies and the economic activities of the union are therefore subject to the workings and constraints of the economic system and are consequently amenable to economic analysis regardless of the precise way in which the policies themselves are formulated. In short, if we take the union's internal decision-making process and resulting economic objectives and policies as given, it is perfectly legitimate to employ the tools of economics to analyse the consequences and outcomes of these policies and of the union's economic activities.

UNION OBJECTIVES

The Neutralisation of Monopsony Power

Considerable attention has been devoted to the construction of theories of union objectives and behaviour. Perhaps the simplest view of the objectives and role of trade unions is that they exist to neutralise the monopsony power of employers (Burkitt, 1975, pp. 8–22; Mulvey, 1978, pp. 51–2). The perfectly competitive labour market, which we considered in previous chapters, is *atomistic*, in the sense that there exist large numbers of unorganized individuals on both the buyers' and sellers' sides of the market. The case of monopsony was considered in Chapter 4, and we noted that this situation can arise through labour-purchasers' combining to form an employers' association to act as a single purchasing unit in the labour market. Alternatively, monopsony can occur on a local basis when a firm is the sole purchaser of the type of labour in question in a local labour market. As we have seen, the monopsonist faces an upward-sloping labour-supply curve and maximises his profits by equating his marginal labour cost (MLC) to labour's marginal revenue product (MRP), with the consequence that his equilibrium levels of employment and wages are each lower than the corresponding, perfectly competitive values. Look again at Figure 4.4, and recall that the monopsonist's equilibrium level of employment is e workers, which falls short of the competitive equilibrium employment level by $(e' - e)$ workers, at wage w, which is $(w' - w)$ units below the competitive wage.

When discussing monopsony, we saw how the imposition of a minimum wage above the monopsonist's equilibrium level can, over a certain range of wages, result in an increase in employment. Accordingly, this 'neutralisation of monopsony power' view sees the objectives of trade unions as the establishment of a union minimum wage above the monopsonist's equilibrium value in order simultaneously to achieve increases in wages and employment. The analysis here is exactly the same as that of minimum wage imposition considered in Chapter 4. In so far as the union membership supports the minimum wage policy, the union establishes a perfectly elastic section to the labour supply curve at the official union wage rate, and the monopsonist can hire any amount of union labour at this rate up to the point where this section meets the original labour-supply curve. If, for example, the union were able to set the wage rate in Figure 4.4 at w', the labour supply curve facing the monopsonist would be $w'CL_S$. The monopsonist would maximise profits at point C by employing e' workers at wage w', and the union would have succeeded in increasing both wages and employment to their perfectly competitive levels. Notice that a union wage in excess of w' can only be achieved at the expense of contracting employment below its perfectly competitive level. However, provided that the union wage is set at a level no greater than w_A in Figure 4.4, employment will still be higher than in the absence of union action. If, for example, the union wage were set at w_m, the resulting equilibrium level of employment would be e_m workers as compared to the e workers that would be employed in the absence of union action.

Early Maximising Models

In the early literature there was, as we have seen, a marked tendency for economists to view unions as being economic agents analogous to firms. It was frequently argued that in the same way that a rational firm seeks to maximise a single variable, its profits, so too a rational union must possess some single maximand. Various suggestions were put forward as to precisely which variable trade unions could reasonably be assumed to be seeking to maximise, and a number of these are summarised below.

Wages. A very simple view of the objectives of trade union wage policies is that these aim to maximise wage income per member. Given the existence of a downward-sloping demand curve for union labour, this objective implies that the union will seek to raise wages to such a level that the bulk of its members will be forced out of employment.[5] As we have seen, workers tend to withdraw from unions on becoming unemployed, and so the pursuit of this objective implies in addition that the bulk of existing members will subsequently leave the union. According to this specification, the union's objective is actually achieved by pushing the wage rate so high that only one member remains in employment and by implication the union – clearly a highly implausible prediction. If this objective is reformulated to be the maximisation of the average wage income of the original members, the prediction is ultimately the same, except that employment and membership are contracted more slowly (i.e. at the rate at which members retire, resign or die). If one views the union as an institution, with goals of its own, the prediction of this model of union wage policy becomes even more implausible, for it implies that the union has no interest in either the employment of its members or the size of its membership and hence no interest in its own survival.

Employment. At the other extreme is the view that unions aim to maximise the employment of their members, and this specification implies that the union will seek to move down the demand curve for union labour, trading lower wages for increased employment of its members. Given the existence of a downward-sloping demand curve for union labour, this objective will be achieved when the union has succeeded in pushing its members' wages as low as possible.

Consider the case of an individual firm (with no monopsony power) employing only union labour, and assume the existence of a negatively sloping demand curve for union labour. Assume also that all workers hired by the firm are accepted into union membership and that all workers leave the union on becoming unemployed, so that we can talk of changes in employment and changes in union membership as being synonymous. This situation is shown in Figure 5.1, where L_S denotes the perfectly elastic labour-supply curve that it is assumed the firm would face in the absence of the union and where L_D is the firm's demand (*MRP*) curve for union labour, measured, for simplicity, in this and subsequent figures, in terms of numbers of members employed.

If the union in this example were an employment-maximiser, it would achieve its objective by setting wages at the level w, to give employment of e members. This wage is the competitive one that would prevail in the absence of unionisation, and the employment of e members is the maximum attainable, as presumably workers would withdraw from the union if membership required them to take a wage less than that which they could obtain without unionisation. Under this latter condition the labour supply curve represents a constraint that sets a lower limit on the wage rate (equal to w) at any particular employment level (Cartter, 1959, p. 82).[6] In the absence of any such supply constraint, the employment-maximising model of union wage policy implies that the union will seek to push its members' wage down to zero.

The wage-maximising formulation gives the implausible prediction that the union has no concern about its members becoming unemployed and subsequently leaving the union and, therefore, about its remaining in existence as an organisation. The employment-maximising formulation, however, gives the equally implausible prediction that the union seeks the lowest wage possible, by aiming to increase its members'

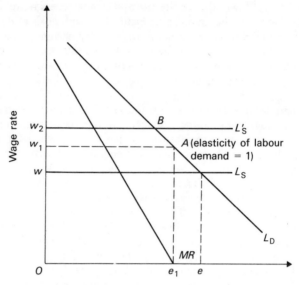

Figure 5.1   Union objectives

employment up to the point where they are no better off than they would be without a union. In addition, if one adopts a Ross (1948) type view of the union as an institution, it is difficult to see how such a membership maximisation policy can survive. To the extent that existing members are able to exert greater pressure than potential members on the union leadership, it is not easy to see how the leadership can continue to pursue such a maximisation policy, which sacrifices the wages of existing members in the cause of increasing the numbers of members employed.

The Wage Bill. Clearly, it is more satisfactory to argue that unions are concerned with both their members' wages and the size of their membership, and as a consequence the product of the members' wage rate and employment (i.e. the *wage bill*) has been put forward as a likely union maximand.[7] At any point on the union labour-demand curve the wage bill is given by the area of the wage–employment rectangle lying under the curve at the point in question. The wage bill is maximised at the point where the elasticity of the union labour-demand curve is equal to unity, and this is shown in Figure 5.1 by point A, where employment is e_1 members and the wage is w_1. If we think of the union in Figure 5.1 as a seller of labour facing the downward-sloping demand curve L_D, we can draw the marginal revenue (MR) curve corresponding to this labour demand curve to show the addition to the total union wage bill that arises when the wage is lowered by an amount sufficient to allow employment to be increased by one member. Notice in the usual way that the wage bill, as the union's 'total revenue', is maximised at the point where marginal revenue equals zero. Notice also from Figure 5.1 that, if the wage that would prevail in the absence of the union were above w_1 at, say, w_2 (i.e. if the labour supply curve that the firm would face in the absence of unionisation were L'_S) then by the reasoning of the previous section it follows, because of supply constraints, that the maximum wage bill actually achievable is at the non-unionised wage–employment combination at point B.

Although the wage-bill maximisation hypothesis has the attraction of combining both wage and employment dimensions into a single maximand, it is unsatisfactory because it gives the unrealistic prediction that, in cases where the demand for union labour is elastic (i.e. to the left of employment e_1 in Figure 5.1), the union will seek to achieve wage cuts! However, in cases where the wage is initially low, this hypothesis can simply be interpreted as not seeking to raise it above w_1 in Figure 5.1. As under the employment maximisation hypothesis, the union in this model sacrifices the wages of its already employed members in order, in this case, to increase the wage bill. As in the employment maximisation specification, it is not easy to see how such a policy, if pursued, could survive, as existing members would be unlikely to be willing to continue to subscribe to a union policy that persistently sacrificed their own interests. In addition, the plausibility of the wage-bill maximisation model can be further questioned, because it implies that the wage of a given type of union labour will differ both within and between relevant employments according to the elasticity of labour demand – a prediction that does not appear to be borne out in practice, since uniform rather than varied union wage rates are typically observed for homogeneous groups of labour (Mulvey, 1978, pp. 31–2).

The Monopoly Analogy. In the search for a union objective function it has been suggested that the union can be viewed as a monopoly seller of the labour services of its members and that it can therefore be assumed to behave in a manner analogous to a product market monopolist. It has therefore been argued that, in the same way as a product market monopolist is assumed to set his sales so as to equate marginal cost to marginal revenue, it is reasonable to assume that the trade union as a monopoly seller of labour seeks to equate the marginal revenue from the sale of its members' labour to their supply price. This situation is

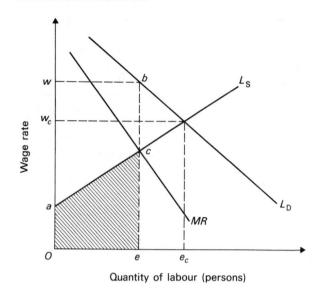

Figure 5.2   The union-monopoly analogy

shown in Figure 5.2, where L_D is the firm's downward-sloping demand curve for union labour and L_S is the upward-sloping supply curve for labour that it is assumed the firm would face in the absence of unionisation. The union's demand curve for its 'product' (L_D) is its average revenue (AR) curve and since this is downward sloping, the union monopoly can (in the absence of price discrimination) only gain additional units of employment at the expense of a lower wage rate. The curve MR in Figure 5.2 is the marginal revenue curve corresponding to the labour demand curve (L_D).

Acting as a monopolistic seller of labour, the union, according to this model of its wage policy, seeks to equate the marginal revenue from the sale of its members' labour services (or, as it is sometimes called, the marginal demand for labour; Marshall *et al.*, 1976, p. 330) with its supply price at employment e in Figure 5.2, demanding a wage of w. Notice that this wage is above the level (w_c) that would prevail in a perfectly competitive market with the same labour demand and supply curves but that this gain in wages is achieved only at the expense of ($e_c - e$) units of employment. Notice also from Figure 5.2 that, in the case where there is a perfectly elastic labour-supply curve, at a wage of zero (i.e. the analogue of a monopolistic firm with zero marginal cost) this formulation reduces to the wage-bill maximisation model considered above.

The problem with the monopoly analogy arises on the supply side. In discussing the behaviour of monopolistic firms, it is usually assumed that they aim to maximise their profits and, therefore, that they equate their marginal cost to the marginal revenue from the sale of their output. The union, however, does not produce the labour services of its members but acts instead as their agent, therefore, unlike a firm, it does not incur production costs. The labour supply function (L_S in Figure 5.2) is not a marginal cost function analogous to that of a monopolistic producer but illustrates, as we saw in Chapter 2, members' work–leisure preferences at various wage rates. Therefore, according to the monopoly analogy, the union is seen as attempting to maximise an *economic rent*, namely, the surplus of its members' total wage income over and above the total of their individual marginal supply prices or their transfer earnings, where the latter is shown by the area lying under the labour supply curve at the employment level in question. In Figure 5.2 the union-monopoly's equilibrium level of employment is *e* members, and at this point its membership's total transfer earnings are given by the shaded area under L_S; the surplus of the membership's total wage income over their transfer earnings, which is maximised here, is shown by the area *awbc*.

The union-monopoly model, derived by analogy with the monopolistic firm, is therefore a dubious one, because the union possesses nothing analogous to the cost functions that underlie the firm's supply curve, with the consequence that the maximum implied by this analogy (i.e. the economic rent accruing to union labour) is a quantity that is unlikely in itself to be of particular concern to the union (Reder, 1952). In addition, as Rees (1973, pp. 128–9) pointed out, this formulation implies that the union will restrict employment to *e* members (presumably by some form of job-rationing device) in order to obtain the wage *w*, which is in excess of each employed members' supply price. However, the wage gains and employment losses that arise from such a policy accrue to different people, with employed members obtaining wage gains at the expense of the employment of others. Given that the union leadership in its policy formation must presumably balance pressures for work from any remaining unemployed members against pressures for improved wages from employed workers, it is (in the absence of any mechanism for redistributing the gains from the pursuit of such a policy from employed to unemployed members) only by mere chance that this political balancing exercise will lead to the maximising solution predicted by this model.

The Membership Function. A variant of the employment maximisation model considered above was put forward by Dunlop (1944). Suggesting that unions attempt to maximise their membership, Dunlop argued that the number of workers who will be allied to the union is a function of the wage rate. Accordingly, Dunlop constructed a *membership function* showing union membership as an increasing function of the union wage rate and suggested that this should be substituted in place of the conventional labour-supply curve, which, as we have seen, reflects the income–leisure preferences of workers rather than their allegiance to the union. In cases where union membership is required in order to work (i.e. the *closed* or *union shop*[8]), the labour supply and membership functions will be identical for any unionised firm, although notice that these need not necessarily coincide with the labour supply curve that the firm would face in the absence of unionisation, as some workers may choose to work or to search for employment elsewhere rather than join the union. In other cases the membership function will lie to the left of the conventional labour-supply schedule, with its displacement to the left of the latter indicating the number of workers who will not be union members at the wage rate in question.

In Figure 5.3 L_S is the labour supply curve, assumed to be upward sloping, faced by a unionised employer, and the curve MF is the membership function, showing the number of employees who will be union memberss at any given wage rate. If the union's objective is to maximise its membership (the analogy in the theory of the firm being the sales-maximising producer), it will seek the wage rate w (where the membership function intersects its MRP curve[9]) in order to achieve its maximum membership level of N workers. In the case shown in Figure 5.3, the union membership function lies to the left of the labour supply curve, with the consequence that the maximisation of membership is not synonymous with the maximisation of employment. The union would have maximised employment at the competitive wage rate of w_M, but in so doing it would have lost $(N - Q)$ members.

Although the membership function approach has the advantage of explicitly recognising the distinction between employment and the size of union membership, it suffers from the same sort of defect as the other simple maximising formulations, in that it implies that the union is willing and able to sacrifice the wages of its employed members in order to maximise its membership. In addition, the specification of union membership as a function of only the union wage rate is an oversimplification, because, as we have seen, a variety of other economic factors have been shown to exert significant influences on union membership.

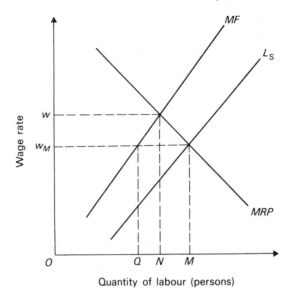

Figure 5.3 Union membership function

Utility-Maximising Models

In view of the difficulties encountered in the specification of a single union maximand, it is perhaps most reasonable to argue that trade unions are concerned at least with increasing both the wages and employment of their members, but to accept that the precise weights attached to these two objectives differ both between unions and over a given union's life cycle. Presumably, closed (or craft) unions place relatively large weight on the wage increase objective, while open (or industrial and general) unions attach particular weight in their policies to employment, because of the influence that this has on the size of their membership.

Trade-Union Preference Functions. As a development of this approach, a number of more recent writers have analysed trade union wage policy within a utility-maximising framework. Cartter (1959), developing Fellner's (1951) earlier analysis, specified a utility function according to which a trade union's utility is an increasing function of two variables: its members' wage rate and their level of employment. Given this utility function, it is possible to employ the standard techniques of indifference curve (or, as these are often called in the present context, preference function) analysis to analyse the union's wage–employment objectives. Although unions in practice may be concerned with a variety of issues (including the length of the working day, the amount of paid holidays and other factors relating to the conditions of work), this simple two-variable formulation serves to illustrate the nature of the trade-offs and constraints faced by the union.

In the extreme case where the union's utility is a function of only its members' wage rate (i.e. the wage maximisation case considered above), the union's indifference-mapping will consist of a series of horizontal lines on the usual wage–employment diagram (with the wage on the vertical axis and the level of employment on the horizontal one), and utility-maximising behaviour, given the existence of a downward-sloping demand curve for union labour, implies that the union will seek to move to the top point of the labour demand curve in order to reach the highest possible indifference curve. At the other extreme is the case where the union's utility is a function of only the level of its members' employment (i.e. the employment maximisation case considered above). In this case the union's indifference map is a series of vertical lines, and utility-maximising behaviour implies that the union will seek to increase employment to the maximum level possible, given the constraints imposed by the labour supply schedule. These two extreme cases are discussed in more detail in Cartter (1959, pp. 86–8).

As already noted, it is much more plausible to argue that unions are concerned with both the wages and employment of their members and therefore to specify union utility as an increasing function of both these arguments. Given such a utility function, we can construct, in the usual way, a mapping of union indifference curves, each of which is the locus of combinations of wage rates and employment levels that yield a given level of utility to the union. Figure 5.4 shows an example of an indifference map of a union for which wages and employment are the only arguments entering its utility function.[10] Since wages and employment are unlikely to be perfect substitutes for one another, the union's indifference curves are drawn convex to the origin on the basis of the usual assumption of a diminishing marginal rate of substitution between them.

The precise form of the union's indifference map, in terms of both the shape and the configuration of its indifference curves, will vary from case to case according to its utility function. However, it is generally argued that the union attaches a special significance to the prevailing wage–employment combination, with the consequence that its indifference curve is likely to be sharply kinked about this combination, indicating that, once a union is enjoying a particular wage–employment combination, it will take a considerable increase in wages to compensate for even a small decrease in employment and a large

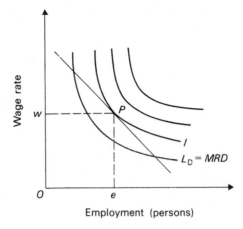

Figure 5.4   Union indifference map

increase in employment to compensate for any wage reduction. The argument here is that any worsening of the situation relative to the *status quo* will generate internal political pressures within the union, which threaten its existence, with the consequence that any reduction in wages (or employment) must be accompanied by a large increase in employment (or wages) in order to maintain union utility at a constant level. Such an indifference curve is shown by *I* in Figure 5.4, where point *P* denotes the existing wage–employment combination.

The Union's Equilibrium Assuming that the employer has no monopsony power, the demand (*MRP*) curve for union labour represents a constraint, since it shows the quantity of union labour that the employer will seek to hire at each particular wage rate. In the same way that the consumer's equilibrium is found by superimposing his budget constraint on to his indifference map, it follows that, with a given labour-demand curve, the union's utility is maximised at the point where this curve is tangential to an indifference curve. In Figure 5.4 the union is in equilibrium at point *P*, where the slope of its indifference curve (i.e. the marginal rate of substitution of wages for employment) is equal to the slope of its labour demand curve, and this utility-maximising model therefore predicts that the union will seek the wage *w* and an employment level of *e*.

Dynamic Considerations: The Wage Preference Path. The utility maximisation approach can be extended to allow analysis of the union's reactions to shifts, over time, in the position of its short-run

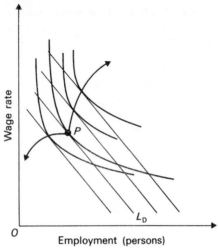

Figure 5.5   The wage preference path

labour-demand curve. Many writers (e.g. Lewis, 1963) have noted that trade unions do not react in a symmetrical manner to increases and decreases in the conditions of labour demand. Confronted with an increase in the conditions of labour demand, unions are likely to exhibit a higher order of preference for improvements in wages than for increases in employment, but when confronted with a decrease in labour demand conditions, they are likely to resist any reduction in money wages despite the resulting contraction in employment. Notice that such downward rigidity in the money wage is a feature central to the supply side of the labour market in the Keynesian macromodel.[11]

In Figure 5.5 point P denotes the union's equilibrium position, given an initial demand curve for union labour (L_D). In this diagram various levels of labour demand both greater than and less than the initial level are shown, and given these we are able to trace out the locus of utility-maximising wage–employment combinations or tangency points between labour demand and indifference curves. This path, which can be thought of as analogous to a firm's expansion path or a consumer's income–consumption curve, indicates the path that the utility-maximising union would seek to follow if the conditions of labour demand were to change from their initial level at L_D, and it is known as the union's *wage preference path*.

The wage preference path shown in Figure 5.5 illustrates the observed asymmetrical response of unions to upward and downward changes in the conditions of labour demand. The path is sharply kinked

at the prevailing equilibrium (P), and its shape indicates the different
weights attached by the union to improvements in wages and employment for potential increases or decreases in the conditions of labour
demand. As shown in Figure 5.5, the union uses an increase in labour
demand conditions primarily to secure wage increases and only accepts
increased employment for substantial upward shifts in labour demand.
When there is a decrease in the conditions of labour demand, the union
resists money wage cuts, despite the resulting inroads into its members'
employment, and it continues to do so until the decrease in labour
demand becomes substantial.[12]

NOTES ON FURTHER READING

The literature covering the economic analysis of trade unions is very
extensive, and much of this is summarised at a fairly elementary level in
Burkitt (1975), Rees (1977), Mulvey (1978) and Burkitt and Bowers
(1979). A useful short history of trade unionism in Britain is to be
found in Pelling (1971), and the literature on the theory of union
growth is surveyed in Bain and Elsheikh (1976, pp. 5–57). There are
marked interindustry variations in the degree of unionisation and the
determinants of such variations in postwar Britain are analysed in Bain
and Elsheikh (1979). The problems encountered in the specification of
an economic model of the union are conveniently summarised in
Cartter (1959, pp. 77–94) and Rees (1977, pp. 46–64), and the early
works by both Dunlop (1944) and Ross (1948) contain much of
interest.

Wage Determination Under Collective Bargaining and the Effects of Unions

The analysis of the previous chapter was concerned with the union's objectives in respect of the wage rate and employment of its membership. In order to analyse wage determination in the presence of trade unions, it is necessary also to consider the employer's equilibrium levels of wages and employment, and since these will, as we shall see, typically differ from those of the union, it is necessary to consider the union–employer negotiating or *collective-bargaining* process, which occurs in order to determine the wage that the union will actually receive.

WAGE DETERMINATION UNDER TRADE UNIONISM: THE BILATERAL MONOPOLY FORMULATION

Traditional neoclassical analysis treats the problem of wage determination in the presence of trade unions as a particular case of *bilateral monopoly*. According to this formulation, the union is assumed to behave as a monopolistic seller of labour, while the employer is assumed to be a monopsonistic purchaser of labour. The monopoly model of union behaviour was considered in the previous chapter (see pp. 93–95), and the case of a monopsonistic purchaser of labour was considered in Chapter 4 (see pp. 62–64). Figure 6.1 brings together the models of the union-monopoly seller and the employer-monopsony purchaser (considered above in Figures 5.2 and 4.4 respectively) in order to illustrate the bilateral monopoly formulation.

As we have seen, the monopsonistic purchaser of labour faces an upward-sloping labour-supply curve, and in order to maximise his profits he equates the marginal labour cost (*MLC*) to the marginal revenue product (*MRP*) and therefore seeks to employ e_1 units of

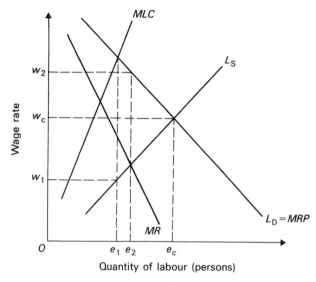

Figure 6.1   Bilateral monopoly formulation

labour at wage w_1. According to the labour monopoly model (the limitations of which were discussed above; see p. 95), the union is assumed to aim to equate the marginal revenue (*MR*) from the sale of its members' labour services to their supply price, and it therefore seeks to have e_2 members employed at wage w_2.

According to this model, the employer attempts to restrict employment below the competitive level e_c in order to maximise his profits, while the union likewise seeks to restrict the sale of its members' labour services in order to maximise the collective rent of its membership. The bilateral monopoly formulation, which is based on the usual assumptions of rational maximising behaviour, is unable to yield a unique prediction of the wage settlement that will be established; rather, it is only able to delineate a *range of indeterminacy* within which the outcome can be expected to lie. In Figure 6.1 the union seeks the wage w_2 and the employer the lower wage w_1, but the actual wage rate is left indeterminate meaning that, while it can be argued that the wage rate will lie somewhere between w_1 and w_2, the analysis is unable to predict the actual wage that will be established between these limits. Given that this analysis predicts that the actual wage will lie somewhere in the range of indeterminacy w_1 to w_2, it is usually argued that its precise value within this range will be determined as the outcome of a process of collective bargaining between the union and the employer.

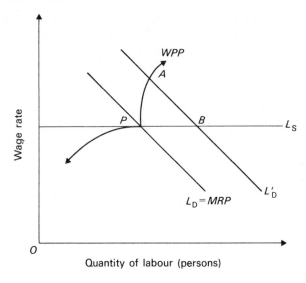

Figure 6.2   The union's wage preference path and the bargained wage

This formulation, however, does not provide any theory of the bargaining process that is presumed to operate between these limits or any prediction of its outcome. Notice from Figure 6.1 that the competitive wage (w_c) lies between the employer's and the union's desired wage levels and that this can conceivably arise as the outcome of the union–employer collective-bargaining process.

The Wage Preference Path and the Wage Bargain

The bilateral monopoly model can be criticised for the reasons considered in our discussions of the union-monopoly model, principally because of the questionable nature of the maximand implied by the analogy and the fact that the union does not possess costs functions analogous to those underlying the firm's supply function. The absence of such cost curves was one of the reasons that led Cartter (1959, pp. 92–4), in his development of Fellner's (1951) earlier analysis, to put forward the union's wage preference path as being a more appropriate concept than a labour supply curve of the conventional sort in the analysis of unionised labour markets.[1] In cases where wages are determined by collective bargaining, the wage preference path (*WPP*) analysis gives us much the same conclusion as the bilateral monopoly formulation, namely, that market forces are primarily important in establishing boundaries, within which the levels of wages and employment can be expected lie.

In order to consider the determination of the union wage within the utility-maximising framework offered by the *WPP* analysis, let us assume for simplicity that there is perfect competition among purchasers of labour, so that the individual purchaser of labour faces a perfectly elastic labour-supply curve. Assume also that the initial wage–employment combination coincides with the perfectly competitive equilibrium. This situation is shown in Figure 6.2, where L_S denotes the labour supply curve faced by the employer in question, L_D is his short-run labour-demand curve and P denotes the initial wage–employment combination.

At point P the firm is maximising its profits, given initial conditions, because the wage is equated to labour's marginal revenue product, and we assume, in addition, that the union is maximising its utility subject to the constraint imposed by the initial labour-demand curve at this point. Suppose now that there is an increase in the conditions of labour demand, such that the labour demand curve shifts from L_D to L_D'. Given this shift, the union will seek to move along its wage preference path from P to its new utility-maximising position at point A, while the employer will seek to move along the perfectly elastic labour-supply curve to point L_S, where his profits will be maximized given the new labour-demand conditions. In this case the employer seeks to absorb the increased conditions of labour demand solely in increased employment, while the union seeks to absorb this mostly in the form of a wage increase.

According to this formulation, the union seeks the wage–employment combination shown by A, while the employer seeks that at B, and since the labour demand curve shows the quantity of labour that the profit-maximising firm will seek to employ at any given wage, the new wage–employment combination will, in the case where the employer is free to adjust employment once a wage is agreed, lie somewhere along the new labour-demand curve between A and B.

Therefore, this analysis, like the bilateral monopoly formulation, does not provide a determinate solution; instead, it is only able to predict a range within which the union wage can be expected to lie. Once again it is argued that the actual wage–employment combination within this range will be determined by a process of collective bargaining, within which the conflicting preferences of the union and employer are resolved, but the analysis gives no theory of the collective-bargaining process and no prediction as to where the final outcome will lie. While the *WPP* analysis is easily generalised to cases where the initial wage–employment combination does not coincide with the perfectly competitive equilibrium, and to cases where there is a decrease rather than an increase in the conditions of labour demand, its conclusion that the union wage is indeterminate within some range remains unaltered (see Cartter, 1959, pp. 92–4).[2]

Indeterminacy and the Bargaining Process

As we have seen above, the traditional tools of microeconomic analysis have proved unable to provide a unique prediction of the wage that will be determined in unionised labour markets; instead, they have only been able to delineate a range of indeterminacy within which the outcome is predicted as lying. Faced with this indeterminacy, many writers have been content to follow the spirit of Edgeworth's famous pronouncement of the so called classical view that 'contract without competition is indeterminate' (1881, p. 20) and to dismiss the determination of the precise outcome of the bargaining process within the range of indeterminancy as being beyond the realms of economic analysis.[3,4]

SOME THEORIES OF THE COLLECTIVE-BARGAINING PROCESS

The classical conclusion that the outcome of the bargaining process is indeterminate within some range was challenged in the late 1920s, and since this date an extensive literature of theories offering determinate solutions has evolved. In this section we consider the contribution of this literature to the analysis of collective bargaining, as the process by which the union and the employer resolve their conflicting preferences and reach agreement on the actual value of the union wage within the range of indeterminacy bounded by their respective preferences.

Basic Concepts

It is usual to model the bargaining process within the distributional framework as the problem of the determination of the quantities of fixed initial endowments of some homogeneous good that will be exchanged between isolated individuals. While bargaining situations can involve any number of parties, it is usual to treat union–employer negotiations as a case of two-party exchange, on the implicit assumption that each involved party behaves in the manner of a perfectly co-ordinated individual.[5]

Basic to the theory of bargaining is the concept of a *threat*, which is defined as a committment to a definite course of action that is conditional on the demand associated with the threat not being met. Bargaining situations can be subdivided into fixed and variable threat cases. In *fixed threat bargaining* a failure to reach agreement has the unique consequence of no trade, so that each bargainer has only one possible (fixed) threat, namely, his refusal to trade. In the more general case of *variable threat bargaining*, each bargainer possesses a choice among several possible threats, each characterised by varying degrees of non-participation, so that there are various possible states of conflict.

It is, however, usual to treat union–employer bargaining as a case of fixed threat bargaining, on the basis of the (often implicit) assumption that, from among the various threats open to them, the union and the employer each elects to adopt a single (or pure) threat, these being respectively the threat of an indefinite strike and the threat of an indefinite lock-out.[6]

To formalise things, let bargainer 1 be the union and bargainer 2 the employer, and let w denote the wage rate. Assume that the union's utility is an increasing function of only the wage rate and that the employer's is a decreasing function of the wage. We can therefore write the bargainers' respective utility functions as

$$u_1 = u_1(w) \text{ and } u_2 = u_2(w)$$

where

$$\frac{du_1}{dw} > 0 \text{ and } \frac{du_2}{dw} < 0$$

Bargaining theorists focus attention on the *utility frontier*, which is the mapping on to the utility space of the contract curve[7] and which is generally assumed to be concave to the origin.[8] The point with co-ordinates that are the utilities of the two bargainers when fixed threats are implemented is defined as the *threat point*, and the utility frontier that is obtained by placing the origin at the threat point (i.e. by adjusting the bargainers' utility functions so that the utility that each obtains in the event of disagreement is zero) is termed the *utility increments frontier*. (In technical terms, this frontier represents the boundary of the first quadrant of the outcome set when the origin is placed at the utility combination corresponding to disagreement.)

Zeuthen's Theory

The first determinate theory of the bargaining process was proposed by Zeuthen in 1928 and first published in English in 1930. Zeuthen's is a theory of two-person bargaining, which is cast in terms of union–employer wage negotiations, and recognising the sequential nature of the bargaining process Zeuthen treated it as a problem of risk. In his initial analysis Zeuthen made the assumption, which was later relaxed, that the demand for union labour is perfectly inelastic, so that bargaining over the wage rate is equivalent to bargaining over the wage bill, and

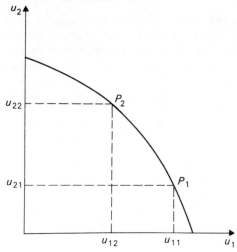

Figure 6.3   Zeuthen's theory of bargaining

although his own exposition is in money terms, we follow Harsanyi's (1956) reformulation, which is basically a straightforward translation of Zeuthen's analysis from money into utility terms.[9]

The essence of Zeuthen's theory is that, at each stage of the bargaining process, both players compare the alternative of holding out for their own current demand, at the risk of causing a conflict, with that of immediately accepting their opponent's latest offer.

To illustrate Zeuthen's theory, recall that bargainer 1 is the union and bargainer 2 the employer, let u_{ij} denote the utility to the ith bargainer of the outcome demanded by the jth and transform the bargainer's utility functions, so that the utility that each obtains at the threat point is zero. Consider the utility increments frontier shown in Figure 6.3, and assume that bargainer 1 opens the negotiations with the demand shown at P_1, which would give him u_{11} and offer his opponent u_{21}, and that bargainer 2 opens with the demand at P_2, which would given him u_{22} and offer his opponent u_{12}.

If bargainer 1, for example, were to accept his opponent's offer, he would obtain the outcome u_{12} with certainty. However, if he were to hold out for his own current demand at P_1, he would expect to achieve the higher utility u_{11} with some probability. If r_1 denotes bargainer 1's estimate of the probability that his insistence on this outcome would result in conflict,[10] his expected utility from pursuing this course of action is given by $(1 - r_1)u_{11}$.[11] According to Zeuthen, bargainer 1 compares this expected utility with that which he could obtain with certainty by settling on the terms of his opponent's current offer at P_2 (i.e. u_{12}). Zeuthen argued that it is rational for bargainer 1 to hold out for his own current demand (i.e. to insist on his opponent's complete capitulation) and to incur any risk of disagreement (r_1) such that

$$(1 - r_1)u_{11} \geqslant u_{12} \tag{6.1}$$

since the net expected utility gain from so doing is, say,

$$\Delta u_1 = (1 - r_1)u_{11} - u_{12} \geqslant 0$$

By a parallel route Zeuthen argued that bargainer 2 will incur any risk of disagreement (r_2) such that

$$(1 - r_2)u_{22} \geqslant u_{21} \tag{6.2}$$

Rearranging these conditions, we obtain

$$r_1 \leqslant \frac{u_{11} - u_{12}}{u_{11}} \tag{6.3}$$

$$r_2 \leqslant \frac{u_{22} - u_{21}}{u_{22}} \tag{6.4}$$

Therefore, Zeuthen argued, the highest risk of disagreement to which bargainer 1 will rationally expose himself in holding out for his preferred outcome is that value of r_1 for which the net expected utility gain from this course of action is zero (i.e. the value at which bargainer 1 is indifferent between pressing for his own claim at P_1 and accepting his opponent's offer at P_2). This probability, denoted by $r_1^{\max}$, is termed the *risk willingness* of bargainer 1 and is obtained by solving condition (6.3) as an equation, giving

$$r_1^{\max} = \frac{u_{11} - u_{12}}{u_{11}} \tag{6.5}$$

Similarly, bargainer 2's risk willingness is given by

$$r_2^{\max} = \frac{u_{22} - u_{21}}{u_{22}} \tag{6.6}$$

Crucial to Zeuthen's theory is the behavioural assumption that, at each

stage of the bargaining process, the bargainer with the smallest risk willingness (i.e. the one who will rationally expose himself to a smaller
maximum probability of conflict) will make some concession. From
(6.5) and (6.6) the condition for bargainer 1 to make a concession is

$$\frac{u_{11} - u_{12}}{u_{11}} < \frac{u_{22} - u_{21}}{u_{22}} \qquad (6.7)$$

which can be rearranged to give

$$u_{11}u_{21} < u_{22}u_{12} \qquad (6.8)$$

Conversely, bargainer 2 will make a concession if $r_2^{\max} < r_1^{\max}$, i.e. if

$$u_{11}u_{21} > u_{22}u_{12} \qquad (6.9)$$

Finally, in cases where $r_1^{\max} = r_2^{\max} > 0$, Zeuthen assumed that both
bargainers will make concessions, as conflict in such a case would be
'the greater evil to each' (1930, p. 119).

Noting that $u_{11}u_{21}$ is the value of the utility product u_1u_2 proposed
by bargainer 1 and that $u_{12}u_{22}$ is the value proposed by bargainer 2, it
follows, given the usually assumed non-convexity to the origin of the
utility increments frontier, that each concession raises the utility product proposed by the conceding player. Such a concession need not be
total, in the sense of a complete acceptance of the opponent's last
offer; rather, it must be large enough to reverse the inequality sign in
the relevant expression (6.8) or (6.9). It then becomes the other
bargainer's turn to concede, and thus this process of successive concessions proceeds, until further concessions can no longer increase the
utility product u_1u_2, so that agreement is reached at the point where
u_1u_2 assumes its maximum value. Harsanyi (1956, p. 148) argued that,
because indivisibilities (of the smallest monetary unit and of a psychological nature) set a lower limit to the size of admissible concessions,
this point will be reached after a finite number of steps. At the point
where u_1u_2 is maximised, $u_{11} = u_{12}$ and $u_{22} = u_{21}$, and we see from
(6.5) and (6.6) that $r_1^{\max} = r_2^{\max} = 0$.

Zeuthen's conception of, and solution to, the bargaining problem
is easily illustrated by superimposing on to Figure 6.3 a family of
rectangular hyperbolas given by

$$u_1u_2 = nK$$

where K denotes the Harsanyi lower limit of the admissible size of

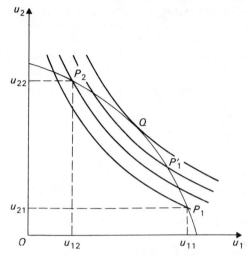

Figure 6.4   Zeuthen's solution to the collective-bargaining problem

concession (say £1 when a weekly wage is being negotiated) and $n = 1, 2, 3, \ldots$. Figure 6.4 shows a number of such hyperbolas, and from this we see that, for demands at P_1 and P_2, inequality (6.8) is satisfied, so bargainer 1 concedes, moving around the frontier to a hyperbola above that passing through P_2 (say to point P_1'). Since inequality (6.9) is now satisfied, it becomes bargainer 2's turn to concede, and so on, with settlement being achieved (in the next step in this simple example) at point Q, where a hyperbola is tangential to the utility increments frontier.

It is important to recognise that Zeuthen's solution to the bargaining problem is the point on the utility increments frontier at which its elasticity equals -1. To show this, write the frontier as

$$u_2 = g(u_1)$$

and notice that the utility (increments) product is maximised when[12]

$$\frac{d}{du_1}(u_1 u_2) = \frac{d}{du_1}[u_1 g(u_1)] = u_1 \frac{du_2}{du_1} + u_2 = 0$$

At this point the frontier's elasticity is

$$\frac{du_2}{du_1} \cdot \frac{u_1}{u_2} = -1 \qquad (6.10)$$

Although a detailed critique of Zeuthen's theory is outside the scope of the present section, it is nevertheless useful to notice that most existing criticisms fall into two groups. First, there are the criticisms that centre on the plausibility of Zeuthen's crucial behavioural assumption that the bargainer with the lower risk willingness is the one to concede.[13] Secondly, there are the criticisms of what Saraydar (1965, p. 805) termed Zeuthen's *full concessions assumption*. According to this assumption, both bargainers' expected utility and risk willingness calculations are based on the expectation of their opponent's total capitulation (i.e. they involve the assignment of zero probabilities to all offers involving less than total concession), yet in Zeuthen's theory these calculations provide the basis for determining the bargainer who is to make a concession that itself is not total but merely of sufficient magnitude to make it the opponent's turn to concede.[14] Since expected utility and maximum risk calculations continue to be made at each round of the collective-bargaining process on the basis of expectations that are limited to the opponent's full concession, even though modified offers have occurred in previous rounds, Saraydar argued that Zeuthen's theory also involves the questionable implicit assumption of 'ineducable bargainers'. To these we can add a third criticism, namely, that neither Zeuthen nor Harsanyi offered any explanation as to how the respective bargainers arrive at their subjective conflict probabilities.

However, despite these criticisms Zeuthen's theory is important, because it explicitly recognises the sequential nature of, and uncertainty inherent in, collective bargaining and because by so doing it is able to yield a unique prediction as to the wage rate that will result from the collective-bargaining process, namely, that wage at which the utility increments product is maximised.[15]

Nash's Theory

The theory of games has been extensively used in the construction of theories of the bargaining process.[16] Basic to the game-theoretic approach is the assumption that each bargainer possesses a von Neumann–Morgenstern utility function,[17] and given these utility functions it is usual to treat the bargaining problem as a non-zero-sum co-operative game.[18] Of special importance in the game-theoretic literature is the determinate theory of the bargaining problem proposed by Nash (1950).

Nash's theory of fixed threat bargaining is axiomatic in nature, consisting of the specification of a set of conditions that the outcome of the bargaining process can be 'reasonably' expected to satisfy and on the basis of which he was able to demonstrate the existence of a unique solution.[19] Nash argued that there are four axioms that a solution of the bargaining problem can be expected to satisfy:[20]

Axiom 1: Pareto optimality. The solution lies on the utility increments frontier.

Axiom 2: Symmetry. If the outcome set is symmetric with respect to the line $u_1 = u_2$, the solution gives equal utility increments to each party, so that the solution does not depend on the labelling of the bargainers.

Axiom 3: Transformation invariance. The solution is invariant with respect to any order preserving linear transformation of either player's utility function; that is, the solution is independent of the units and origins of the utility functions.

Axiom 4: Independence of irrelevant alternatives. If the outcome set of a bargaining game is restricted (i.e. unfavourably altered) in such a way that the threat point remains unaltered and the new set contains the solution point of the original game, this point will also be the solution of the new game.

Nash proved that the only solution that satisfies these four axioms is the one at which the product of the players' utility increments from the threat point is a maximum. Although Nash's proof is set theoretic, it is possible to derive his solution by simple geometry.[21]

Placing the origin at the threat point, let us consider the straight-line utility-increments frontier with slope of -1, shown by AB in Figure 6.5. Axiom 1 requires the solution to lie on AB, and axiom 2 requires it to be on the line $u_1 = u_2$, so that in this case these first two axioms are sufficient to determine a unique solution at N (i.e. the midpoint of the frontier AB) – a solution that yields the respective bargainers the utility pay-offs u_1^* and u_2^*, where $u_1^* = u_2^*$.

Now, any straight line boundary in the utility space, such as AF in Figure 6.5, can be transformed into one with slope of -1 by a suitable adjustment of the units in which one bargainer's utility is measured, with the origin unchanged. According to axiom 3, the solution is invariant with respect to such a transformation; therefore, since the other bargainer's utility scale is unaltered, he must obtain the same utility (u_2^*) from the solution point on the original frontier as from that on the transformed one (AB). Consequently, by projecting the line $u_2^* N$ leftwards, we see that the solution on the original frontier must be at its midpoint (M). Therefore, in all cases where the utility increments frontier is linear, the solution lies at its midpoint, and since the maximum

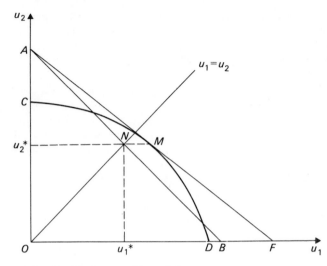

Figure 6.5   Nash's theory of bargaining

area of rectangle that can be inscribed within a right angle triangle bisects its hypotenuse, this solution is immediately recognisable as being the point at which the utility increments product is maximised.

Finally, axiom 4 allows transition to appropriately shaped non-linear frontiers. According to this axiom, any restriction on the outcome set of the bargaining game that leaves the threat point unchanged, and is such that the original solution is a possible outcome of the restricted game, leaves the solution unchanged. For example, if the bargaining game that has the linear frontier AF in Figure 6.5 is restricted in such a way that the curve CMD, which is everywhere concave to the origin, becomes its utility increments frontier, the solution remains unchanged at point M. Therefore, since it is always possible with a concave frontier to find a straight line that is tangential to the frontier such that it is bisected at the point of contact, it follows that Nash's solution is the point on this frontier at which the utility increments product is maximised.

Despite his different approach it is clear that Nash's solution is the same as that predicted by Zeuthen's theory, which, as we have seen, is that point on the utility increments frontier at which its elasticity equals -1. But notice that, by the nature of its argument, Nash's fixed threat formulation has nothing to say about the passage of the bargaining process to settlement.

In a later paper Nash (1953) extended his treatment to the more general case of variable threat bargaining. With the specifications of two additional axioms, Nash provided a solution to the bargainers' problem of selecting optimal threats (showing that these always consist of pure and not mixed threat strategies and that this pair possesses saddle point properties) and demonstrated that, once these have been selected and therefore the threat point determined, the solution is given in exactly the manner of his fixed threat theory as the point where the utility increments product is maximised.

A large number of alternative theories of the bargaining process exist in the literature, and perhaps the best known of these are Hicks' theory and Cartter's (1959) development of Chamberlain's (1951) theory.

Hick's Theory

Hick's theory of collective wage bargaining appeared only shortly after Zeuthen's, being first published in 1932 (see Hicks, 1963, pp. 136–58). Perhaps the most important feature of this theory is its explicit recognition of the role of the strike threat in collective bargaining as a weapon by which pressure can be put upon the employer to pay a higher wage than he would otherwise do. Hicks saw the union's ability to obtain such improvements in wages and other conditions as being derived from the threat of imposing on the employer a cost even greater than that associated with such a settlement and saw this as providing the compulsion towards agreement. The essence of Hicks' theory is that both the employer's tendency to concede and the union's to resist are functions of the *expected* length of the threatened strike.

According to Hicks, the employer chooses between the two alternatives confronting him (namely, pay the higher wage or take the strike) in light of his assessment of the costs involved in each. Accordingly, Hicks constructed the 'employer's concession curve' shown in Figure 6.6, which relates the highest wage that the employer will be willing to pay in order to avoid a strike to the expected length of the threatened strike. At points on this curve, the expected cost of the strike and the expected cost of concession, suitably discounted, are equal, so that at any lower wage demand the employer will prefer to settle and avoid a strike whereas at any higher wage he will prefer a strike to take place.

The intercept of this curve on the vertical axis (OZ) is the wage that the employer would pay in the absence of union pressure, and the curve is assumed to have a positive slope, because the expected cost of the threatened strike is positively related to its expected length and the expected cost of concession is positively related to the wage demanded. Finally, Hicks argued that this curve cannot rise above some upper limit

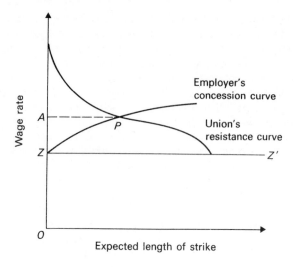

Figure 6.6   Hicks's theory of collective bargaining

imposed by the wage at which the employer will prefer to close down, so that the slope of the employer's curve must eventually become a decreasing function of expected strike length.

Similarly, Hicks constructed the 'union's resistance curve', which shows the minimum wage that the union will accept rather than undergo a strike as a function of the expected length of the strike. Since this curve shows the length of time for which the union members will be willing to stand out rather than allow their wage rate to fall below any particular level, Hicks argued that it will have a negative slope, because the 'temporary privations' (1963, p. 142) that they will be willing to endure to prevent the wage rate falling below a particular level are a decreasing function of the wage level in question. Finally, Hicks pointed out that the resistance curve must cut ZZ' at some finite distance along it, indicating the maximum time for which the union can organise a stoppage, whatever the offered wage, and that it generally intersects the vertical axis, indicating a wage sufficiently high that the union will not seek to go beyond it.

Given that these two functions have opposite slopes, Hicks assumed that there will be a unique point of intersection (P in Figure 6.6) and argued that the wage corresponding to this intersection point 'is the highest wage which skilful negotiation can extract from the employer' (1963, p. 144). If the union demands a wage in excess of OA, the employer will refuse it, because he calculates that a strike designed to achieve this demand will not last long enough to compel him to concede. If the union demands a wage below *OA*, the employer will concede, offering little resistance, but the union will have done badly for its members, since more 'skilful' negotiating could have resulted in a more favourable settlement. Hicks then argued that the union, given only imperfect knowledge of the employer's curve, will prefer to begin bargaining by setting its initial claims high, to be subsequently modified once some indication of the employer's attitude has begun to emerge during bargaining.

Although a detailed critique of Hicks's theory is outside the scope of the present survey, it is important to notice that there exists something of a confusion in the literature as to whether or not Hicks's theory is determinate (i.e. whether it predicts the wage *OA* as the outcome of the bargaining process).[22] The truth of the matter is that Hicks's own exposition seems in effect to embody two versions of his theory. In the first there is the assumption of perfect knowledge, the presence of which 'will always make a settlement possible' (1963, p. 147) – a settlement that Hicks's theory predicts will be at the wage corresponding to the intersection of his curves. Relaxing the assumption of perfect knowledge on the part of the union but not the employer,[23] Hicks presented the indeterminate version of his theory, in which he conceived of negotiations as the process by which a 'skilful' bargainer extracts information about his opponent's (curve's) position. In discussing this version Hicks considered what happens to his curves during a strike, should one occur, arguing that the union's resistance curve is likely to shift to the left as the strike proceeds and its budget constraint becomes eroded and that the employer's concession curve may also shift in response to alterations in the 'prospects of trade'.[24]

In view of the uncertainties associated with the shape and position of one's opponent's Hicksian curve and the volatility of the curves in the event of a strike occurring, it is advisable to regard Hicks's formulation from the viewpoint of bargaining *ex ante* (Bronfenbrenner, 1971, p. 240) and to interpret Hicks's curves not as the loci of the bargainers' positions but rather as the boundaries of the sets of combinations of wage rates and expected strike lengths that are acceptable to the respective parties (Cross, 1969, p. 33).[25]

The Cartter–Chamberlain Theory

It is frequently argued that the precise outcome of the collective-bargaining process within the range of indeterminacy depends on the *bargaining power* of the union relative to that of the employer. Chamberlain provided an explicit definition of the bargaining power of a bargainer (say A) as 'the cost to B of disagreeing on A's terms relative to the cost of agreeing on A's terms' (1951, pp. 220–1). In his reformulation of Chamberlain's analysis, Cartter (1959, p. 117), however, preferred to interpret the above definition in terms of B's *bargaining attitude* rather than A's bargaining power. Thus, according to these definitions we have:

Union's bargaining power (or employer's bargaining attitude) $= \dfrac{\text{Cost to employer of disagreeing with union's terms}}{\text{Cost to employer of agreeing with union}}$

Employer's bargaining power (or union's bargaining attitude) $= \dfrac{\text{Cost to union of disagreeing with employer's terms}}{\text{Cost to union of agreeing with employer}}$

For each party the cost of disagreeing with its opponent's current offer at any stage of the bargaining process is the income loss that would arise from the work stoppage that would follow the opponent's implementation of his fixed threat. Within this framework the costs of disagreement to the union and the employer are respectively the wage income and profits foregone during a strike or lock-out. It is important to notice that neither the employer's profit loss nor the workers' wage income loss during a work stoppage is likely to correspond exactly to the value of lost production and wage payments respectively. As a number of writers have pointed out, an employer's foregone profits during a strike will diverge from lost production for a number of reasons, including savings in variable cost expenditures, sales from stocks while the stoppage is in progress and the possibility of recouping sales once a settlement has been reached. Similarly, from the workers' viewpoint receipts of a variety of benefits results in a divergence between foregone wages (net of tax and other deductions) and actual income foregone. Examples of such receipts are union strike pay, earnings from temporary alternative employment during the stoppage, and entitlements to state social security and other benefits, particularly tax rebates (Durcan and McCarthy, 1974; Hunter, 1974; but see also Gennard, 1977).

To each party the cost of agreeing to its opponent's current offer at any stage of the collective-bargaining process is the difference between the present values of its future income flows on its own and its opponent's current terms. The union's cost of agreement is therefore the difference between the wage income flows, suitably discounted, that would arise from agreement on its own and the employer's current terms, and similarly, the employer's agreement cost is the difference between the present values of the profit flows that would arise on the basis of the wage that it is currently offering and the wage that the union is currently demanding.

It is important to notice that, given the absence of perfect knowledge, each party's assessment of its own and its opponent's bargaining power must be based, at least implicitly, on some estimates of the relevant cost components. Each party's estimate of agreement costs will be influenced by the length of time for which it expects agreement, once reached, to last (i.e. the *contract duration*), while each bargainer's calculations of disagreement costs will be based on its expectations regarding both the disagreement costs per unit of time and the likely length of stoppage necessary to make its opponent accept its own terms (Cartter, 1959, pp. 117–20).

According to this theory, each bargainer evaluates its bargaining attitude at each stage of negotiations as the ratio of the cost of disagreeing with its opponent's current offer by holding out for its own, to the cost of agreeing by immediate acceptance of this offer. The attitude ratio of each party will undergo change as negotiations proceed, according to each party's demands, and the bargainers are assumed to be cost-minimisers, which each therefore will accept the current offer when its attitude ratio is greater than, or equal to, unity and otherwise reject it in favour of continued pursuit of its own objective. In cases where both bargainers' ratios are less than unity, a strike will occur. Within this framework collective wage bargaining is seen as the process in which each party adopts tactics designed to raise its opponent's ratio to unity or above, while simultaneously adopting tactics of a defensive nature that are designed to keep its own ratio less than unity.[26] This process continues, through a strike should one occur, until the point where the ratio of one or both parties rises to unity and an agreement is reached.

Some Comments

It is important to notice the similarity between the solutions predicted by the various theories of the collective-bargaining process reviewed above. Despite the considerable differences in the reasoning and hypotheses underlying the Nash and Zeuthen theories, we have seen that they both predict that the outcome of the collective-bargaining process will be such that the utility increments product is maximised. In addition, it has been shown (Cross, 1969, pp. 29–31, but see Sapsford, 1979, p. 33) that, if one looks beyond the interplay of the two ratios in the Cartter–Chamberlain formulation, this model too predicts the Nash–Zeuthen solution, and indeed it can also be shown that Hicks's theory, with its still different underlying reasoning, converges in the limit on the Nash–Zeuthen solution (Crossley, 1973, p. 216).

While there is a danger of imputing too much significance to this result by overestimating the importance of what Pen called 'an affinity of form' (1959, p. xii), it should also be noted that the majority of the large number of theories of the bargaining process that exist in the literature in addition to those considered above can also be shown to predict outcomes that are always identical, or identical in special cases, to the Nash solution (see de Menil, 1971, p. 15, and Sapsford, 1979, pp. 36–9). This solution equivalence result has elevated the Nash solution (i.e. the maximisation of the utility increments product) to a position of special importance in the theoretical literature, and although there is further theoretical work still to be done in this area, it is relevant to notice that formal models of the bargaining process have made some significant contributions in a number of areas, including the study of money wage movements (de Menil, 1971; see Chapter 7).[27]

UNIONS AND RELATIVE WAGES

A question that has attracted particular research interest over recent years is the extent to which trade unions are able to raise the wages of their members relative to those of comparable non-union workers. In estimating the impact of unions on wages, one would ideally like observations on what the earnings of a union member would be in the absence of unionisation, but since this is clearly not possible, it is necessary to compare the wages of union and non-union workers who are as much alike as possible. Notice, however, that, in cases where the union affects the wage paid to non-union labour, the impact of unions on the wages of union relative to non-union labour will differ from their impact on union wages relative to those prevailing in the absence of unions altogether. There are two ways in which unions can influence the non-union wage and cause it to diverge from the wage that would prevail in the absence of all unions. First, there is the *threat effect*, which raises the non-union wage, as non-union employers raise the wages of their employees in order the reduce the probability of their becoming unionised (Rosen, 1969). Secondly, there is what can be called a *displacement effect*, according to which the non-union wage may fall if, in response to the higher wage paid in the union sector, less union labour is demanded and if those losing their jobs in the unionised sector seek employment in the non-union sector, thereby increasing the supply of non-union labour and depressing the non-union wage.

Theoretical Framework
The methodology for estimating the influence of unions on relative wages was developed by Lewis (1963), and following his analysis we

may express the observed average wage in industry or occupation i (W_i) as a geometric weighted average of the wage rates prevailing in the unionised and non-unionised sectors of this market (denoted by W_i^u and W_i^n respectively.) Thus, we have

$$\ln W_i = U_i \ln W_i^u + (1 - U_i) \ln W_i^n$$

where U_i denotes the proportion of the labour force in i that is unionised. Rearranging this expression, we obtain[28]

$$\ln W_i = \ln W_i^n + U_i \ln (1 + r_i) \qquad (6.11)$$

where

$$r_i = \frac{W_i^u - W_i^n}{W_i^n}$$

measures the relative wage effect of trade unions or the *union/non-union differential*.

Equation (6.11) is the basic equation employed in estimating the size of the union/non-union differential from cross-section data by industry or occupational groups, but in some studies estimates are made from a sample of individual workers, in which case the subscript i stands for the ith individual and U_i takes the value 1 if the individual is a union member and zero otherwise.

Expression (6.11) is an identity that must hold by construction, and if W_i^n as well as W_i and U_i were directly observable, it would be a matter of simple algebra to calculate the union/non-union differential. However, although we can generally observe W_i and U_i from published sources, W_i^n is not directly observable, and so it is necessary when estimating the union/non-union differential to replace the non-union wage term in (6.11) by a vector of variables that are hypothesised as determining it. Let X_i denote a vector of the observable determinants of the non-union wage. Then, writing

$$\ln W_i^n = f(X_i) + e_i'$$

and letting

$$\ln (1 + r_i) = \ln (1 + r) + e_i'',$$

where r is the mean union/non-union differential[29] and e_i' and e_i'' are stochastic disturbance terms (see Haines, 1978, pp. 19–22), equation (6.11) can be written as

$$\ln W_i = f(X_i) + \beta U_i + e_i$$

where

$$e_i = e'_i + e''_i$$

$$\beta = \ln (1 + r)$$

Given observations on W_i, X_i and U_i, estimates of the magnitude of the union/non-union differential can be obtained by applying standard regression methods to this form of expression (Pencavel, 1974, Mulvey, 1976). However, it is important to notice that various statistical problems do arise when estimating the union/non-union differential in this way, and these are discussed in depth in Lewis (1963) and at a more elementary level in Pencavel (1974) and Metcalf (1977). Notice that particular problems arise if union wage levels and membership are simultaneously determined (see Reder, 1965, and Johnson, 1975).

Determinants of the Non-Union Wage
So far we have distinguished between the wages paid to union and non-union workers and noted that the latter can deviate from the wage rate that would prevail in the industry or occupation or for the individual in question in the absence of all unions because of the threat and displacement effects. Consider first the wages that would prevail in the absence of unions throughout the economy. The theory of wage differentials (which is examined in Chapter 9) predicts a number of economic variables as influencing the structure of wages between industries, occupations and individuals, and when estimating the relative wage effects of trade unions researchers have typically included these variables as components of the so called *adjustment vector*, which is specified to incorporate all other variables besides unionism that influence wages. The precise specification of the set of independent variables included in the vector varies from study to study and according to whether industry, occupational or individual data are being analysed. (For a tabular survey of the explanatory variables employed in some recent UK studies, see Metcalf, 1977, p. 160.) However, these typically include such variables as a measure of skill mix (on the grounds that the interindustry structure of wages will vary with the occupational composition of the industry's labour force), a measure of industrial concentration (on the grounds that monopolies tend, other things being equal, to pay their workers more than competitors do), sex and age mix variables (on the grounds that average wages will tend to be lower the higher is the proportion of women and young workers, because these workers tend, *ceteris paribus*, to be paid

less than males and older workers), educational variables (on the grounds that an individual's earnings tends to rise with the level of his/ her educational achievement), and so on. These factors are considered in more detail in Chapter 9 in the context of wage differentials.

Having specified the variables hypothesised as determining the wage rates that would prevail in the complete absence of unions, it is necessary when estimating the size of the union/non-union differential to allow for differences between these and the wages actually paid to non-union members. Different writers have approached this question in different ways. Pencavel (1974, pp. 195–6) treated the movements in the difference between the wage paid to non-unionists and the wage that would prevail in the complete absence of unions as part of the variations in the disturbance term of his regression equation, whereas Metcalf (1977, p. 173) and Nickell (1977, p. 195) specified this discrepancy as depending only on the extent of unionism within the industry or occupation in question. An alternative approach is to use, when available, data that relate not to union membership but rather to *union coverage* (i.e. to the numbers of workers, both union members and non-union members, who are covered by collective agreements and thus paid the union rate). The use of coverage rather than membership data is preferable, because these data directly measure the proportion of workers (both members and non members) in receipt of the union wage in the industry or occupation in question, and in order to obtain some indication of the extent of the divergence between these two series it should be noted that it has been estimated that in 1973 at least one-quarter of the manual workforce in UK manufacturing was paid at the union rate despite not being union members (Metcalf, 1977, p. 159). In the UK, data on the coverage of collective agreements recently became available from the Department of Employment's New Earnings Survey of 1973, and a number of writers, including Mulvey (1976), have used these data to estimate the size of the differential between union and non-union wages.

Estimates of the union/non-union differential
The earliest estimates of the impact of trade unions on relative wages were made in the USA between 1950 and 1960, and these studies were reviewed in considerable depth by Lewis (1963), whose conclusion that unions had raised the average wage rate of union workers by 10–15 per cent above that of their non-union counterparts has served as a benchmark for further study. Some of these early studies provided estimates of the union relative-wage effect for particular industries and occupations, while others provided economy-wide estimates. Although the precise estimates obtained from these studies varied quite considerably

between studies, the general order of magnitude of union relative-wage effects for particular industries and occupations in the USA during the interwar period that emerged was something under 25 per cent, while economy-wide estimates placed the union/non-union differential in the USA during the immediate postwar years in the range 4–25 per cent (Mulvey, 1978, pp. 108–9). Lewis provided his own estimates of the impact of unions on relative wages in the USA between 1920 and 1958, and these implied a union/non-union differential that varied considerably over time in response to the level of economic activity, ranging from 2 per cent in the period between 1945 and 1949 to 46 per cent between 1930 and 1934. We return to the relationship between the size of the union/non-union differential and the level of economic activity below. Economy-wide studies subsequent to Lewis's work estimated the US differential for the early 1960s as around 30 per cent (Throop, 1968; Rosen, 1969), while later studies based on individual data provided somewhat lower estimates. Weiss (1966), for example, estimated the 1960 US differential as 20 per cent, while Stafford (1968) provided estimates of the US differential in 1966 that showed an inverse relation between skill level and the differential and placed the differential in the range 24–52 per cent.

The first study of the impact of unions on relative wages in the UK was due to Pencavel (1974), who analysed data covering twenty-nine industries in 1964. Using union membership data, Pencavel estimated that for manual workers unions raised the hourly earnings of their members relative to those received by non-members by amounts ranging from zero (in industries that did not engage in a significant degree of bargaining at the plant level) to 14 per cent (in industries that did engage in a significant degree of plant bargaining). More recently, data on the coverage of collective agreements in Britain has become available from the 1973 New Earnings Survey, and a number of estimates of the union/non-union differential have been made using these data. These recent British studies have analysed samples that variously included male, female, manual and non-manual labour, and with few exceptions their results suggest that the 1973 differential was in the range 16–26 per cent. (For summaries, see Metcalf, 1977, pp. 159–62, and Mulvey, 1978, p. 112.)

A finding of particular importance that emerged from the US work of Lewis (1963) and others was the existence of a significant inverse relationship between the size of the union/non-union differential and the level of economic activity as this affects the state of the labour market. Lewis interpreted this result as giving support to what he termed the Rees–Friedman *wage rigidity hypothesis*, according to which non-union wages are relatively more sensitive to changes in demand conditions than are union wages. This effect is suggested as arising because, while trade unions are able to prevent union wages from falling during periods of depressed product and labour-demand conditions (giving rise to a high differential during depressed periods), they actually prevent wages from rising during upswings as rapidly as they would otherwise do (thus giving rise to a low differential during boom periods). This wage rigidity effect is seen as arising because of the rigidities and lags that are introduced into the wage adjustment process by the existence of collective bargaining. Thus, since collective agreements typically last for a year or more, unionised workers may be at a disadvantage during periods of rapid cyclical upswing and inflation, as non-union employers who are not 'locked in' to collective agreements may raise wages more frequently than union employers, and as union employers making agreements during such periods become reluctant to make unusually large wage increases in case the period of buoyant demand turns out to be only short lived. In a recent study Demery and McNabb (1978) re-estimated Pencavel's (1974) model and introduced into this the role of demand factors in order to measure the impact of non-zero excess demand on the effects of unions on relative wages in the UK. By so doing they found evidence to suggest the presence of a wage rigidity effect of the above sort in UK industries characterised by widespread plant bargaining.

UNIONS AND RESOURCE ALLOCATION

The extent to which unions, via their influence on relative wages, affect the allocation of resources within the economy is a question of some importance. This problem was considered by Rees (1963), whose analysis is discussed below, but more recently it was approached at a more advanced level by Johnson and Mieszkowski (1970) within a general equilibrium framework.

Rees considered an economy with a perfectly inelastic supply of homogeneous labour and assumed that the economy is divided into two sectors, say N and U, both of which are initially non-unionised. This situation is shown in Figure 6.7, where S is the supply curve of homogeneous labour, D_u and D_n are the labour demand curves in sectors U and N respectively and D_t is the total demand for labour, obtained by horizontal summation of D_u and D_n. In the initial situation there is no unionisation, and it is assumed that the wage in both sectors is set competitively at W_c. At this wage, employment in sector U is E_0 and in sector N it is N_0, giving total employment of $(E_0 + N_0)$.

Assume now that the union enters the stage and organises sector U. If the union, through collective bargaining, succeeds in raising the wage

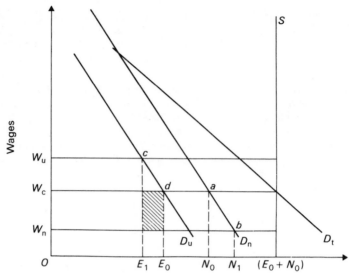

Figure 6.7   The effects of union wage differentials on resource allocation

in its sector to W_u, employment in this sector declines from E_0 to E_1 as employers and consumers substitute against union labour and union-made products. On the assumption that the workers who have lost their jobs in sector U prefer to work in sector N at the non-union wage in preference to remaining unemployed, the supply of labour to the non-union sector is increased by the amount $(E_0 - E_1)$ to, say, N_1. This displacement of workers from the unionised to the non-unionised sector increases employment in N from N_0 to N_1 and depresses the non-union wage (which is still competitively determined) from W_c to W_n.

A welfare or output loss arises from this displacement of workers from the union to the non-union sector, because workers are now being employed where their marginal productivity is lower than before. Since the labour demand curve for each sector is its marginal revenue product (*MRP*) schedule, the area below each curve up to the employment level in question measures the total product or output of the sector. In order to measure the decrease in the total output of the economy that arises because the union wage is raised above the competitive level, it is necessary to measure the difference between the area under D_u from E_0 to E_1 and the area under D_n from N_0 to N_1. In the non-union sector output increases by the amount aN_0N_1b, and in the union sector output decreases by cE_1E_0d. The difference between these areas (i.e. the output loss due to the union wage increase) is the area of the shaded rectangle between E_0 and E_1, and in the particular case where the demand schedules are parallel, it is easy to show by elementary geometry that

$$\text{Output loss} = \tfrac{1}{2}(W_n - W_u)(E_0 - E_1)$$

or one-half of the absolute union/non-union wage differential times the difference in employment.

On the basis of Lewis's (1963a) estimate of the size of the elasticity of union relative to non-union employment with respect to the union/non-union wage differential of approximately -1, Rees (1963) made a rough estimate of the size of the welfare loss caused by the effects of unions on earnings and employment in the USA in 1957 as being approximately 0.14 per cent of gross national product. Although the findings of more recent studies suggest that Lewis's estimates of the effects of unions on relative wages may be on the low side, Rees's analysis does suggest that the losses caused by the misallocative effects of unions are very small indeed — a general conclusion that is supported by the findings of the Johnson and Mieszkowski (1970) study. Notice, however, that Rees's analysis takes as its initial situation the case of a perfectly competitive labour maket. If instead, as may well occur in practice, the initial situation is one characterised by monopsonistic imperfections, the analysis may overstate the output losses due to unionisation, which may even prove to be negative in such circumstances, in the sense that unionisation may result in a structure of relative wages that conforms more closely than the initial situation to those which would be found in a competitive market (King, 1972, p. 48).

NOTES ON FURTHER READING

The economic analysis of the collective-bargaining process was considered in some depth by Coddington (1968) and Cross (1969) and surveyed by Sapsford (1979). A thorough survey of the theoretical and econometric issues involved in the estimation of the relative wage effect of trade unions, together with an extensive survey of early US empirical work, is to be found in Lewis (1963), and Metcalf (1977) provided a useful survey of recent UK studies. The standard analysis of the effects of unions on resource allocation, discussed in the text, is due to Rees (1963), but a more complete and theoretically advanced approach to the effects of unionisation on income distribution, which is suitable for those with a knowledge of general equilibrium analysis, was developed by Johnson and Mieszkowski (1970).

Part Three

FURTHER TOPICS

Chapter 7

Wage Inflation

In this chapter we consider the forces that determine the rate of increase of the general level of money wages or *wage inflation*. Throughout the chapter emphasis is placed on explaining wage inflation in the UK, but in a number of places reference is made to relevant research findings from other countries and to the relationships between wage and price inflation.

THE FACTS TO BE EXPLAINED

Figure 7.1 shows movements in the annual proportional rate of wage inflation ($\dot{w}$) in the UK between 1948 and 1978. Wage inflation, like price inflation, reached a peak during the Korean War period, and between 1952 and 1960 there was a slight downward trend in the rate of wage inflation; this gave way to a slight upward trend, which continued until about 1969. After this date the rate of wage inflation rose from 9.9 per cent in 1970 to just under 14 per cent in 1972, and after remaining at about this level during 1973 it rose rapidly to reach its peak of 29.5 per cent in 1975. After 1975 the rate of wage inflation fell sharply to 6.5 per cent in 1977, but at the time of writing in 1979 there were signs of its increasing again, as it had risen to 14 per cent in 1978.

THE PHILLIPS CURVE

In 1958 Phillips published a paper that quickly became a focal point in the study of wage inflation. The principal finding of Phillips's study was the existence of a stable inverse and non-linear relationship between the annual proportional rate of change of money wage rates ($\dot{w}$) and the unemployment rate (u) in the UK between 1861 and 1957.[1] Figure 7.1 shows the fluctuations in the unemployment rate that occurred between 1948 and 1978, and the inverse relation between $\dot{w}$ and u can be seen during the period up to 1967. However, after 1967 the previous inverse relationship was severely disrupted – a point that we return to below. This inverse relationship between the rate of wage inflation and

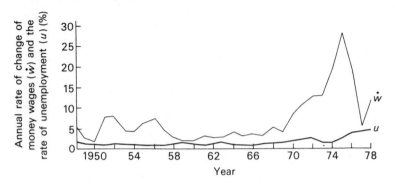

Figure 7.1   UK wage inflation, 1948–78

Notes:
(1) Percentage changes in wages per year ($\dot{w}$) were constructed using data of basic weekly wage rates of manual workers in all industries and services (31 July 1972 = 100) as

$$\dot{w}_t = \frac{w_t - w_{t-1}}{w_{t-1}} \, 100$$

(2) Unemployment rates (u) show the numbers unemployed expressed as a percentage of the appropriate midyear estimate of total employees (i.e. employed plus unemployed).
Sources:
(1) *Economic Trends: Annual Supplement* (London: HMSO, 1979).
(2) *The British Economy: Key Statistics, 1900–1970* (London: Times Newspapers), and *Economic Trends: Annual Supplement* (London: HMSO, 1979).

the rate of unemployment became known as the *Phillips curve*, and this is shown in Figure 7.2.[2]

Phillips's basic argument was demand pull in nature. It was that excess demand in the labour market is the triggering force of wage inflation and the factor that determines its speed. Phillips argued that the extent of excess demand in the labour market can be proxied by the percentage of the labour force that is unemployed, and he interpreted his findings as supporting the hypothesis that excess demand pressure in the labour market determines the rate of wage inflation. The argument underlying the hypothesised relation between excess labour demand and wage inflation is derived from a straightforward application of traditional price theory to the perfectly competitive labour market.

Consider the competitive labour market shown in Figure 7.3. The equilibrium wage or price of labour is w_e, given by the point where the labour demand and supply curves intersect. At wages above w_e there is an excess of labour supply over demand, while for wages below w_e

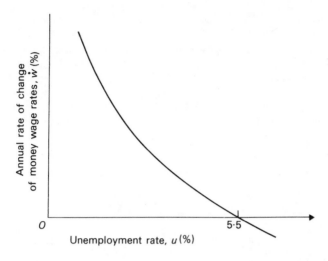

Figure 7.2 The Phillips curve

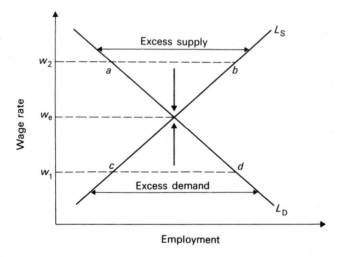

Figure 7.3 Wage adjustment and the labour market

there is an excess demand for labour. If the wage is below equilibrium at, say, w_1 (because this was an equilibrium wage in the previous period perhaps), there will be excess demand for labour equal to cd, and there will be a tendency for wages to rise from this disequilibrium level towards the equilibrium wage w_e, as employers bid up money wages in order to attract relatively scarce labour. In addition, it is usual to assume that the speed with which the wage rate converges on the equilibrium value is greater the larger is the excess demand for labour. Conversely, at wages above equilibrium there will be an excess supply of labour (equal, for example, to *ab* at wage w_2) and a resulting tendency for wages to fall towards equilibrium, with the speed of adjustment towards equilibrium being greater the larger is the excess of labour supply over demand.

LIPSEY'S THEORY OF THE PHILLIPS CURVE

While the existence of an inverse relationship between inflation and unemployment was not a new discovery, with Fisher (1926) apparently being the first to investigate such a relation, Phillips's findings quickly attracted considerable interest. In a further analysis Lipsey (1960) sought to provide a sound theoretical basis for the statistical relation observed by Phillips. Lipsey explicitly considered the proxy-taking assumptions of Phillips's analysis and argued that the observed inverse relation between wage inflation and unemployment derived from the two behavioural relations shown in Figure 7.4. These relations refer to a single micro labour market. The first illustrates a positive relation between the rate of money wage change and the magnitude of excess

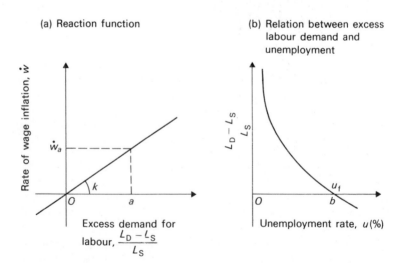

Figure 7.4 Lipsey's theory of the Phillips curve

demand for labour, and the second illustrates an inverse non-linear relation between excess labour demand and unemployment.

Lipsey assumed that the rate at which the wage level rises during any period is positively related to the proportionate excess demand for labour, that is, the greater is the proportionate excess demand for labour the more rapid is the adjustment towards the equilibrium wage level. Denoting the quantities of labour demanded and supplied by L_D and L_S respectively, we can write this relation or *reaction function* as

$$\dot{w} = f\left(\frac{L_D - L_S}{L_S}\right)$$

where $f' > 0$, or, adopting Lipsey's assumption of linearity,

$$\dot{w} = k\left(\frac{L_D - L_S}{L_S}\right)$$

where k is some positive constant. This reaction function is shown in Figure 7.4(a) by the straight line with slope k passing through the origin. At the origin excess demand is zero and the money wage is at its equilibrium level (w_e in Figure 7.3), so that $\dot{w} = 0$. To the right of the origin there is positive excess demand for labour (i.e. the wage is below its equilibrium level of w_e), so that money wages are rising, while to the left of the origin there is a negative excess demand (or an excess supply) of labour, with the consequence that money wages are falling. For example, if the level of excess demand were a, wages would increase at the rate $\dot{w}_a (= ka)$.

Because the excess demand for labour is not directly observable, it is necessary to select an appropriate proxy variable for purposes of testing the wage inflation–excess demand hypothesis. With this objective in mind, Lipsey examined the relation between the excess demand for labour and the unemployment rate and assumed that this will be negative and non-linear, as shown in Figure 7.4(b). The negative slope of this relationship reflects the assumption that the higher is the level of excess demand for labour the lower is the level of unemployment. When excess demand for labour is zero, the labour market is in equilibrium (at wage w_e in Figure 7.3), but we cannot infer from this the absence of unemployment; rather, we can infer that the number of job vacancies equals the number of job-seekers. In a given labour market the demand for labour comprises the sum of two components: the number of workers employed (say E) and the number of vacancies that employers are unable to fill (denoted by V), while the supply of labour is likewise given by the sum of the numbers of workers actually in employment and the numbers searching for employment (i.e. the unemployed, denoted by U). The labour market will be in equilibrium when the demand for labour (L_D) equals the supply of labour (L_S), i.e. when

$$L_D = E + V = L_S = E + U$$

or when

$$V = U$$

The unemployed compatible with zero excess demand (i.e. with equilibrium in the individual labour market) is termed *frictional unemployment*, and this is shown by rate u_f in Figure 7.4(b). As we see in the following chapter, frictional unemployment arises because the process of matching unfilled vacancies with unemployed workers is not instantaneous.

Lipsey argued that the unemployment–excess demand relation will be negatively sloped to the left of point b, because an increase in excess demand means that jobs will become easy to find and that less time will be taken in moving between jobs, and so it will reduce u, provided that there is not a completely offsetting increase in the number of persons moving between jobs.[3] Lipsey argued that this relation will be non-linear to the left of point b, because, while positive excess demand for labour will decrease the unemployment rate below the frictional level (u_f), it can never fall below zero however high is the level of excess demand. Consequently, he assumed that, as excess labour demand increases, u approaches zero, or some small positive value, asymptotically.

Combining the two relations shown in Figure 7.4, Lipsey obtained a Phillips curve of the form shown in Figure 7.2 for a representative individual micro labour market.[4] The aggregate Phillips curve is derived by aggregation of the individual curves, and Lipsey showed that the dispersion of aggregate unemployment between the individual micro labour markets determines the position of the aggregate Phillips curve. (For discussion of Lipsey's aggregation procedure, see Peston, 1971, pp. 128–9, and Trevithick and Mulvey, 1975, pp. 47–50.)

Some Subsequent Developments

The publication of Phillips's original paper and Lipsey's subsequent analysis stimulated a great deal of research activity, and very soon a large number of studies appeared in which Phillips-type curves were fitted to data relating to other countries, time periods and levels of aggregation. In the extensive literature that has resulted from this activity, Phillips's original relationship has been modified in a number

of ways. Its functional form has been simplified, variables have been
added to the original specification for a number of purposes (including
the representation of inflationary expectations), more adequate proxies
for excess demand for labour have been sought, and additional
equations have been specified to make it part of a simultaneous
equation system explaining price as well as wage inflation. Although a
number of aspects of the Phillips curve literature are considered below,
a detailed survey is beyond the scope of the current chapter. A number
of comprehensive surveys are, however, available elsewhere. See, in
particular, Burton (1972), Goldstein (1972), Gordon (1975), Frisch
(1977), Santomero and Seator (1978) and, at a more elementary level,
Marin (1972).

COST PUSH OR DEMAND PULL?

The demand-pull/cost-push distinction is a well-known one in the
analysis of inflation. The *demand pull* school sees inflation as being
initially triggered by the emergence of excess demand in the product
market at the ruling price level. This results in an increase in the general
level of product prices, which subsequently leads to an increase in the
conditions of derived demand for labour (i.e. to a rightward shift in the
labour demand or marginal-revenue-product curve). This shift gives rise
to excess demand for labour at the prevailing wage rate, with the result
that money wages tend to increase. In short, the demand pull school
sees inflation as arising initially from forces operating on the demand
side of the product market, with feedback effects on the labour market.
Notice that the initial excess demand in the goods market can arise in
either the *Keynesian* inflationary-gap manner or in *monetarist* manner
from too few goods being chased by too much money.

In contrast, the *cost push* school sees the reverse causal chain, with
the initial inflationary push or 'shock' emanating from the supply side
in the form of increased import prices, greater profit margins or higher
wage costs, forced up by monopolistic trade unions. These increased
costs, given the assumption of mark-up pricing, subsequently feed into
the general level of prices, as producers pass them on in the form of
higher product prices. Particular attention is most frequently placed on
so called *wage-push inflation*, where, in its most extreme form, unions
are assumed to be able to push up money wages irrespective of the level
of excess demand in the labour market. Less extreme is the so called
bargaining-power approach (Burton, 1972, pp. 18–20), which sees a
union's ability to influence money wages as being influenced by various
economic conditions, such as the pressure of excess demand in the
labour market. (See, for example, Eckstein and Wilson, 1962.) While

this form of cost push theory, like the demand pull model, predicts that the pace of wage inflation will be positively related to the pressure of excess demand in the labour market, it offers very different explanations of the underlying mechanisms involved. The bargaining power approach sees wages as being determined as the outcome of a collective-bargaining process of the sort considered in Chapter 6, whereas the demand pull formulation sees wages as being determined by supply and demand adjustments in a competitive labour market.[5]

Phillips interpreted his findings as providing strong support for the demand pull hypothesis, and it is true that the existence of a significant inverse relation between wage inflation and unemployment appears to refute the cost push hypothesis in its extreme form where the role of excess labour demand is ignored. However, as Lipsey (1960) pointed out, the existence of a Phillips curve is perfectly consistent with the less extreme bargaining-power type of cost push theory, according to which the wage rate is determined by a process of collective bargaining, the outcome of which is influenced by the pressure of excess labour demand.

POLICY IMPLICATIONS FOR WAGE AND PRICE INFLATION

The discovery of the Phillips curve attracted considerable interest from the policy viewpoint, primarily because of the implications of the relationship for price inflation. The existence of a significant inverse relation between the rate of wage inflation and the unemployment rate appeared to present policy-makers with a *trade-off* (i.e. less wage inflation at the cost of higher unemployment, or lower unemployment but only at the cost of higher wage inflation). Given the linkage between fluctuations in wages and fluctuations in the prices of goods and services (look again at Figure 1.2), the existence of the Phillips relation appeared to provide policy-makers with a similar trade-off (or 'menu' of policy choices) between price inflation on the one hand and unemployment on the other.

In order to consider the implications of the Phillips curve for policy decisions regarding the rate of price inflation, it is necessary to make certain assumptions regarding the influence of wages upon prices. The simplest assumptions to make are: first, that average productivity (or output per man-hour) is growing at a constant proportional rate; and second, that prices are set by firms applying a constant mark-up on unit labour costs. On the basis of these two assumptions, the rate of price inflation (say $\dot{p}$) equals the difference between the rates of growth of money wages ($\dot{w}$) and labour productivity (say $\dot{q}$).[6] For each value of the unemployment rate, we can therefore calculate the rate of price inflation ($\dot{p}$) by merely subtracting the rate of productivity growth ($\dot{q}$) from the rate of wage inflation ($\dot{w}$) given by the Phillips curve. Diagrammatically, we transform the Phillips curve to show the relation between the rate of price inflation and unemployment by merely displacing downwards the original Phillips curve by a vertical distance equivalent to the (assumed) constant rate of productivity growth. In Figure 7.5 curve *WW* denotes the Phillips trade-off between wage

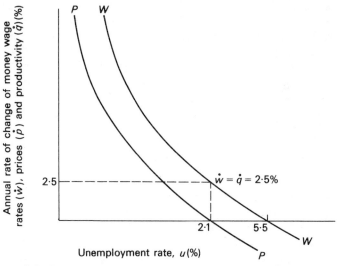

Figure 7.5 Wage and price inflation

inflation and unemployment, and the curve *PP* shows the relation between the rate of price inflation and the unemployment rate, on the assumption that labour productivity is growing at a rate of 2.5 per cent per year.[7] Phillips's own estimates implied that a zero rate of wage inflation was consistent with an unemployment rate of just under 5.5 per cent (see Figure 7.2), and with productivity rising at 2.5 per cent per year these estimates implied that a zero rate of price inflation was attainable with an unemployment rate of 2.1 per cent.

As can be seen from Figure 7.5, a productivity growth rate ($\dot{q}$) of 2.5 per cent per year allows wages to rise at the same rate with prices remaining stable. Curve *PP* shows that a reduction in the rate of unemployment below 2.1 per cent can only be achieved by sacrificing price stability, while a decreasing price level can only be achieved at the cost of an increase in unemployment rate above 2.1 per cent. Curve *PP* shows combinations of u and $\dot{p}$ that can be attained by varying the level of aggregate demand and can be thought of as a constraint facing government policy-makers. While combinations of price inflation and unemployment lying on curve *PP* are attainable, those represented by points lying below the curve (signifying lower rates of both unemployment and inflation) are not.

The problems faced by policy-makers in selecting the optimum inflation–unemployment combination can be analysed with the aid of the techniques of indifference curve analysis. Consider the case where the policy-maker is prepared to trade some increase in the rate of inflation in return for a reduction in the unemployment rate, and assume that he possesses a preference function that gives rise to a set of indifference curves that are ordered in such a way that higher utility is attained by moving towards the origin. Since both inflation and unemployment are 'bads' (i.e. undesirable), it is usual to assume these indifference curves to be concave to the origin, as shown in Figure 7.6.

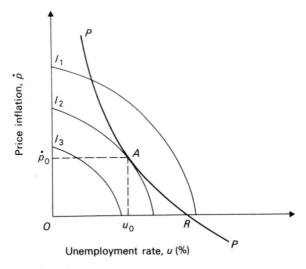

Figure 7.6 Inflation–unemployment trade-off

Assuming that policy-makers are utility-maximisers, they will select the inflation–unemployment combination represented by point *A* in Figure 7.6, since at that point the trade-off curve *PP* is tangential to an indifference curve. *A* denotes the policy-makers' optimum inflation–unemployment combination and indicates the point at which aggregate demand policies will be aimed. If the initial position on *PP* were, say, point R, the reduction in the unemployment rate below R to its optimal level u_o is achieved at the cost of an inflation rate of $\dot{p}_o$ – a cost that is acceptable to the policy-makers, given their preference function.[8]

TRADE UNIONS AND WAGE INFLATION

Hines's theory

As already noted, the existence of a Phillips curve can be interpreted either as a manifestation of the workings of competitive markets or as representing the operation of a wage-bargaining process, the outcome of which is not independent of the level of excess demand in the labour market. In a series of papers, Hines (1964, 1968, 1969, 1971) produced evidence that appeared to suggest that trade unions had pushed up money wages independently of excess demand for labour. In putting forward this theory of wage push via union strength, Hines argued that earlier writers had either dismissed the possibility that unions may influence the rate of change of money wages independently of excess demand or used unsatisfactory indices to measure the impact of unions. Hines postulated that the rate of wage inflation depends directly on trade union *pushfulness* and that pushfulness itself can be proxied by the rate of change of the percentage of the labour force that is unionised, denoted by $\Delta T_t (= T_t - T_{t-1}$, where T_t denotes the percentage of the labour force unionised in period t). The proxying of union pushfulness by ΔT is justified by the assumption that, when unions are being aggressive (or militant), they simultaneously increase their membership and exert upward pressure on wage rates.

Hines (1964) tested the hypothesis that the rate of change of money wages can be explained by union pushfulness against UK data for various periods since 1893. He found strong statistical support for this, particularly for the years from 1921 onwards, during which period excess demand, as measured by the rate of unemployment, did not appear to exert a significant influence on the rate of change of money wages. In a later disaggregated study Hines (1969) found corroboration for his conclusion that union pushfulness, as measured by ΔT, is more important than the unemployment rate in determining movements in money wages.

Hines's Critics

Hines's analysis has been criticised on a number of fronts, particularly by Purdy and Zis (1974), and was defended with equal ferocity by Dogas and Hines (1975). Hines's proposition that ΔT is an index of the intensity of union activity or militancy, which manifests itself simultaneously in increased union membership and in increased upward pressure on money wage rates, was criticised by Purdy and Zis on the grounds that it is not derived from any formal model of union behaviour, that it pays insufficient attention to the strength of employer resistance to union wage *claims* and that fluctuations in ΔT may occur for reasons unrelated to militancy (such as the reallocation of labour from non-unionised employments to employments covered by existing closed-shop arrangements). In addition, Purdy and Zis argued that Hines selected his data series badly, using an inappropriately defined labour-force series and inconsistent definitions of variables. Re-estimating Hines's model to take account of their various criticisms, Purdy and Zis found that the influence of ΔT on the rate of change of money wages is much reduced but still statistically significant and that, once such corrections have been made, the unemployment rate, as a proxy for the excess demand for labour, reappears as a significant determinant of the rate of wage inflation from the mid 1920s onwards.

Two other problems arise: first, that ΔT may itself be related to the strength of excess demand for labour, and second, that the direction of causation may not run from ΔT to $\dot{w}$, as suggested by Hines, but instead, or in addition, may run from $\dot{w}$ to ΔT. If the first of these possibilities were true, ΔT would be proxying the pressure of excess demand in the labour market and Hines's results would not imply that union pushfulness is an independent force in the determination of the rate of wage inflation; instead, they would imply that unions are only able to push wages up in circumstances when demand conditions are favourable and they would be rising in any case. Hines was aware of this possibility but could find no significant relationship between ΔT and the rate of unemployment, either current or lagged, or other indices of demand pressure – a result that has been treated with suspicion by subsequent writers because of its inconsistency with the findings that have emerged from the literature on the history and determinants of union growth. As we saw in our discussion of the theory of union growth (see above, pp. 86–7), evidence has been produced by Bain and Elsheikh (1976) to suggest that the unemployment rate did exert a significant negative influence on the rate of growth of union membership in the UK between 1893 and 1970.[9]

Turning now to the second possibility, it has been suggested that causality may not run from ΔT to $\dot{w}$ but rather from $\dot{w}$ to ΔT, because the willingness of non-union members to become union members is directly related to the union's apparent success at the bargaining table. For example, workers may mistakenly credit increases in wages to unions rather than to the existence of excess labour demand and may join unions as a reward for services rendered or to ensure that they will receive any future gains that the union may achieve, or perhaps workers join unions during periods of rising wages simply because their wage increases provide them with the financial ability to meet the costs of union membership. Alternatively, there is the possibility that causation may run in both directions, with unions initially pushing up wages according to Hines's hypothesis and additional workers then joining unions, either because they now have the financial resources to meet membership subscriptions or because they now estimate, in view of the union's current success in increasing wages, that the benefits of union membership, in the form of current and expected future improvements in wages and conditions of employment, are sufficient to outweigh membership fees. In view of the possible simultaneity between changes in money wage rates and union membership, some investigators have constructed simultaneous equation models in which wage inflation and union growth are jointly determined. (See, for example, Ashenfelter and Johnson, 1972; Ashenfelter *et al.*, 1972; and Schmidt and Strauss, 1976.)

The Role of Unions: Some Subsequent Developments
The debate over the exact role played by trade unions in the inflationary process continues, with no general consensus yet emerging as to whether unions exert an independent influence on the rate of wage inflation or whether they are merely responding to the demand pressures that are generated in the labour market by forces of demand pull or excess demand in the goods market and doing, at least in part, the work that would in any case be done by these excess demand pressures in the labour market. At least two strands have developed in the recent literature in attempting to shed light on this question. The first consists of a search for a more satisfactory index of union pushfulness than that proposed by Hines, while the second consists of attempts to construct and test theoretical models of the actual process of collective wage bargaining that operates in unionised labour markets.

Alternative Pushfulness Proxies
Several writers (e.g. Godfrey, 1971; Knight, 1972; Taylor, 1972; Godfrey and Taylor, 1973) have used measures of strike activity to proxy union pushfulness, but the use and interpretation of such variables are fraught with almost as many difficulties as Hines's index. Strike activity in the UK, as elsewhere, has been shown to be positively related to the level of economic activity (Pencavel, 1970; Sapsford, 1975) and hence inversely related to unemployment, so that it is possible that strike variables act as a proxy for labour-market

demand pressure. In any case the volume of strike activity is not solely a manifestation of union behaviour, since it depends not only on unions' propensity to push or threaten but also on the interaction that takes place between this and employer resistance (Sapsford, 1978). In addition, there are at least three possible alternative measures of strike activity: the frequency of strikes, the number of workers involved and the number of working days lost, with no single one emerging as the obvious contender for the role of pushfulness proxy. In addition, empirical work has shown the significance of such proxies to be highly erratic and sensitive to the precise measure and definition chosen (Ward and Zis, 1974; Zis, 1977).

Other investigators have inserted profit variables into wage equations to proxy union pushfulness or militancy, on the basis of the assumption that unions become more militant and therefore push more vigorously for higher money wages the higher is the level of profit. While Lipsey and Steuer (1961) found only a weak association between wage changes and profits in their study of UK data at the industry level, both Bhatia (1961) and Perry (1964) found in US studies that profits exert a significant influence on the rate of wage inflation. However, collinearity between profits and demand pressure makes it difficult to interpret this result as definitely showing the effects of pushfulness as opposed to those of excess demand. In addition, there is a difficulty in this sort of model in identifying to what extent an observed relationship between profits and the rate of change of money wages indicates the presence of forces of the union push type and to what extent it indicates an increased willingness and ability on the part of employers to grant wage increases during periods when profits are high (see Kaldor, 1959).

Two Bargaining Models

Dissatisfied with the 'adhocery' associated with the grafting of various bargaining and pushfulness variables on to Phillips-type relations, de Menil (1971) set out to specify and test a model of the wage determination process operating in labour markets characterised by a high degree of organisation on the employers' and employees' sides, and to do this he began with the firmest theoretical foundations currently available, namely, the formal theory of the bargaining process as summarised briefly in the previous chapter.

De Menil's model is basically an application of Nash's (1950) fixed threat theory of bargaining (see above, pp. 112–15) to money wage determination under bilateral monopoly at the level of the firm. As we have seen, Nash's theory of bargaining predicts that the outcome of the bargaining process will be such that the product of the two bargainers' utility increments from the threat point is maximised. On the assumptions that the employer's utility is an increasing function of his profit level and that the union's utility is an increasing function of the difference between the real wage bill and what the real wage bill would be if its members earned non-union wages, de Menil (1971, pp. 21–43) used Nash's theory to derive the equilibrium union wage rate. He showed that this depends on: (1) revenue net of capital costs per unit of labour, (2) the going non-union wage level, and (3) some index of demand pressure in the industry in question. After making an additional assumption about the dynamics of the process by which actual wages adjust towards equilibrium, de Menil derived a testable wage-change equation, which, as he pointed out, can be interpreted as a Phillips style relation to which 'bargaining' variables (derived not from *ad hoc* arguments but from a formal theory of the bargaining process) have been added. He then tested the bargaining wage-change equation thus derived against time series data relating to eight, highly unionised, US industries between 1954 and 1969. The results of this analysis give considerable support to the bargaining wage-change equation and in particular lead to the rejection of the null hypothesis that the bargaining variables add nothing to the explanatory power of a simple industry-level Phillips curve. In view of these results, a replication of de Menil's analysis for the UK would certainly be a worthwhile exercise.

An alternative theory of wage determination in unionised labour markets was proposed by Johnston (1971, 1972a) and subsequently tested against UK data by Johnston and Timbrell (1973). Building on Hieser's (1970) earlier analysis of wage determination under bilateral monopoly, Johnston constructed a model that is probabilistic in character and that explicitly recognises the uncertainties involved in, and the sequential nature of, the process of collective wage bargaining. In this model a distinction is made between the pre- and poststrike stages of the negotiating process, and the costs of agreement and disagreement to each party are considered. After making some assumptions about the way in which the employer generates his estimate of the probability that a given wage offer will result in a strike, Johnston derived the employer's expected cost function. On the assumption that the employer is an expected cost-minimiser, Johnston derived his optimal final prestrike offer and, to be used if this fails, his optimal strike-settling offer and showed that each of these values is in general unique.

In a subsequent empirical analysis of aggregate UK annual data between 1952 and 1971, Johnston and Timbrell (1973) found support for this model and produced evidence to suggest that it provides a more adequate explanation of money wage movements over the sample period than that offered by a conventional Phillips curve.[10] While Johnston's model provides some important insights into the collective-bargaining process, particularly as regards questions of uncertainty, it suffers from a major deficiency, in that it ignores the union's behaviour during bargaining. What Johnston's model provides is not a theory of wage determination under collective bargaining but only a theory of the employer's optimal response to the union's claim, the size and determination of which is left unexplained. Rabinovitch and Swary (1976) noted this deficiency in the Johnston model and extended it to take account of simultaneous optimising behaviour on the part of the union. By so doing, they showed that an essentially symmetrical approach also allows derivation of the union's own optimal prestrike demand.

THE DEMISE OF THE PHILLIPS CURVE?

The relationship that Phillips discovered in 1958 appeared to have remained stable as far back as data went, for nearly a century.[11] However, from about 1967 onwards the UK Phillips curve (and that of other major industrialised countries) has broken down and lost its explanatory power. Contrary to the prediction of the Phillips curve, the UK experience since the late 1960s has generally been one of a high rate of wage inflation accompanied by a high rate of unemployment. As can be seen from Table 7.1, which compares the actual rate of wage inflation in various years during the postwar period with the rates predicted by Phillips's own estimates, there has been a marked tendency from 1967 onwards for the Phillips curve to underpredict the actual percentage change in money wages. Diagrammatically, the post 1967 breakdown of the Phillips curve has taken the form of a rightward shift (or shifts) in the relationship, illustrating that a given level of unemployment appears to have been associated with a higher or rising rate of wage inflation.

There have been a number of attempts to explain this shift in what appeared, prior to 1967, to rank among the stablest of economic relations, and these fall into two main categories: first, those that see it as arising from some shift (or shifts) in one or both of the relations underpinning the Phillips curve (i.e. the reaction function, and the relation between excess demand and unemployment), and second, those that follow from the argument that the Phillips curve is in fact *mis-specified*, because the dependent variable should be the rate of change of real wages and not money (or nominal) wages.

Unemployment as an Index of Excess Demand for Labour
The possibility of the Phillips curve's shifting in response to shifts in

Table 7.1 *Actual and predicted rates of wage inflation in the UK,*[a] *selected years 1950–78 (%).*

Year	Annual rate of wage inflation predicted by Phillips's estimates[b]	Actual rate of wage inflation	Predicted minus actual rate of wage inflation[c]
1950	4.6	1.8	+ 3.2
1955	6.6	6.9	− 0.3
1960	3.7	2.5	+ 1.2
1965	4.6	4.2	+ 0.4
1967	1.8	3.9	− 2.1
1970	1.5	9.9	− 8.4
1973	1.6	13.7	− 12.1
1974	1.8	19.8	− 18.0
1975	0.5	29.5	− 29.0
1978	0.0	14.0	− 14.0

Notes:
(a) This table was constructed by using the wage inflation and unemployment series shown graphically in Figure 7.1.
(b) Phillips's estimated equation is given in note 2, and the predicted rates of wage inflation were obtained by substituting into this the rate of unemployment for the year in question.
(c) The last column shows the discrepancy between the predicted and actual rates of wage inflation, so that a negative sign indicates underprediction and a positive sign overprediction.

the reaction function is considered in a later section in our discussions of the influence of incomes policies. A number of investigators have sought to rescue the UK Phillips curve by arguing that the underlying relationship between the rate of wage inflation and the extent of excess demand in the labour market (i.e. the reaction function) still holds good and that what has happened has been some change in the relation between excess demand for labour and unemployment, which has meant that unemployment has ceased to be an adequate indicator of the level of excess demand for labour. As we saw above, the demand for labour in a particular labour market is equal to the sum of the numbers employed (E) and the number of unfilled vacancies (V), while the supply of labour is given by the sum of numbers employed and the numbers of job-seekers (i.e. the unemployed, U). Therefore, the excess demand for labour, $(L_D - L_S)/L_S$, can be written as

$$\frac{(E + V) - (E + U)}{E + U} = \frac{V - U}{E + U} = v - u$$

where v and u denote the rates of unfilled vacancies and unemployment respectively, that is, they represent the numbers of unfilled vacancies and unemployed workers each expressed as a proportion of the total labour force (i.e. the employed plus the unemployed).

From this we see that a direct measure of excess demand for labour is given by the difference between the rates of unfilled vacancies and unemployment. However, since data series on unfilled vacancies are generally thought to be unreliable, because many vacancies are simply not notified to official agencies and hence go unrecorded, Phillips, Lipsey and the majority of subsequent investigators have taken the aggregate unemployment rate (or some transformation of this) as a proxy for the excess demand for labour.[12] Now, provided that there exists a stable relationship between the rates of unemployment and unfilled vacancies, their difference can be reduced to a function of only the unemployment rate (Hansen, 1970), and this function of the unemployment rate can be used to proxy excess labour demand. As we see in the next chapter, such a stable relationship between the unemployment rate and the rate of unfilled vacancies did exist on the UK up until late 1966, after which time it too became unstable and began to move rightwards on the u/v plane, indicating that a given rate of vacancies became associated with a higher rate of unemployment. While a number of competing explanations of this shift in the unemployment-vacancies relation have been put forward (see above, pp. 180–185, for a survey), what is of relevance here is that, because of this shift, there will be an outward movement in the relation between excess demand and unemployment and hence an outward movement in the Phillips curve, even when there has been no change in the underlying reaction function relating wage inflation to the level of excess labour demand.[13]

A number of investigators have sought to rescue the Phillips relation by explaining its instability in terms not of a breakdown in the underlying relation between excess demand and wage inflation but in terms of changes that occurred in the relations between various labour-market variables in the UK in the late 1960s and that rendered the unemployment rate inadequate as an index of the pressure of excess demand in the labour market. In consequence, a number of improved excess-demand proxies have been put forward. (For a brief survey, see Trevithick and Mulvey, 1975, pp. 65–7, 75–8.) Apart from the unemployment–vacancies shifts, a number of writers have questioned the adequacy of the officially published unemployment series as an index of excess labour demand, on the grounds that it excludes hidden unemployment (i.e. as we saw in Chapter 2, the numbers of persons who are not in employment but who are willing and able to work, although not searching for employment under prevailing economic conditions) and labour-hoarding (i.e. labour that is retained by employers but is surplus to their current requirements). By augmenting official unemployment data to take account of estimates of these, Taylor (1974) had some success in reviving the UK Phillips curve during the period up to 1971.

THE ROLE OF PRICE EXPECTATIONS

Friedman's theory

The second class of explanation offered for the instability of the Phillips curve is attributed principally to Friedman (see, for example, Friedman 1968), although a closely related analysis was presented by Phelps (1968). The essence of Friedman's argument is that the Phillips curve, relating the rate of change of *money wages* to the unemployment rate as a proxy of excess labour demand, is incorrectly specified, because it is the *real wage* that responds to disequilibrium in the labour market. During periods when prices are changing, these two concepts are not interchangeable, and so it is argued that it is necessary to introduce the rate of price inflation into the analysis. Further, since money wages are typically fixed on a discrete rather than a continuous basis (generally on an annual basis in the UK at the time of writing in 1979), it follows that it is not the current price level that is important when money wages are being fixed but the price level that is expected to prevail for the duration of the agreement. It is therefore argued that it is necessary to introduce the expected rate of price inflation into the analysis.

In the interest of simplicity, let us assume that labour productivity remains unchanged, so that, given the assumption of a constant mark-up pricing policy by firms, the rate of price inflation in any period ($\dot{p}_t$) will equal the rate of wage inflation ($\dot{w}_t$). Friedman assumed that neither employers nor employees suffer from money illusion and argued that expected or anticipated changes in the price level will be fully incorporated into money wage settlements, with the consequence that the rate of change of money wages will be a function of both the unemployment rate (in Phillips curve manner) and the anticipated rate of change of prices. Thus, with an additional assumption about the formation of expectations regarding the rate of price inflation, we can summarise Friedman's model by the following three-equation system:

$$\dot{w}_t = f(u_t) + \alpha \dot{p}_t^e \qquad (7.1)$$

$$\dot{p}_t = \dot{w}_t \qquad (7.2)$$

$$\dot{p}_t^e = \dot{p}_{t-1} \qquad (7.3)$$

where $\dot{p}_t^e$ is the expected rate of price inflation in period t.

Equation (7.1) has become known as the *expectations-augmented Phillips curve*, and this says that the rate of change of money wages is equal to the sum of some function, $f(u_t)$, of the current rate of unemployment (i.e. the original Phillips relation) and some proportion (α) of the expected rate of change of prices. Friedman's hypothesis that there is full compensation for expected inflation implies that α enters this equation with a value of one, while Phillips's original relation implies a value of α equal to zero. If there is only partial adjustment for expected inflation, with people perhaps subject to some degree of money illusion, then $0 < \alpha < 1$.

Equation (7.2) follows from the assumption of zero productivity, growth and mark-up pricing and states that in any period the rate of price inflation will be equal to the rate of wage inflation. If, however, productivity were growing at some constant proportional rate (say $\dot{q}_t$), we would simply replace equation (7.2) with the equation

$$\dot{p}_t = \dot{w}_t - \dot{q}_t$$

Equation (7.3) concerns the formation of expectations regarding the rate of price inflation and represents what is perhaps the simplest possible hypothesis, namely, that the expected rate of price inflation in period t is equal to the actual rate that occurred in period $(t-1)$. In empirical studies it is usual to replace (7.3) with the assumption that expectations are determined according to the *adaptive expectations mechanism*, with expectations being updated each period by some fraction (i.e. the expectations coefficient) of the discrepancy between last period's actual and expected rates of inflation. The assumption that expectations are generated according to this scheme is equivalent to assuming that the current expected rate of inflation is a geometrically declining weighted average of all previous actual values of the inflation rate, and it is easy to show that (7.3) is the special case where the expectations coefficient equals unity (Solow, 1969, p. 4).[14]

A Long-Run Trade-Off?

Friedman's theory of the Phillips curve can be demonstrated by setting α in equation (7.1) equal to one. If the expected rate of inflation is zero, equation (7.1) reduces to the original Phillips curve, where the rate of wage inflation is a function of only the unemployment rate; this is shown by curve A in Figure 7.7. Suppose now that the expected rate of inflation ($\dot{p}^e$) is equal to some positive value (say 5 per cent). Then,

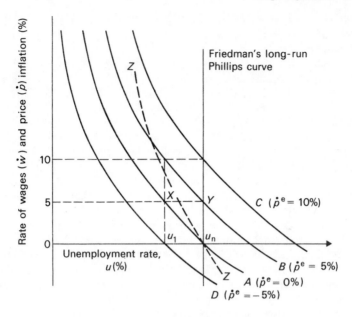

Figure 7.7 Expectations-augmented Phillips curve

according to (7.1), the rate of wage inflation corresponding to any particular value of the unemployment rate will equal that given by the zero expected-inflation Phillips curve plus the anticipated rate of price inflation of 5 per cent. For example, if the unemployment rate were equal to u_n in Figure 7.7, there would be zero wage inflation (and by our assumptions zero price inflation) in the case where $\dot{p}^e = 0$. However, in the case where the anticipated rate of price inflation equals 5 per cent, the rate of inflation corresponding to unemployment of u_n will be 5 per cent, because according to (7.1) there will be full compensation in current wage changes for expected inflation. Similarly, for any other rate of unemployment, the rate of inflation will equal that shown by the zero expected-inflation Phillips curve plus the full 5 per cent expected inflation rate. Therefore, an anticipated inflation rate of 5 per cent gives rise to the new Phillips curve shown by B in Figure 7.7, which lies above the zero expectations curve by a vertical distance equal to the 5 per cent expected inflation rate. If the expected rate of inflation were 10 per cent, we would obtain the curve C, while an expected fall in the price level at a rate of 5 per cent would give rise to curve D, which lies below the original zero-expectations curve by a vertical distance equal to 5 per cent. Thus, according to

Friedman's theory we obtain not a single Phillips curve but a whole family of Phillips curves, with one corresponding to each expected inflation rate.

Consider now the case where the expected rate of inflation in the initial period (t) equals zero, so that curve A in Figure 7.7 applies, and suppose that the initial rate of unemployment equals u_n and that the government, by either fiscal or monetary means, seeks to achieve and maintain a rate of unemployment below u_n. Curve A shows the unemployment–inflation trade-off that applies in period t, and from this we see that the consequence of a policy designed to reduce the rate of unemployment below u_n to, say, u_1 is an increase in the inflation rate in the first period from zero to 5 per cent. However, the story does not end here, because the current period's inflation will influence the next period's expected rate of price inflation, which will in turn influence next period's rates of wage and price inflation, and so on.

The dynamic implications of Friedman's theory can be illustrated by considering equations (7.1) to (7.3). In our example the expected rate of price inflation in the initial period ($\dot{p}^e_t$) equals zero, and with an unemployment rate of u_1, money wages and (from equation 7.2) prices increase at a rate of 5 per cent. Consider now what happens in the following period if unemployment is held at u_1. Equation (7.3) shows that the rate of price inflation expected in period ($t + 1$) is equal to the actual rate of the previous period (i.e. 5 per cent), and so in this period, with $\dot{p}^e_{t-1} = 5$ per cent, the Phillips curve B in Figure 7.7 becomes applicable. According to (7.1), the rate of wage inflation during this period equals the rate shown by the zero expected-inflation curve A (i.e. 5 per cent) plus the rate of price inflation expected during this period (i.e. 5 per cent), giving a total rate of growth of money wages during this period ($\dot{w}_{t+1}$) equal to 10 per cent. According to (7.2), prices rise during this period at a rate of 10 per cent, so that (from 7.3) the expected rate of inflation in the following period ($t + 2$) rises to 10 per cent, giving rise to wage and price inflation during period ($t + 2$) of 15 per cent. So the process continues, with an ever rising rate of inflation: 5 per cent in the initial period, 10 per cent in the second period, 15 per cent in the third, and so on.

The preceding argument predicts that any policy that holds the unemployment rate permanently below u_n will result in an ever accelerating inflation. Conversely, if the government were to keep the unemployment rate above u_n, the process would operate in reverse and result in the price level's falling at an ever increasing rate. In short, Friedman's theory predicts that the only way in which unemployment can be permanently held below u_n is by an ever accelerating inflation.

Notice that, if the government were to implement policies in the second period to hold the inflation rate constant at 5 per cent (in preference to holding the unemployment rate at u_1 at the expense of a continually increasing inflation rate), the expected rate of inflation would, according to (7.3), turn out to be equal to the actual rates and the economy would revert to the original unemployment rate (u_n), but with an inflation rate of 5 per cent (at point Y on curve B in Figure 7.7) as compared with the original zero inflation rate at this same level of unemployment. Therefore, in this case Friedman's theory predicts that the only consequence of the initial attempt to decrease unemployment below u_n is an inflation rate of 5 per cent.[15]

Friedman's theory predicts that there is no trade-off between steady inflation and unemployment in the long run. What we have instead is a whole series of short-run Phillips unemployment–inflation trade-offs, each corresponding to a different expected rate of inflation, but with only one unemployment rate (u_n in Figure 7.7) being consistent with a constant rate of inflation. Notice that the unemployment rate u_n is compatible not only with a zero rate of inflation but also with any constant rate. If the expected rate of inflation were, say, x per cent and the unemployment rate were equal to u_n, the actual rate of price inflation would turn out to be equal to the expected rate of x per cent. This is because unemployment of u_n would result in a zero rate of wage inflation in the case where the expected rate of price inflation was zero, so that, with expected price inflation of x per cent, the rate of wage inflation would be equal simply to x per cent. In terms of equation (7.1), the term $f(u)$ represents the original Phillips or zero expected-inflation relation (curve A in Figure 7.7), and its intercept on the unemployment axis shows that, with a zero expected rate of price inflation, an unemployment rate of u_n results in zero wage inflation. Using (7.2), we see, since $f(u_n) = 0$, that

$$\dot{w}_t = \dot{p}_t^e = \dot{p}_t$$

when the unemployment rate equals u_n. This shows that at this unemployment rate the actual rates of price and wage inflation are equal to the expected rate of price inflation of x per cent. Because inflationary expectations have turned out to be correct (i.e. because inflation has been perfectly anticipated), they remain unchanged in the next period at x per cent (from equation 7.3), so that in this as in each subsequent period the rates of wage and price inflation remain constant at x per cent, giving rise to a long-run equilibrium position of a constant x per cent inflation at the unemployment rate u_n.

Since the argument applies for any value of expected rate of inflation, we see that long-run equilibrium can be established at the unemployment rate u_n with any constant actual rate of inflation, the value of which will be equal to the expected rate of price inflation. The locus of these possible equilibrium points gives rise to a vertical long-run Phillips curve, as shown in Figure 7.7. Friedman's analysis therefore predicts that in the long run, when the actual rate of inflation is equal to the expected rate, the inflation–unemployment trade-off vanishes, and the Phillips curve becomes vertical.

The Natural Rate of Unemployment

The rate of unemployment that is compatible with any constant, as distinct from varying, rate of inflation (u_n in Figure 7.7) was termed the *natural rate of unemployment* by Friedman.[16] This is the unemployment rate that corresponds to the level of aggregate demand at which there is neither upward nor downward pressure on the rate of inflation. Friedman argued that its magnitude will be determined independently of the expected rate of inflation by existing real conditions in the labour market, principally the existence of *frictions* (or obstacles) of various forms, which determine the speed of adjustment of supply to demand in the labour market. The factors that determine the natural rate of unemployment include the extent to which the geographical distribution of the unemployed is matched to that of job vacancies and the way in which the skill mix required to fill vacancies is matched by that of the unemployed. It is therefore influenced by such things as the educational characteristics of the labour force and the presence of barriers to geographical mobility of labour and jobs as well as barriers to the acquisition of new skills. Friedman stressed that the natural unemployment rate is not some irreducible minimum of unemployment; rather, it is the rate that is consistent with existing real conditions in the labour market, and it can be lowered by removing obstacles in the labour market (i.e. by reducing frictions) and increased by introducing additional obstacles.[17]

Empirical Evidence on the Long-Run Phillips Curve

Friedman's theory, with its prediction that there is no inflation–unemployment trade-off in the long run, depends crucially on the hypothesis that α in equation (7.1) takes the value unity (i.e. that expected inflation is fully incorporated into current wage changes, so that there is an absence of any long-run money illusion). If α takes the value zero, the wage change equation reduces to Phillips's original formulation, so that there is only one curve (A in Figure 7.7), regardless of price expectations.

In between these two polar cases is the one where $0 < \alpha < 1$, meaning that there is partial but not complete compensation for anticipated inflation. This case implies that there is a long-run Phillips curve (such as *ZZ* in Figure 7.7), which, although more steeply sloped than the short-run ones, is not vertical, meaning that there is some trade-off between unemployment and inflation in the long run. (For a derivation of the long-run Phillips curve *ZZ*, see Brooks and Evans, 1978, pp. 78–80.)

A number of investigators have sought to test Friedman's theory by estimating the size of α (see Turnovsky, 1974, pp. 326–7, for a survey and Friedman, 1975, pp. 24–8, for a critique of such studies), and the majority of such studies have come up with values of α in the range 0.3–0.8, implying the existence of a negatively sloping long-run Phillips curve. In one such study of British inflation, Solow (1969) estimated α to be significantly less than unity and interpreted his findings as suggesting that, while people are rational and do adjust to inflation, they are subject to some degree of (dynamic) money illusion and do not therefore fully adjust to inflation. However, such findings need not necessarily imply the presence of money illusion. In cases where the wage is determined by collective bargaining, workers may for some reason be prevented from fully incorporating their inflationary expectations into money wage settlements. For example, Rees (1970) argued that the *transactions costs* involved in continuously adjusting the real wage under inflationary conditions may be of sufficient magnitude to discourage complete adjustment for expected inflation.[18]

The Formation of Price Expectations
It should be noted that, because price expectations are not generally directly observable, it is necessary to make some assumptions about their formation. Most of the above tests of Friedman's theory have assumed that expectations are generated according to the adaptive expectations mechanism, which, as we have seen, implies that current expectations are equal to a weighted average (with weights declining geometrically as one goes further back in time) of past rates of inflation and nothing else. The plausibility of this assumption has, however, been challenged in the recent literature, and a number of studies employing Muth's (1961) concept of *rational expectations*, the basic idea of which is that expectations are formed on the basis of an economic model of the determination of the variable in question rather than on the basis of a weighted average (with fixed weights) of past values of the variable alone, have been undertaken and have produced results more favourable to Friedman's theory. (For surveys, see Laidler and Parkin, 1975, pp. 770–4, and Santomero and Seater, 1978, pp. 525–9.)

WAGE INFLATION AND INCOMES POLICIES

In cases where inflation is caused by an excess of aggregate demand for goods and services over their supply, it can be controlled by aggregate demand policies (i.e. by deflationary monetary and/or fiscal policies), with the precise policy mix presumably reflecting the policy-makers' perception of the source of the excess aggregate demand. In cases where inflation originates in the labour market, as wage push inflation, it is frequently argued that it is to be controlled by some form of incomes policy, which is typically accompanied by some form of prices policy designed to change the traditional relationships between wage (and other) costs and prices.

However, the inter-relationships between product and factor markets can mean that there is an apparent role for an incomes policy even when inflation does not have its origins in forces of wage cost push in the labour market. Consider the case where the pressure of excess demand in the derived market for labour arises as a consequence of the emergence of excess demand in the product market and gives rise to increases in money wages, either through wages' being bid up in competitive labour markets, or through some cost push or bargaining mechanism whose outcome is influenced by the pressure of excess labour demand. In such circumstances there may be a role for an incomes policy that seeks to restrain these increases in money wages in order to minimise the ultimate effect of the initial increase in aggregate demand on the general price level by minimising the extent to which increased labour costs feed back, via the price equation, into the supply side of the product market. In addition, in cases where changes in money wages are influenced by changes in the price level (via the latter's influence on the expected rate of inflation), there may be a place for an incomes policy designed to reduce the responsiveness of wages to prices in order to dampen or eliminate the *price–wage spiral* that would otherwise exist.

The existence of some form of prices and incomes policies at various times over the postwar period has been an important feature of the UK economy and that of many other Western nations, and in this section we examine briefly the theory and evidence that surround the effects of such policies on the rate of wage inflation.[19]

Shifting the Phillips Curve

As we have seen, the Phillips curve presents policy-makers with a trade-off, showing that lower wage and (given appropriate assumptions about price formation) price inflation is available but only at the expense of increased unemployment. In cases where the terms of this trade-off have been considered unacceptable, policy-makers have sought to shift the whole Phillips curve leftwards towards the origin, so that each particular rate of unemployment becomes available at a lower rate of inflation. Regional and manpower policies have been advocated as methods of achieving such shifts. By transferring excess demand for labour to areas of excess supply, and vice versa, and by improving geographical and occupational mobility as well as flows of information in the labour market about unfilled vacancies, such policies can cut down adjustment lags by reducing market frictions and cutting down periods spent in job search. If successful in those objectives, such policies result in a lower rate of unemployment at each level of excess labour demand, thus bringing about a leftward shift in the relation between excess labour demand and unemployment (Figure 7.4(b)) and, therefore, a leftward shift in the Phillips curve.

The Effects of Incomes Policies

The other method by which governments attempt to alter the terms of the inflation–unemployment trade-off embodied in the position and shape of the Phillips curve is through the operation of some form of incomes or pay policy. Incomes policies in the UK have taken various forms, ranging from voluntary policies, such as Cripps's wage standstill of 1948, through to the Conservatives' compulsory and statutory wage freeze of 1972–3.[20]

The earliest systematic attempts to assess the effects of incomes policies (e.g. Bodkin *et al.*, 1967; Smith, 1968) sought to test the hypothesis that incomes policies cause a leftward shift in the Phillips curve (such as the movement from curve *PP* to curve *QQ* shown in Figure 7.8(b)), indicating that during *policy-on* periods there is a lower rate of wage inflation for each given value of unemployment and its other determinants. Tests of this shift hypothesis typically took the form of the insertion of shift (or intercept) dummy variables into estimated Phillips curves (to allow for possible changes during policy-on periods in the intercept term of the relationship, with the other coefficients remaining unchanged), and the results of such studies suggest that incomes policies had succeeded in shifting the Phillips curve inwards. For example, the results of Smith's (1968) study of 1948–67 UK data indicate little consistency in the effects of incomes policies in successive periods but do suggest that, on average, incomes policies had succeeded in lowering the rate of increase of weekly wage rates to about 1 per cent below the level that was otherwise expected.[21]

The Lipsey–Parkin Analysis

In a detailed discussion of the way in which incomes policies may influence wage inflation, Lipsey and Parkin (1970) argued that they can have the effect not of shifting the Phillips curve to the left but of flattening it. In the extreme case where incomes policy succeeds in making the Phillips curve horizontal, it will allow the economy to operate at full employment without any increase in the rate of inflation.

To illustrate the Lipsey–Parkin argument, consider the following wage equation, which is a slightly simplified version of the one used in their original paper:

$$\dot{w} = a_1 + a_2[f(u)] + a_3\dot{p}^e + a_4S$$

where S denotes some measure of union aggressiveness and all other variables are as above.

This wage equation consists of a straightforward Phillips-type curve (where $\dot{w}$ is related to some function of the unemployment rate), on to which have been grafted price expectations and union pushfulness terms. An incomes (or, more precisely, a wages) policy seeks to reduce w below the level that it would otherwise be, given the level of aggregate demand and hence the rate of unemployment, and Lipsey and Parkin argued that such a policy may affect the wage equation in three ways:

(1) by changing the values of the independent variables in the wage equation other than u (as this will be controlled by aggregate demand as opposed to incomes policies);
(2) by changing the coefficients attached to the independent variables, and
(3) by substituting a new relation in place of the existing wage equation.

Under (1) Lipsey and Parkin argued that the only available policy is that of reducing union aggressiveness.[22] If policy leads to a general decrease in all dimensions of aggressiveness, there will be a corresponding fall in the variable chosen to proxy S. If, however, policy results in a decrease in aggressiveness (or pushfulness) in wage bargaining but nothing else, policy will lead to a decline in the coefficient a_4 attached to the chosen aggressiveness proxy – a case falling under heading (2). For example, the various versions of the Labour government's 'social contract', which operated between 1974 and 1978, were examples of policies designed in part to persuade unions to adopt less aggressive stances in wage bargaining. In return for moderation in wage claims and adherence to various wage guidelines, the government agreed to implement a number of social and industrial policies that were considered desirable by the union movement.

Under (2) incomes policies may have the goal of reducing or eliminating the responsiveness of wages to expected price changes, in order to eliminate or weaken any wage–price spiral that would otherwise exist. Such an effect would result in a fall in the coefficient a_3, attached to the expected inflation rate, and a completely successful policy in this regard would drive a_3 down to zero. We have already seen the way in which the coefficient of the union aggressiveness proxy can fall if policy results in the channelling of aggressiveness away from pushfulness in wage bargaining, and it should be noted that slope and not shift or intercept dummies, as used in early studies of the effects of incomes policies, are the appropriate vehicles for capturing these effects.

Consider now a policy that changes the relation between the unemployment rate, as a proxy for excess demand for labour, and $\dot{w}$, and assume that the reaction function before the implementation of this policy is SS, as shown in Figure 7.8(a). Notice that this reaction function indicates that, in the absence of excess demand in the labour market, money wages will be rising at the rate $\dot{w}'$. This occurs because of the influence of the other explanatory variables included in the wage equation, namely, inflationary expectations and union pushfulness, which are assumed in the specification of the wage equation to exert influences on the rate of wage inflation independent of the level of excess labour demand. In cases where the rate of wage inflation is a function of only the level of excess demand in the labour market, it is usual to assume that the reaction function passes through the origin, indicating that, in the absence of excess labour demand (i.e. when the labour market is in equilibrium), money wages remain stable (Figure 7.4(a) above). Notice also that changes in either the values or coefficients of the independent variable in the wage equation, other than unemployment, result in shifts in the reaction function, analogous to the shifts in demand functions that occur as a result of changes in the conditions of demand.

An incomes policy that succeeded in reducing, by exhortation or force, the upward effect on the wage rate of excess demand pressure in the labour market, would result in a flattening of the reaction function to, say, TT in Figure 7.8(a), indicating a decrease in the rate of wage inflation associated with any given (positive) level of excess labour demand. The effect of such a policy would be to flatten or pivot the Phillips curve to, say, RR in Figure 7.8(b). Notice that, at each rate of unemployment in excess of u_1, the rate of inflation becomes *higher* as a result of the operation of incomes policy.

Finally, under heading (3) the policy-makers seek to break the relationship described by the existing wage equation and to substitute some alternative in its place. The simplest possibility is that they seek

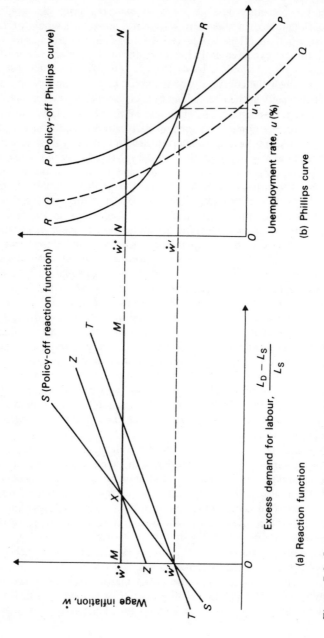

Figure 7.8 Incomes policies and the Phillips curve

to substitute a constant *wage norm* in its place. If $\dot{w}^*$ is the norm for wage increases, then, assuming that it is fully enforced as a maximum as well as a minimum, the reaction function, which is originally *SS*, becomes horizontal at $\dot{w}^*$, as shown by *MM* in Figure 7.8(a). Consequently, the Phillips curve becomes horizontal, as shown by *NN* in Figure 7.8(b).

Lipsey and Parkin also argued that, in cases where there is a wage norm that, although designed as a maximum, is treated in some sectors of the economy as a minimum, other sectors may be encouraged to give higher money-wage increases for given levels of excess demand than they would otherwise do, in order to maintain their relative wage position. If this is the case, and if the norm fails to be a fully effective ceiling but instead exerts some restraining effect when wage increases would otherwise exceed the norm, the reaction function for some sectors of the economy becomes *MXZ* and for others *ZXZ*. Under such circumstances it can be shown from Figure 7.8(a) that the implementation of incomes policy results in the Phillips curve's pivoting in a manner like that shown in Figure 7.8(b).

The Evidence

The Lipsey–Parkin analysis suggests that the possible effects of incomes policies on the wage determination process are too complex to be captured by the insertion of simple shift or intercept dummies into the wage equation. By testing the stability of the wage equation as between policy-on and policy-off periods, they found support for the hypothesis that incomes policies had had some significant effect on the *slope coefficients* of the wage equation. In addition, their findings produced support for the pivoting Phillips-curve hypothesis and suggested that the implementation of incomes policy had resulted in a pivot occurring at an unemployment rate of about 1.8 per cent and an annual wage inflation rate of about 4 per cent. They obtained estimates of the effects of incomes policies on the rate of wage inflation by comparing the actual rates of wage inflation during policy-on periods with those predicted by their estimated policy-off equation, and these estimates suggested that only one period of incomes policy (that operated by Cripps between 1948 and 1950) had exerted a significant average downward influence on the rate of wage inflation.

As to the precise effects of incomes policy on the wage equation, Lipsey and Parkin's evidence suggested that incomes policy had been highly successful in weakening the relation between wage changes and unemployment, replacing it by a constant, with the estimated coefficient of the unemployment term proving not significantly different from zero in the policy-on period. In addition, their results suggested that incomes policy had weakened the feedback effect from (expected) price changes to wage changes and interestingly created a near significant relation between wage inflation and union aggressiveness (as proxied, following Hines, by ΔT) where none existed before.

However, these findings have been seriously challenged by a number of subsequent writers (e.g. Godfrey, 1971; Wallis, 1971; Burrows and Hitiris, 1972) because of Lipsey and Parkin's failure to take adequate account of simultaneous equation and autocorrelation problems, and these later studies have shown that, once proper account is taken of these considerations, Lipsey and Parkin's findings evaporate. Indeed, on the basis of a detailed survey of the current literature, Parkin, Sumner and Jones, summing up the present state of knowledge, concluded that incomes policy apparently has little effect either on the wage determination process or on the average rate of wage inflation (1972, p. 13).[23]

NOTES ON FURTHER READING

The literature on wage inflation is very extensive, but a number of useful surveys are available. See, in particular, Burton 1972; Goldstein, 1972; Gordon, 1975; Laidler and Parkin, 1975; Trevithick and Mulvey, 1975; Frisch, 1977, and Santomero and Seater, 1978. The original articles by Phillips (1958), Lipsey (1960) and Hines (1964) are well worth reading, and useful discussion of Phillips's original estimates can be found in Desai (1975) and Gilbert (1976). Friedman's theory of the Phillips curve has appeared in a number of places since its debut in Friedman (1968), and concise summaries are to be found in Friedman (1975, 1976). Since the late 1960s a number of important studies, aiming to provide a firm theoretical microeconomic underpinning to the Phillips relation, have appeared, and this literature has become known as the *new microeconomics* of inflation and employment theory. Such studies stress the role of imperfect information in the labour market, and a number of the most important papers in this area are available in Phelps *et al.* (1971). The readings edited by Parkin and Sumner (1972) contain much of interest on the effects of incomes policy on inflation, and the readings edited by Johnson and Nobay (1971), Laidler and Purdy (1974) and Parkin and Sumner (1978) contain much that is of interest.

Chapter 8

Unemployment and Unfilled Vacancies

An unemployed worker is one who is unable to find employment under prevailing economic conditions. Although any factor of production can be unemployed, economists have placed particular emphasis on unemployment of labour, primarily because of the mental (and some-times physical) sufferings and hardships experienced by the unemployed and their dependents.

A distinction is sometimes drawn between voluntary and involuntary unemployment. *Involuntary unemployment* occurs when workers who are willing to work at current wage levels are unable to find jobs. *Voluntary unemployment* refers to those workers who are thought to be capable of taking a job but prefer to remain unemployed, perhaps to enable themselves to continue their search for a better paid or otherwise more desirable job than those currently on offer. In cases where the wage ruling in a particular labour market is for some reason above the equilibrium or market-clearing level, there will be an excess of labour supply over labour demand, and the workers comprising this excess supply are said to be involuntarily unemployed, as they are seeking but are unable to attain employment at the prevailing wage rate.[1]

TYPES OF UNEMPLOYMENT

It is usual to distinguish between several types of unemployment, and the fourfold classification, discussed by Beveridge (1944), of total unemployment into frictional, structural, seasonal and cyclical cate-gories appears at first sight to provide a straightforward subdivision. *Frictional unemployment* is the unemployment that results from workers' moving between jobs. As long as people change jobs, and as long as it takes a finite time to move from one job to another, some positive amount of frictional unemployment will exist at any moment in time. Frictional unemployment is a consequence of the short-run changes in the labour market that constantly occur in a dynamic economy in response to changes in the pattern of demand for, and supply of, goods and services, and it arises because labour supply does not adjust instantaneously to changes in labour demand.

Structural unemployment is caused by long-run changes in the structure of the economy, which give rise to changes in the demand for labour in particular industries, regions and occupations, and it arises because, although workers are available for employment, their skill or locations do not match those of unfilled vacancies. The distinction between frictional and structural unemployment is by no means a clear-cut one. While most writers see the distinction as being one of degree rather than kind, with structural unemployment being essentially a longer-term or more stubborn form of frictional unemployment, others have sought to clarify the distinction by explicitly considering the nature of unfilled job vacancies. Perlman (1969, p. 168), for example, defined a worker as structurally unemployed if a job vacancy exists that he is not qualified to fill and as frictionally unemployed if a vacancy that he is qualified to fill exists and remains unfilled.[2]

Seasonal unemployment is that which results from the lower level of economic activity that occurs in certain sectors of the economy at particular times of the year. Agricultural and building workers, as well as those involved in the tourism industry, who are out of work during the winter months, are said to be seasonally unemployed. However, the most significant group of seasonally unemployed workers in the UK in recent times has been unemployed school-leavers, who join the unemployment register at particular times of the year and generally (at least until very recently) pass off it quite rapidly. Since seasonal unemployment is viewed as reflecting normal seasonal variations, unemployment data are frequently presented in a seasonally adjusted form, sometimes with school-leavers excluded.

Cyclical or demand-deficient unemployment is that which is associated with a lack of aggregate demand. This type of unemployment was discussed by Keynes (1936) in the *General Theory*, and its cure lies in policies that succeed in increasing the level of aggregate demand. Some more recent writers (e.g. Reynolds, 1978, p. 126) have differentiated between this and *growth gap unemployment*, which they see as a longer-term secular version of demand-deficient unemployment that occurs not so much due to cyclical factors but when the economy's growth potential exceeds its actual rate of growth, so that part of its productive capacity remains unutilised.

JOB SEARCH

Frictional unemployment arises because the process of matching unfilled vacancies with unemployed workers is not instantaneous, and recent developments in the analysis of the microeconomic foundations of unemployment theory have explicitly considered the search processes undertaken by both workers and employers in order to bring about such matching (Holt, 1971). Such models dispense with the conventional assumptions that perfect information is available at zero cost and that there is instantaneous costless adjustment. Instead, they consider behaviour in labour markets characterised by conditions of imperfect information about available job vacancies and offered wages and about available labour and its asking prices.

In the absence of perfect knowledge about available job vacancies and the wages and conditions of employment being offered by employers, an unemployed worker or one contemplating a job change has the incentive to search the market. Similarly, an employer who has a vacancy to fill will be uncertain about the available workers, their quality and their asking prices and therefore has an incentive to engage in a search of the market. Although some employments are flexible enough (or offer enough paid holidays) to allow workers to engage in on-the-job search, others are not, and some workers find it expedient to quit their existing jobs in order to engage in a period of full-time job search to overcome the various difficulties that can arise in searching outside of normal working hours (e.g. because of the fact that company and state employment offices may open, and prospective employers hold interviews, only during normal working hours).

Job search is the process by which an unemployed worker gathers information about the unfilled vacancies and associated wages and conditions that are on offer, but it is not a costless process. It involves foregone earnings (net of any benefits to which an unemployed searching worker is entitled) and various out-of-pocket expenses, and a rational worker will continue his search up to the point where the expected gain from further search (in the form of expected improvements in wages and other conditions of employment, including job security, fringe benefits, promotion prospects, pleasant working conditions, and so on) is equal to the additional costs involved. At this time he will accept the best previous offer that is still open.

More specifically, a newly unemployed worker is assumed to possess some *reservation wage*, or wage aspiration level, below which he is unwilling to accept a job offer. The magnitude of this wage is assumed to be negatively related to the duration of search or unemployment. There are several reasons for this.[3] First, it is initially set high to avoid the risk of the worker selling himself short by accepting the first offer, unless it is a very good one. Secondly, search will begin with firms known to pay good wages, so that the reservation wage gradually declines as search turns towards less attractive occupations, firms and localities. Thirdly, financial and psychological hardships are likely to rise with continued unemployment and with the depletion of family resources, so that income becomes increasingly attractive. Similarly, the employer with unfilled vacancies is assumed to possess a reservation wage, and it is assumed that this is revised upwards, or his hiring standards are lowered, as the duration of the vacancies increases, with the process continuing until he fills his vacancies. Thus, the search process results in a matching of vacancies and unemployed workers through a convergence of the wage aspirations of buyers and sellers of labour. Notice, however, that the analysis does not imply that the parties to a given 'hire' have been searching for the same period of time. It is possible both for newly occurring vacancies to be filled by workers who have been unemployed for a long time and for newly unemployed workers to accept jobs that have been vacant for a long time.

STRUCTURE OF UNEMPLOYMENT IN THE UK

On 12 July 1979 unemployment in the UK, excluding school-leavers and seasonally adjusted, amounted to 1.279 million or 5.3 per cent of the total number of employees (employed plus unemployed). Including school-leavers and without seasonal adjustment, it totalled 1.464 million, equal to a rate of 6.1 per cent of all employees.

What do the official UK unemployment statistics measure?
Some aspects of the adequacy of official statistics of the number of *registered unemployed* as an index of the number of workers seeking paid employment were discussed in Chapter 2 (see above, p. 16). In the UK, official statistics of unemployment are based on the concept of seeking work, and there is a monthly count of the registered unemployed; these are those persons registered for employment at local employment and careers offices or at job centres who, on the day of the count (now the second Thursday of the month), have no job and are classified, according to standard rules, as being 'capable of and available for work'.[4]

There are two reasons why men and women join the unemployment register: first, to become eligible for cash benefits, such as unemployment and supplementary benefits, and second, to obtain assistance in their job search. The adequacy of the official unemployment statistics has been seriously questioned in recent years on the grounds that they exclude certain groups of workers who are in practice capable of, and available for, work and include others who are not.

Workers falling into the first of these categories are sometimes termed the *unregistered unemployed*, and two principal groups of such workers can be singled out. First, there are those who are seeking work but do not register because they are ineligible, or think themselves to be ineligible, for cash benefits and who prefer to conduct their job search through non-official channels, such as pursuing newspaper advertisements, registering with private employment agencies, direct contact with possible employers or simply personal contacts. Possibly the largest group here is married women not eligible for unemployment benefit because they opted not to pay full National Insurance contributions while previously at work. However, since this option was phased out in April 1978, we can expect this source of unregistered female unemployment to decline in importance in the future. From an analysis of data gathered for census purposes and data provided by the General Household Surveys, the Department of Employment has estimated that in Britain during the period 1971–3 the numbers of unregistered unemployed ranged from 70 to 100,000 men and from 160 to 200,000 or more women (as compared to the average number of registered unemployed over this period of 615,000 men and 119,000 women), with most of the women being married and not eligible for unemployment benefit.[5] In addition, it was felt that a significant proportion of male unregistered unemployment could be accounted for by those who were between jobs and either did not bother to claim benefit for a short period (perhaps a week or two) or were not entitled to benefit as they had left their previous job voluntarily (thus disqualifying themselves from receiving benefit for six weeks). Secondly, there are the *hidden unemployed* who, as we have seen, are willing to work at current wage rates but have abandoned their job search as hopeless; unless they are entitled to benefits, the hidden unemployed will not bother to register. Some indication of the extent of under recording in the official data due to this source is given by the estimates of hidden unemployment discussed in Chapter 2 (see above, pp. 20, 25–6).

While the above considerations point to a potentially serious underestimation in the official unemployment statistics, others suggest an overestimation. Since registration is in general a necessary condition for receipt of cash benefits, it is generally argued that the total number of workers registered as unemployed includes some proportion who are not capable of, and available for, work. These 'registered non-unemployed' workers include those fraudulently collecting benefit when in employment, the 'workshy', older workers who are in receipt of an occupational pension but who register in order to have their National Insurance contributions credited to them, so as to be entitled to a full state pension on reaching the official retirement age, and those who are, due to their mental or physical characteristics or disabilities, effectively

unemployable under normal circumstances. However, there is little
detailed evidence available regarding the magnitude of these categories.

As there are potential sources of both overstatement and understate-
ment in the official unemployment statistics, and as the likely order of
magnitude of each of these opposing biases is not known with any
degree of precision, it is not possible, given the present state of knowledge, to say with confidence whether on balance the official data
represent an under- or an overstatement. In any case it seems likely that
the extent of both under- and overestimation will vary over time in
response to changes in various economic variables.

Unemployment in the UK: Historical Background
Between 1948 and 1966 registered unemployment in the UK, expressed
as a percentage of the total number of employees, ranged from a low of
1.2 per cent in 1951 and 1955 to a high of 2.6 per cent in 1963 and
averaged only 1.7 per cent. The magnitude of unemployment in the
above period contrasts dramatically with that experienced during the
interwar years. Between 1921 and 1939 the percentage of insured
workers who were unemployed only once fell below 10 per cent (to
9.7 per cent in 1927) and reached 22.1 per cent in 1932, with the
average over this period being 14 per cent.[6] During the period prior to
the First World War, the percentage of members unemployed in certain
trade unions between 1881 and 1914 ranged from 2 per cent in 1899 to
10.2 per cent in 1886 and averaged 4.6 per cent.[7]

Since 1966 there has been an upward trend in unemployment in the
UK, with the unemployment rate rising fairly steadily from 1.6 per cent
in 1966 to 5.7 per cent in 1978 (see Figure 7.1). To an extent this
increase in the rate of registered unemployment during recent years
can be accounted for by the relatively depressed state of aggregate
demand (which resulted in a failure of employment opportunities to
expand in line with the rising labour supply).[8] However, there were, as
we shall see, other forces at work. The incidence of unemployment in
the UK has varied markedly between different regions, industries,
occupations and age groups, as well as between the sexes, and it is to
these aspects of the current unemployment situation that we now turn.

Industrial, Occupational and Regional Aspects of UK Unemployment
The uneven spread of unemployment across different industries,
occupations and regions in the UK is not a new phenomenon. For
example, in 1932 in the depths of the interwar depression, when UK
unemployment was 22.1 per cent of all insured workers, unemployment rates among insured workers ranged on an industry basis from
6.1 per cent in tramway and ombibus services up to 61.7 per cent in

shipbuilding and repairing. In 1937, when the aggregate unemployment rate among UK insured workers was 10.8 per cent, the rate in Wales was 22.3 per cent, while that in London was only 6.3 per cent. In the same year unemployment rates among insured workers ranged on an industry basis from 3.1 per cent in electrical engineering to 27.5 per cent in docks, harbour and canal services.

The high unemployment rates experienced in the interwar years were the consequence of a combination of severe cyclical or demand-deficient factors, resulting from the worldwide depression of the 1920s and 1930s and various structural changes, including changes in world consumption patterns, technical progress and a decline in the UK's comparative advantage in shipbuilding, iron and steel, coal-mining and textiles − industries that are in any case particularly susceptible to cyclical forces. Together, these factors gave rise to very high unemployment rates in these industries and in the regions (such as the North and North-East of England, Wales and Scotland) where these industries have traditionally been concentrated. In addition, the high value of the sterling–dollar parity exerted a depressive effect on the UK's exports.

Table 8.1 shows the structure of unemployment in 1979 across different regions and industries. The variation in unemployment rates between regions is an important dimension of the regional problem, and the regional pattern in UK unemployment has remained stubbornly stable despite the various regional policies implemented over the post-war period. The regional and industrial structures of unemployment are clearly related via the prevailing location of industry, and in July 1979, when the aggregate rate of UK unemployment was 6.1 per cent, rates varied from a low of 3.8 in South-East England to a high of 12.7 per cent in Northern Ireland. On an industry basis unemployment varied from 2.2 per cent in gas, electricity and water up to 11.3 per cent in construction.

Considerable variability in unemployment is also present between different occupations, with a negative relationship existing between skill level and the incidence of unemployment. For example, in June 1979 some 2.8 per cent of the total numbers of unemployed were classed as belonging to 'other non-manual occupations' (i.e. selling, security and protective service occupations) and 7.9 per cent to the 'managerial and professional' classification, while 43.3 per cent were 'general labourers'. The observed inverse relation between unemployment and skill is consistent with the analysis of fixed employment costs discussed in Chapter 4 (see above, pp. 71–3), which predicted greater employment stability in occupations requiring high levels of skill and education, because in such cases the employer's investment in

Table 8.1 *Industrial and regional distribution of UK unemployment, 1979*

Standard region	Unemployment rate[a] (%)	Industry and SIC order	Unemployment rate[b] (%)
South-East	3.8	Agriculture, forestry and fishing (I)	5.4
East Anglia	4.4	Mining and quarrying (II)	6.4
South-West	5.8	Manufacturing (III–XIX)	4.2
West Midlands	6.1	Construction (XX)	11.3
East Midlands	5.0	Gas, electricity and water (XXI)	2.2
Yorkshire and Humberside	6.1	Transport and communications (XXII)	3.7
North-West	7.6	Distributive trades (XXIII)	4.4
North	9.2	Financial, professional and miscellaneous services (XXIV–XXVI)	2.9
Wales	8.4	Public administration and defences (XXVII)	4.4
Scotland	8.3	All unemployed	5.1
Northern Ireland	12.7		
United Kingdom	6.1		

Notes:
(a) Data relate to 12 July 1979, are seasonally unadjusted and include school-leavers.
(b) Data relate to Great Britain only, in May 1979. School-leavers are excluded, data are seasonally unadjusted and classification is by industry in which last employed.
Source: Department of Employment Gazette (August 1979), tables 106 and 108.

the employee is highest. The observed negative relation between skill and unemployment will in addition reflect demand side forces, and the fact that skilled workers who do become unemployed find it easier to find a new job reflects, amongst other things, a growth in the demand for their skills relative to the available supply.

Unemployment by Sex and Age

The incidence of unemployment also varies both between the sexes and across different age groups. For example, the 1.464 million workers registered as unemployed in the UK on 12 July 1979 comprised 980,500 men and 483,500 women (176,000 of whom were married), so that, while the unemployment rate was 6.1 per cent for all workers, the rates were 6.8 per cent and 4.9 per cent for men and women respectively. Looking at the trends in unemployment, we see that over recent years registered unemployment among females has grown much more rapidly than that among males. For example, between July 1974 and July 1979 the unemployment rate among males in Great Britain grew from 3.4 per cent to 6.6 per cent (an increase of 94 per cent), while over the same period that among women grew from 1 per cent to 4.8 per cent (an increase of nearly 400 per cent). This rapid increase in female unemployment may in part be attributable to the equal pay and opportunities legislation, which became fully operational in 1976. This is because such legislation may be expected to have increased female attachment to the labour force, while simultaneously decreasing female employment opportunities by encouraging employers to substitute male labour or capital in place of female labour, which is now more expensive. However, it seems likely that there have been other forces at work, including various demographic changes and an increased propensity of women to return to work after having children. These factors together contributed to the rapid increases in female activity rates observed between 1974 and 1978 (see Moore *et al.*, 1978, pp. 24–5).

Table 8.2 presents some official estimates of the unemployment rates of different age groups in 1978, and from this it can be seen that rates for both women and men vary widely between different age groups. The most striking feature of these estimates is the very high incidence of unemployment, for both men and women, among the under-18 age group. This age group encompasses most school-leavers, and the peak in the under-18 unemployment rate in July reflects the end of the school year. Although unemployment of the under-18s dropped considerably by October, as some school-leavers took up their first jobs, it still remained higher than that for any other age group. As already noted, the numbers of unemployed school-leavers are sometimes excluded from official data on unemployment, on the grounds that their unemployment is essentially a temporary phenomenon, with school-leavers soon passing off the register to take up their first employment.

Table 8.2 Estimated unemployment rates by age and sex in Great Britain 1978 (%)

Age group	Total			Males			Females		
	January	July	October	January	July	October	January	July	October
Under 18	14.5	27.6	13.4	13.4	27.5	12.5	15.8	27.8	14.5
18–19	11.0	11.2	10.6	11.1	11.2	10.4	10.9	11.3	10.7
20–24	9.5	8.3	8.5	10.3	8.7	8.7	8.3	7.7	8.2
25–34	6.1	5.3	5.3	7.2	6.0	6.0	4.1	3.9	4.2
35–44	4.3	3.7	3.7	6.0	5.0	5.0	2.0	1.9	1.9
45–54	3.8	3.5	3.5	5.0	4.5	4.5	2.1	2.1	2.1
55–59	4.6	4.5	4.6	6.0	5.7	5.9	2.7	2.7	2.8
60 and over	7.4	7.0	7.1	10.2	9.7	9.9	0.2	0.2	0.2
All ages	6.3	6.4	5.8	7.5	7.3	6.7	4.4	5.0	4.4

Source: Department of Employment Gazette (1979), p. 40.

While it is true that as recently as 1973 (when total unemployment numbered just over half a million or 2.6 per cent of all employees) there were only 23,000 unemployed school-leavers on the register in the summer peak (August 1973) and as few as 2,000 left on the register by December of that year, the picture seems to have changed dramatically since that date. In 1978 there were 243,000 school-leavers on the unemployment register at the summer peak (July rather than August because of changes in the school-leaving regulations since 1976), while at Christmas, including a few new school-leavers, there were still 43,000 left on the register, and even in March 1979 there were still over 30,000 remaining. Because the number of school-leavers remaining on the unemployment register has tailed off much more slowly in recent years, a number of writers have seriously questioned the exclusion of school-leavers from the official unemployment figures. For further discussion of unemployment among school-leavers, see Dean (1976).

The occurrence of high levels of unemployment in recent years among young workers is a phenomenon that has affected not just the UK but most other Western industrialised countries too. In a recent study of youth unemployment in Britain, it was shown that, when unemployment rises, youth unemployment among both males and females rises, but to a much greater extent than total unemployment. The evidence suggests that an increase of 1 percentage point in the unemployment rate for all males results, *ceteris paribus*, in a rise of 1.7 percentage points in the unemployment rate for males under 20 (excluding school-leavers), while a unit increase in the unemployment rate of females of all ages results, *ceteris paribus*, in an increase of almost 3 percentage points in the unemployment rate of females under 20 (excluding school-leavers).[9,10]

Duration of Unemployment

The pool of unemployed workers is a *stock*, the size of which at any moment is determined by two factors: the rate of *flow* into unemployment, and the *duration* of the unemployment spells experienced by individual workers. As can be seen from Table 8.3, the rate of inflow into unemployment in Britain has remained fairly stable since 1967, at about 4 million workers per year. The main reason for the increase in the stock of unemployment, from around half a million workers between 1967 and 1970 to over 1.3 million in 1977, was not an increase in the flow of people into unemployment but an increase in the average duration of unemployment experienced by each individual.

The estimated average duration of spells of unemployment ending during a year has increased quite dramatically since 1970: for men from

Table 8.3   *Stocks and flows of unemployment in Britain, 1967–77*

Year	Annual average no. unemployed, excluding school-leavers and adult students (thousands)		Annual inflow to unemployment (millions)		Estimated average duration of spells of unemployment in year (weeks)	
	Male	Female	Male	Female	Male	Female
1967	413	96	2.99	1.13	7.1	4.4
1968	453	85	3.01	1.03	7.7	4.2
1969	453	78	3.02	0.97	7.7	4.2
1970	485	82	2.97	0.95	8.4	4.5
1971	625	112	2.97	0.96	11.6	6.0
1972	686	130	2.69	0.93	12.1	6.5
1973	488	93	2.58	0.91	9.1	4.9
1974	490	91	2.84	1.02	9.6	4.9
1975	722	169	3.05	1.28	14.1	7.8
1976	941	282	2.92	1.48	16.5	10.5
1977	976	347	2.92	1.65	17.1	11.2

Sources: *Economic Policy Review*, no. 4 (Cambridge: University of Cambridge Department of Applied Economics, 1978), p. 33; based on data taken from *Department of Employment Gazettes* and social security statistics from the Department of Health and Social Security.

8.4 weeks in 1970 to 17.1 weeks in 1977, and for women from 4.5 to 11.2 weeks over the same period. This increase is reflected in an increase in the numbers of long-term unemployed and an increase in the ratio of long-term unemployment to total unemployment. Between July 1970 and July 1979 the total number of people who had been out of work for at least half a year more than trebled, rising from 168,000 in 1970 (30.6 per cent of numbers unemployed) to 552,000 in 1979 (39.7 per cent of numbers unemployed). Between July 1970 and July 1978 the proportion of male unemployed workers in Britain who had been out of work for more than 26 weeks rose from 32.5 per cent to 41.8 per cent, while for women it rose from 19.8 per cent to 28.9 per cent. Further disaggregation of the data shows that the duration of unemployment increases rapidly with age.[11] For example, in July 1978 the median duration of the current unemployment spell for males under 18 was 4 weeks, compared to 48 weeks for those aged 60–64.

In addition, evidence suggests that long-term unemployment itself proves a handicap in getting a job. Evidence from surveys of the characteristics of the unemployed suggests that the prospects of employment decline as duration lengthens, and evidence from an analysis of the 1972 General Household Survey suggests that the conditional probability of obtaining a job declines rapidly after six months' unemployment and falls to very low levels thereafter (Nickell, 1979). However, the extent to which this is due to the individual workers' becoming discouraged and decreasing the intensity of their job search, or due to employers' discrimination against the long-term unemployed, or simply due to the better candidates' finding jobs first, is not yet clear.

IS UNEMPLOYMENT BENEFIT INDUCED?

The question of whether the increase in British unemployment since the mid 1960s has been caused by depressed aggregate demand or by some other forces has given rise to considerable debate. A number of writers (e.g. Gujarati, 1972; Maki and Spindler, 1975) have attributed this increase, at least in part, to increases in the level of unemployment and related benefits,[12] in particular to the introduction of the earnings-related supplement to unemployment benefit in October 1966 and the implementation of the Redundancy Payments Act in December 1965.[13]

There are two ways in which the level of benefit may influence the level of unemployment. Increased benefits can either increase the rate of flow into unemployment by increasing individuals' willingness to give up their jobs and enter into unemployment voluntarily, or they can increase the duration of unemployment spells by enabling individuals to undertake longer periods of search for an acceptable job offer. The ratio of benefits received when unemployed to income earned when employed is sometimes termed the *replacement ratio*. Time series studies of British data have produced estimates of the elasticity of unemployment with respect to the replacement ratio that varies between zero and 2.1, while cross-section studies have produced estimates of the elasticity of the *duration* of male unemployment spells with respect to the replacement ratio of between 0.5 and 0.63. (For a summary, see Nickell, 1979a, pp. 34–6.)

In one study (Maki and Spindler, 1975, p. 449) it was suggested that the introduction of the earnings-related supplement had increased male unemployment rates in Britain by one-third, but this order of magnitude has been challenged on various grounds by a number of subsequent investigators. While the introduction of the earnings-related supplement in 1966 did increase the total benefits for the unemployed from about 60 per cent to 80 per cent of net earnings likely to be obtained in employment, it was only paid to a limited number of men and a very small number of women. For example, between 1966 and 1970 the average number of men in receipt of this supplement was only 100,000. Given that some proportion of these workers would have been unemployed in any case, it is clear that the additional unemployment induced by such benefits must be less than the total number in receipt of benefits.

The fact that the rate of inflow into unemployment has hardly changed since 1967, taken together with the evidence from survey studies, which suggests that few workers choose to leave employment voluntarily to enter unemployment, implies that, if increased benefits have had an impact on the level of unemployment, it is likely that they have worked through an increase in the duration of unemployment spells. An official estimate (Department of Employment, 1976, pp. 9–10) based on the numbers actually in receipt of the earnings-related supplement and also on the extreme assumption that the effect of the supplement was to double the period for which each person remained unemployed, suggests that the effect of the supplement was to increase male unemployment by only 50,000 above the level that it would otherwise have been. Applying this same procedure to the information available for later years, Tarling (1978, p. 34) obtained estimates of 40,000 for 1973 and 100,000 for 1977 – increases in unemployment that are substantially below those which actually occurred (see Table 8.3).

As we have seen, the recent rise in British unemployment has in large part been caused by an increase in the average duration of unemployment, and in a recent study, Nickell (1979a) analysed whether such increases in the duration of unemployment are attributable to changes in the levels of unemployment and supplementary benefits. Results obtained from an analysis of data on unemployed males drawn from the General Household Survey of 1972 show that unemployment duration is significantly affected by the replacement ratio, with an estimated elasticity (defined in household terms) of between 0.6 and 1.0. Between 1964 and 1973 actual unemployment rose by 92 per cent, and the analysis suggests that only 14 per cent of this may be attributed to benefits. As regards the effects of the introduction of earnings-related supplements. Nickell's results suggest that this increased male unemployment between 1965 and 1967 by approximately 9 per cent, as compared with the Maki and Spindler estimate of 33 per cent and the actual observed increase of almost 100 per cent. Thus, while unemployment and supplementary benefits do appear to have exerted significant influences on unemployment duration, they have been able to account for only a small proportion of the observed increases in unemployment.

POLICIES TO REDUCE UNEMPLOYMENT

As we have seen, the existence of some amount of frictional unemployment is inevitable in an economy where workers change jobs and where movement between jobs is not instantaneous. Since frictional unemployment is caused by lags in the adjustment of labour supply to changes in the pattern of labour demand, the numbers frictionally unemployed can be minimised by policies designed to improve the flow of information about unfilled job vacancies and thereby to cut down adjustment lags by decreasing the time spent in job search. The provision by the UK Employment Service of job centres, where vacancies are displayed and trained employment advisers can be consulted, is an example of one such policy measure. Structural unemployment, however, is characterised by a mismatch between available workers and unfilled job vacancies, and it arises because workers are neither occupationally nor geographically perfectly mobile. Long-run changes in the structure of demand and production occur in response to changes in the comparative cost position of different regions and countries, to technical progress, and to changes in tastes and preferences, and they mean that some sectors of the economy will be expanding while others will be contracting. Structural unemployment arises because workers displaced from declining sectors do not have requisite skills or locations for job-openings provided by the expanding sectors. Examples of structural changes giving rise to structural unemployment include the decline of the UK shipbuilding and textile industries. Notice that in both these cases the historic concentration of these industries in particular geographical regions has given rise to a corresponding geographical concentration of structural unemployment. The case of the microprocessor (or 'chip') is an example of a technological development that may give rise to possibly large amounts of structural unemployment in the future.

Since structural unemployment has its roots in the occupational and geographical immobility of labour, it can be reduced by manpower and regional policies. Such policies, which have been widely used in the UK, are designed to assist workers to obtain the skills required by available vacancies (by providing retraining schemes and offering grants for participants), to improve geographical mobility (by providing financial assistance towards relocation expenses and assistance in finding accommodation) and to encourage the movement of vacancies to available workers (by offering employers various financial incentives in the form of grants, tax concessions or low cost premises to move to certain specified areas). In addition, employment subsidies, such as the UK Temporary Employment Subsidy, which was introduced in 1975 and provided firms with a temporary lump-sum subsidy for each job that they maintained, are sometimes applied in an attempt to reduce the number of workers becoming displaced by declining industries (i.e. those becoming structurally unemployed). However, the long-run effects of such subsidies are uncertain, but it is probably true that they provide little more than a temporary reprieve (see Burton, 1977, 1977a).

DEMAND-DEFICIENT VERSUS NON-DEMAND-DEFICIENT UNEMPLOYMENT

Although it is often difficult in practice to distinguish between different types of unemployment, it is nevertheless very important from the policy viewpoint. If the principal cause of unemployment is identified as being demand deficiency, the cure is to be found in appropriate monetary and fiscal policies that increase the level of aggregate demand. If unemployment is diagnosed as being structural and frictional in nature, policies that increase the level of aggregate demand can have serious inflationary consequences (see Chapter 7). The solution to structural unemployment lies in manpower and regional policies that encourage mobility of labour (both occupational and geographic) and of jobs, and that improve training and retraining possibilities. As we have seen, as long as people change jobs, and as long as it takes a finite time to move from one job to another, some amount of frictional unemployment will exist. However, as we have also seen, the amount of frictional unemployment may be reduced, although not entirely eliminated, by policies designed to improve information flows regarding unfilled job vacancies and thereby to cut down lags in the matching of unemployed workers and unfilled job vacancies (i.e. by cutting down the time spent in job search). Therefore, in order to prescribe the correct policies for curing unemployment, it is necessary to know at least two things: first, how the total quantity of unemployment is split as between *demand-deficient unemployment* and *non-demand-deficient unemployment* (i.e. structural, frictional and seasonal unemployment), and second, how far it is possible to decrease non-demand-deficient unemployment without generating inflationary consequences that are in some sense unacceptable (i.e. to define what can be termed the *full employment level of unemployment*).

During the 1960s considerable controversy arose among American economists as to whether the principal cause of the relatively high US unemployment rates of the late 1950s and early 1960s lay in inadequate demand or structural factors. (For surveys of the controversy, see Gitlow, 1971, pp. 359–62, and Marshall *et al.* 1976, pp. 302–6.) An important attempt to clarify the distinction between demand-deficient and structural unemployment was made by Lipsey (1965).

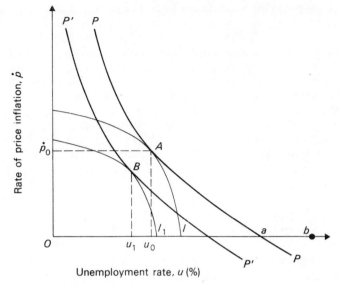

Figure 8.1   Demand-deficient   versus   structural   unemployment: Lipsey's analysis

In this analysis Lipsey stressed the relevance of the Phillips-curve trade-off between inflation and unemployment, and his argument can be illustrated by considering Figure 8.1, which shows the utility-maximising approach to the policy-makers' selection of the optimal inflation–unemployment combination, as considered in the last chapter (look again at Figure 7.6). Curve *PP* is the Phillips curve relating the rate of price inflation to the rate of unemployment, and utility is maximised at point *A*, where *PP* is tangential to indifference curve *I*. If the present rate of unemployment is *b*, unemployment can be reduced to *a* by demand expansion without causing the price level to rise, although clearly any reduction of unemployment below *a* can be achieved only at the cost of a positive rate of inflation. However, utility-maximising policy-makers will aim their aggregate demand policies at point *A*, and since they are willing to accept an inflation rate of $\dot{p}_0$ in order to secure a reduction in unemployment to u_0, Lipsey defined $\dot{p}_0$ as the *acceptable rate of inflation*. With a present unemployment rate of *b*, Lipsey defined the amount $(b - u_0)$ as demand-deficient unemployment, because it is the amount of unemployment that can be removed by increasing aggregate demand without creating unacceptable conflicts with other policy goals.

The only way in which unemployment can be reduced below u_0 without incurring an *unacceptable rate of inflation*, as defined by Lipsey, is for the Phillips curve to be shifted to the left. As we saw above, regional and manpower policies are means by which such a shift may be brought about, but such policies are not costless. If we assume that curve $P'P'$ represents the furthest shift in the Phillips curve that is justified on a social *cost–benefit analysis*, a new equilibrium position is established at B with lower levels of both inflation and unemployment. Lipsey defined the reduction in unemployment of $(u_0 - u_1)$ that can be thus secured as structural unemployment, because it is that which can be removed by structural measures that can be justified on cost–benefit grounds. The remaining amount of unemployment (u_1) was defined by Lipsey as frictional unemployment, because it is that which rational policy-makers do not wish to remove, given the costs and benefits of so doing. In view of this, Lipsey defined unemployment of u_1 as the full employment level of unemployment.[14]

THE RELATIONSHIP BETWEEN UNEMPLOYMENT AND UNFILLED VACANCIES

The relationship between the number of unemployed workers and the number of unfilled vacancies is of the shape shown by curve A in Figure 8.2. The negative slope of this curve indicates that, *ceteris paribus*, an increase in the numbers of unemployed workers is associated with a decrease in the numbers of unfilled vacancies, and vice versa. Suppose, for example, that the level of aggregate demand were initially such that the economy was at point x on curve A. If the government were to introduce policies to decrease the level of aggregate demand, the number unemployed would rise to, say, U_2 and curve A indicates that, *ceteris paribus*, the number of unfilled vacancies would fall to V_2, as shown by point y.

The unemployment vacancies $(U-V)$ relation is assumed to be convex to the origin, because, no matter how many unfilled vacancies exist, unemployment will not fall to zero. As we have seen, as long as people change jobs and as long as job changes are not instantaneous, some frictional unemployment will exist. While the average duration of unemployment tends to fall in tight labour markets as satisfactory jobs become easier to find, the plentiful supply of job vacancies encourages some workers voluntarily to quit their jobs in such circumstances to search for better ones. This factor, together with any structural unemployment that arises because the available unemployed workers do not match the requirements of available vacancies, limits the decline in unemployment as vacancies increase. At the opposite extreme, in

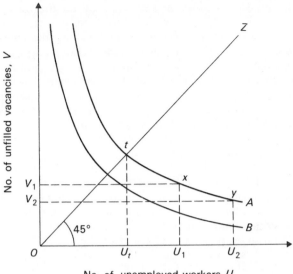

Figure 8.2   The relation between unemployment and unfilled vacancies

situations where unemployment is very high, unfilled vacancies will not
fall to zero, because some undesirable jobs will remain unfilled and
because some vacancies will remain unfilled for structural reasons (i.e.
because they require skills or are in locations that differ from those
possessed by unemployed workers). In addition, some vacancies remain
unfilled for frictional reasons, because, even though there are unemployed workers qualified and available to fill them, these workers have
not yet, given the scarcity of job vacancies, found a suitable one. These
considerations imply that the curve does not touch either axis, and it is
therefore usual to assume that it is everywhere convex to the origin, as
shown in Figure 8.2.[15]

As we have seen, changes in the level of aggregate demand result,
ceteris paribus, in movements around a given U–V curve: leftwards
when aggregate demand increases, and rightwards when it decreases.
However, if policies that improved the functioning of the labour market
(in the sense of reducing the adjustment lags of labour demand to
changes in supply, thereby reducing frictional unemployment) and/or
reduced structural unemployment were introduced, the U–V curve
would move leftwards to, say, curve B in Figure 8.2. This occurs
because, each time that an unemployed worker finds a job, there is a
simultaneous unit decrease in both the number unemployed and the

number of unfilled vacancies, so that such policies give rise to lower numbers of both unemployed workers and unfilled vacancies at each level of aggregate demand. Conversely, any factors that impede the functioning of the labour market and increase frictional unemployment, or that give rise to an increase in structural unemployment, result in a rightward movement of the *U–V* curve. Thus, the nearer the *U–V* curve to the origin, the more effective or, in a broad sense, *perfect* (Brown, 1976, pp. 137–8) are the structure and functioning of the labour market in matching unemployed workers to unfilled vacancies.

A Definition of Full Employment

We have already considered Lipsey's definition of the distinction between demand-deficient and non-demand-deficient unemployment and the associated definition of the full employment level of unemployment. Lipsey's definition sees full employment in terms of the extent to which unemployment can be reduced without creating an unacceptable conflict with the policy goal of price stability.

A commonly used alternative definition of the full employment level of unemployment is provided by *U–V* analysis. According to this approach, full employment (or the absence of a deficiency or excess of labour demand) is said to occur when the number of unemployed workers equals the number of unfilled vacancies, and this is shown in Figure 8.2 by the point where the $45°$ line from the origin (OZ) intersects the relevant *U–V* curve. In the case where curve *A* applies, full employment occurs at point *t*, giving a full employment level of unemployment of U_t. At this point the fact that any persons are unemployed can be ascribed either to their not yet having found some vacancy suitable for them that does in fact exist (frictional unemployment) or to their being in the wrong place or having the wrong skills or personal characteristics to fill an existing vacancy (structural unemployment), so that employment here is full in the sense that total unemployment is wholly attributable to what can be regarded as market imperfections rather than to an excess of the supply of labour over demand.

As we saw in the previous chapter, the labour market under consideration is in equilibrium, with labour demand equal to labour supply and the level of money wages remaining stable, when unemployment equals unfilled vacancies (see above, p. 135). At points along the *U–V* curve to the left of *t*, *V* exceeds *U*, and there is therefore an excess demand for labour, so that money wages tend to rise; conversely, at points to the right of *t*, *U* exceeds *V*, and there is an excess supply of labour, with a resulting tendency for money wages to fall. At points to the right of *t*, there is said to be demand deficiency, because the number unemployed exceeds the number of unfilled vacancies, while to the left of point t there is said to be *overfull employment*. If, for example, the level of aggregate demand were such that we were located at point x on the original curve A, the level of unemployment would be U_1, which exceeds the full employment level by the amount $(U_1 - U_t)$, and according to the current definition this amount can be termed demand-deficient unemployment. The above definition of full employment corresponds to equilibrium and, therefore (on the usual assumptions), to money wage stability in the relevant labour market, whereas Lipsey's definition is cast in terms of the level of unemployment consistent with the attainment of some acceptable rate of price of inflation. Notice that U–V analysis yields not one but a number of possible full-employment positions, with a different one corresponding to each U–V curve (i.e. to each possible structure of the labour market) and curves representing a greater degree of market imperfection (and thus being further from the origin) yielding higher full-employment levels of unemployment.

U–V analysis allows total unemployment in a given labour-market structure to be subdivided into demand-deficient and non-demand-deficient components, but it does not provide a subdivision of non-demand-deficient unemployment into its constituent structural and frictional components. If the labour market were at its full employment position at point t on curve A, the total number of unemployed workers (U_t) would be made up of structural and frictional components. Notice that the composition of the full employment level of unemployment as between structural and frictional elements can depend on the definition of the labour market in question. If we define frictional unemployment as that matched in skill and location by unfilled vacancies and structural unemployment as that not so matched, then it follows that, if a labour market were defined in terms of homogeneous labour in a particular locality, all of full employment unemployment would be frictional. However, if the labour market were more widely defined (e.g. covering a certain geographical region), the skills and locations required by unfilled vacancies might not match those of unemployed workers, with the consequence that some proportion of full employment unemployment would be structural.

Recent British Experience
During the late 1960s it was noticed that the relationship between unemployment and vacancies in Britain, a relationship that had previously appeared to be fairly stable, began to shift outwards (as shown by a movement like that from curve B to curve A in Figure 8.2), indicating that increased unemployment was becoming associated with a given level of vacancies. This increase in unemployment relative to vacancies was apparent for men only and appears to have begun in all

regions in September 1966 (Bowers *et al.*, 1970, p. 52) and to have continued until early 1972. Between 1972 and mid 1975 a new U–V curve appears to have been established, but a further displacement seems to be subsequently occurring. The shift that occurred in the U–V relationship between 1966 and 1974 was equivalent to an increase of approximately 300,000 in the level of male unemployment corresponding to a given level of unfilled vacancies.

Numerous hypotheses have been put forward to explain the observed shift in the British U–V relationship, although no single explanation seems able on its own to offer a completely satisfactory answer. The observed changes in the U–V relationship have been variously attributed: (1) to unemployed workers' being induced, by the introduction of earnings-related unemployment benefit in October 1966 and by the operation of the Redundancy Payments Act, which came into force in December 1965, voluntarily to spend more time in their search for a suitable job than they would otherwise have done (Gujarati, 1972), (2) to an increase in the incentive for those men who became unemployed to register in order to claim benefit, brought about by the introduction of earnings-related unemployment benefit (Evans, 1977), (3) a 'shake-out' (or shedding) of hoarded labour by employers during 1967 and 1968, brought about by business pessimism regarding future product demand, coupled with increased overheads associated with the employment of workers arising from the operation of the Redundancy Payments Act and from levies to the industrial training boards[16] (Taylor, 1972a), and (4) to the increase in the birth rate of the late 1940s, which resulted in a surplus of young and inexperienced workers in the late 1960s (Foster, 1974).

In view of the lack of agreement among economists as to the causes of the observed behaviour of the British U–V relation, the Department of Employment set up a working party in 1974 to consider the evidence for and against the various suggested explanations. Let us consider explanations stemming first from the unemployment side and secondly from the vacancies side. We have already considered the effects of benefits on the level of unemployment, and after an analysis of the numbers receiving benefits and their amount at relevant times, the working party concluded in its final report (Department of Employment, 1976) that the introduction of statutory redundancy payments and earnings-related supplements only accounted for a small proportion of the U–V shift. As we have seen, the shift was equivalent to an increase of about 300,000 in the level of male unemployment corresponding to a given level of vacancies, and the working party estimated that the effect of the introduction of statutory redundancy payments and earnings-related supplements was to increase unemployment only by amounts less than 20,000 and 50,000 respectively. The remainder of the observed increase in male unemployment between 1966 and 1972 was accounted for by a fall in male employment, apparently associated with a lower growth of output over the period, coupled with an increase in the rate of growth of labour productivity. During this period there was also an apparent shift towards a more economical use of labour by employers, with firms appearing to have had greater recourse to holding labour reserves externally than previously, and this apparent shedding (or 'shake-out') of hoarded labour reserves suggested some increase in the level of unemployment corresponding to a given level of vacancies.

On the vacancy side it was necessary to explain why vacancies did not fall during this period as much as would have been expected from the previous $U-V$ relation, and the possible explanations put forward for this occurrence included the existence of some minimum turnover of labour, and thus a minimum level of vacancies, at times of very low demand pressure and an increase in the ratio of recorded to true vacancies. A very rapid increase in vacancies occurred in 1972–3 following reflationary measures, and this was accompanied by a smaller reduction in unemployment than was to be expected, given the previous $U-V$ curve. The explanations suggested for this included the above-noted possible increase in the ratio of recorded to true vacancies and an increase in the mismatch between the skills and locations of the unemployed and those required by these extra vacancies. The postwar birth-bulge hypothesis (Foster, 1974) was, however, largely discounted, because it does not explain why the $U-V$ relationship remained stable for women and not for men.

NOTES ON FURTHER READING

A useful general survey of various aspects of unemployment is given in Parr (1978), and an important series of papers on the concept and measurement of involuntary unemployment have been published in the volume edited by Worswick (1976). Useful studies of the duration of unemployment are to be found in Fowler (1968), Cripps and Tarling (1974), McGregor (1978), Bowers and Harkess (1979) and, at a more advanced level, Lancaster (1979) and Nickell (1979). On the question of benefit-induced unemployment, the studies by MacKay and Reid (1972), Maki and Spindler (1975), Cubbin and Foley (1977) and Nickell (1979a) should be consulted. A useful set of survey results on the characteristics of the unemployed is contained in Daniel (1974), and the study of the unemployment statistics by Wood (1972, 1975) raises a number of important issues. As regards $U-V$ analysis, the paper by Brown (1976) provides a useful survey, the report of the Department of Employment working party (Department of Employment, 1976) surveys and assesses the various explanations put forward to explain the observed shift in the British relation, and other useful references include Bowers, *et al.* (1970, 1972) and Webb (1974).

Chapter 9

Wage Structure

Some facts regarding variations in earnings of individuals were presented in Chapter 1, where it was noted that the wage structure of an
economy, or the composition of wage differentials within it, can be
analysed between different occupations, industries and geographic
regions, as well as between different persons, sexes, age groups and
firms.[1] In this final chapter we examine determinants of the structure
of wages by occupation and industry.

WAGE STRUCTURE BY OCCUPATION

The structure of *wage differentials* between different occupations
provides a convenient starting point for our discussions. In order to
see how occupational differentials can arise and persist, let us consider two occupations (say A and B) and assume that each constitutes
a perfectly competitive labour market, with the labour demand and
supply situation initially prevailing in each occupation being as shown
in Figure 9.1. The equilibrium wage in occupation B is w_B, while that
in A is only w_A, so that there exists an absolute wage differential
between these occupations of $(w_B - w_A)$ or a percentage differential
of $(w_B/w_A - 1)100$. If we also assume that labour in both occupations
is homogeneous and that there is perfect information, with perfect and
costless mobility and the absence of entry barriers, then this differential
between occupations A and B will eventually be ironed out by movements of workers from the low wage occupation (A) to the high wage
occupation (B).

If we assume that such movements have no influence on the labour
demand curves in each occupation, these *interoccupational movements*
of workers will lead to an increase in the conditions of labour supply to
occupation B and to a decrease in the conditions to occupation A, with
in each case an unchanged labour-demand curve. Diagrammatically, we
see that the labour supply curve shifts leftwards in occupation A and
rightwards in occupation B as interoccupational movements occur.
Such movements will continue until supply shifts bring about a
common wage, in which case there is no incentive for additional move-

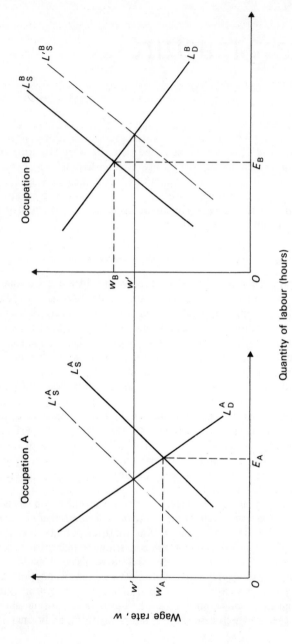

Figure 9.1 Occupational Wage Differentials

ments to occur. In our example migration between occupations A and B continues until the labour supply curve in A is shifted leftwards to L'^A_S and that in B is shifted rightwards to L'^B_S, so that a common wage of w' is established in both occupations. Therefore, in its most basic form (as outlined above) the competitive model predicts that any differences that occur in wages between different occupations will be ironed out by a process of interoccupational movement, in which workers leave the lower-paid occupation and enter the higher-paying one, thus raising the wage in the one while lowering the wage in the other – a process that continues until equilibrium is eventually established at a common wage.

When we come to confront this simple theory with the data, we find the existence and persistence of marked differentials between different occupations. Table 9.1 shows some results obtained from the New Earnings Survey of April 1978 regarding the structure of earnings of full-time men aged 21 and over by broad occupational groups. The first column of figures shows average gross weekly earnings for each occupational group and it should be noted that being earnings data, these include payments made for overtime, as well as payments made under payment-by-results schemes and such payments as shift premia. The second column has been added to provide a measure of earnings for working standard as opposed to overtime hours. It shows average hourly earnings, exclusive of the effects of overtime, and these data therefore provide a measure of hourly earnings during a basic working week.

As can be seen from Table 9.1, earnings on both hourly and weekly bases are highest in the general management occupational group and lowest in the farming, fishing and related group, with the proportional differential between these groups being 139.1 per cent in terms of weekly earnings. When one considers hourly earnings, the differential between these two occupational groups rises to 194.7 per cent – an increase that reflects, among other things, the fact that the general management group is recorded as working on average only 0.1 hours of overtime per week as compared to the 5.5 hours recorded in the farming, fishing and related group.

ECONOMIC THEORIES OF OCCUPATIONAL DIFFERENTIALS

Net Advantages Approach

In the *Wealth of Nations* Adam Smith (1776) suggested a number of reasons why occupational wage differentials may persist. By recognising that different occupations are not homogeneous, Smith argued that

Table 9.1 *Occupational differentials in Great Britain: full-time males aged 21 and over, April 1978 (£)*

Occupational group	Average gross weekly earnings	Average hourly earnings exclusive of effects of overtime
Non-manual		
General management	149.7	3.893
Professional and related in supporting management and administration	117.4	3.129
Professional and related in education, welfare and health	105.5	3.109
Literary, artistic and sports	101.6	2.541
Professional and related in science, engineering, technology and similar fields	105.8	2.658
Managerial (excluding general management)	100.4	2.561
Clerical and related	74.1	1.832
Selling	82.0	2.005
Security and protective services	88.3	1.934
Manual		
Catering, cleaning, hairdressing and other personal services	66.4	1.431
Farming, fishing and related	62.6	1.321
Materials-processing (excluding metals)	80.2	1.727
Making and repairing (excluding metal and electrical)	80.5	1.789
Processing, making, repairing and related (metal and electrical)	87.0	1.866
Painting, repetitive assembling, product-inspecting, packaging and related	79.8	1.771
Construction, mining and related not identified elsewhere	82.8	1.796
Transport-operating, materials-moving and storing, and related	80.4	1.641
Miscellaneous	73.8	1.560
All non-manual occupations	100.7	2.579
All manual occupations	80.7	1.728
All occupations	89.1	2.049

Note: These data refer to those whose pay for the survey period was not affected by absence.

Source: Department of Employment Gazette (1978), pp. 1152–4.

occupational wage differentials will exist and fail to be wiped out by interoccupational mobility because of differences in the advantages and disadvantages of different occupations, and the most widely discussed is the agreeableness or otherwise of the job (including the dangers inherent in, and the social prestige accorded to, the work). Smith argued that the process of movement between occupations under competitive conditions will lead, not to equalisation of the monetary (or pecuniary) advantages of different employments, but to equalisation of their *net advantages* (i.e. the sum of pecuniary and non-pecuniary advantages). Thus, if one occupation is less attractive or agreeable than another in terms of non-pecuniary factors, Smith's net advantages theory predicts that in equilibrium the pay in the former occupation will exceed that in the latter by an amount sufficient just to offset its non-pecuniary disadvantages. Such differentials are known as *compensating differentials,* and their magnitude, according to the net advantages theory, reflects equal and opposite differences in the non-pecuniary advantages of the occupations in question.

When we come to consider the available evidence, we find, however, that many of the most disagreeable jobs are the ones that, contrary to the prediction of the net advantages approach, receive the lowest monetary payments. For example, results from the 1978 New Earnings Survey show that full-time male (21 and over) road-sweepers and dustmen (occupations that most people would rank among the most disagreeable) received average gross weekly earnings of £60.6 and £70.4 respectively and average gross hourly earnings (exclusive of the effects of overtime) of £1.366 and £1.622 respectively, as compared to the corresponding earnings of (say) accountants of £107.4 per week or £2.906 per hour and the average earnings across all occupations of £89.1 per week or £2.049 per hour.

Non-competing Groups
The observation that wage differentials do not serve to equalise net advantages across all occupations led Cairnes (1874) to develop the concept of *non-competing groups*, which recognises that, while competition can be expected to bring about equality in the net advantages of certain occupations, there are others between which mobility is either impossible or occurs on such a limited scale as to have little, if any, equalising effect on net advantages. The essence of the non-competing groups concept is that there are groups of occupations each of which is commonly entered by persons from households in the same socioeconomic grade and within which mobility is high; hence, the net advantages of the different occupations comprising the group tend to equality, so that wage differentials between occupations within a given

group will represent compensation for the various deterrent aspects of the work. However, different groups are non-competing, in the sense that mobility between them is limited, and so there will be little or no tendency for net advantages between occupations from different groups to be equalised.

Intergroup movements are restricted, if not altogether prevented, by several factors (Phelps-Brown, 1977, p. 14): namely, lack of knowledge regarding the net advantages of other occupations and one's own ability to perform such jobs, lack of the means required to meet any migration, search and training costs necessary to enter the relevant occupation, and a lack of natural ability. Notice that this last point suggests that some proportion of the higher income attained by those actually in possession of such abilities may in certain cases be considered as a *rent of ability*. In cases where training is used as a barrier to entry to certain occupations, this presents further impediments to intergroup movements. Some aspects of this problem were considered in Chapter 5 in our discussions of the apparent similarity between the actions of certain professional bodies and craft unions in restricting the supply of entrants (via such means as the enforcement of training standards and the control of training places), thereby keeping the pay of incumbents up. However, as noted there, it is not always possible to be clear to what extent such supply restrictions by either craft unions or professional bodies are the result of a genuine desire to protect the public by maintaining standards or of a desire to keep earnings within the profession or craft up.

Thus, while movements within manual occupations may be expected to result in a tendency for the net advantages of, say, road-sweeping and dustbin-emptying to be equalised (notice the size of the wage differential between these two occupations, as shown above, which may reasonably be taken to represent a compensating differential), neither worker can, even if he does possess the required natural abilities, become, say, a consultant surgeon or a university professor, no matter how attractive he finds these jobs, without undergoing many years of study and training (with all its associated costs, including foregone earnings) in order to attain the relevant professional qualifications and experience. Even then, it is by no means certain that he will be appointed to a consultancy or a university chair.

The non-competing groups approach therefore suggests the existence of two different types of occupational differentials: first, those which occur between different occupations within a given group and which reflect differences in the non-monetary advantages of the different occupations, and second, those differentials which occur between occupations in different groups and which persist because movement between them is prevented for the various reasons set out above.

CHANGES IN THE OCCUPATIONAL WAGE STRUCTURE OVER TIME

The changes that have occurred over time in the occupational wage structures, and the extent to which these can be explained by the various economic theories of occupational differentials, have attracted considerable research interest.[2] Table 9.2, which presents data on

Table 9.2 *Average male earnings expressed as a percentage of average earnings of all male employees: Great Britain, 1913–78.*

Occupational group	1913–4	1922–4	1935–6	1955–6	1960	1970	1978
Unskilled manual	67	71	69	69	63	68	71
Skilled manual	113	100	105	98	94	84	91
Foremen	131	149	147	124	120	98	98
Clerks	105	101	103	82	80	78	77
Managers	213	267	237	233	218	199	168
Higher professional	349	323	341	243	240	172	173

Source: Diamond (1979), p. 81.

average male earnings in various occupational groups expressed as a percentage of the average earnings of all male employees (as shown graphically in Figure 1.4 above), gives an indication of the changes that occurred in the structure of earnings between broad occupational groups over the period 1913–78. As can be seen from this table, there was over the whole period a substantial reduction for each occupational group (other than the unskilled manual group) in the ratio of its average earnings to the average of all employees, signifying a narrowing or compression of occupational differentials. This reduction of occupational differentials was most marked for higher professionals (doctors, dentists, solicitors, etc.) in relation to all other groups.

In the preceding section theories of occupational differentials in general were considered. However, in the UK and other countries two specific dimensions of the occupational wage structure have attracted particular interest, namely, the differentials accruing to skilled as opposed to unskilled occupations, and to white collar as opposed to blue collar (or manual) occupations.

SKILL DIFFERENTIALS

This aspect of the occupational wage structure arises if we differentiate between occupations according to their level of skill and consider the size of the differential accruing to the skilled worker relative to the unskilled one. Table 9.3 gives a summary of the size of the skill differential for male manual workers in a number of British industries between 1963 and 1976. It shows the percentage differentials (for both hourly paid and payment-by-results workers) between skilled and unskilled workers in engineering, shipbuilding and ship-repairing and between craftsmen and general workers in chemical-manufacturing.

Long-run changes in skill differentials in certain industries have been studied in detail. For example, the pay of the craftsman and labourer in building was traced back fairly continuously in southern England from about 1300 to the present day by Phelps-Brown and Hopkins (1955), and their findings show a remarkable constancy in the ratio of the craftsman's wage to that of the labourer, as a measure of the differential for manual skill. In the fourteenth century the relation between these two rates varied, but by 1412, after the doubling of the crafts-man's wage that followed the Black Death, they settled in the ratio of three to two: namely, 6d a day for the craftsman and 4d for the labourer. By the 1890s these rates were 7½d an hour for the craftsman and 5d for the labourer, and by 1914 in central London they were 10½d and 7d respectively – still in the ratio of three to two. From 1914 onwards, however, the differential between skilled and unskilled manual workers in a number of occupations (including building) in Britain and a number of other countries (including the USA) began to contract (Phelps-Brown, 1977, pp. 73–4).

One particular British industry that has been extensively analysed is the engineering industry. Earnings in the British engineering industry during the twentieth century have been fairly well documented (see Hart and MacKay, 1975), and analysis of movements in the ratio of the average weekly earnings of adult male fitters (skilled workers) to the average weekly earnings of adult male labourers (unskilled workers) since 1914 shows three periods of rapid compression in the differential for manual skill. These are the periods during and immediately after the two world wars and the period from 1969 to the present. While neither of the wartime compressions in the engineering skill differential were followed by any rapid restoration of prewar differentials, there is some evidence of a gradual widening of percentage skill margins between 1950 and about 1969, with much of this gradual widening being reversed since 1969 – a pattern also evident in shipbuilding, ship-repairing and chemical-manufacturing (see Table 9.3). The skill dif-

Table 9.3 Skill differentials in Britain: average hourly earnings (excluding the effects of overtime) of skilled full-time adult male manual workers as a percentage of those for labourers in certain industries, 1963–76 (June each year).

Industrial group	1963	1965	1967	1969	1971	1972	1973	1974	1975	1976
Time workers										
Engineering	143	143	145	144	144	141	138	137	132	128
Shipbuilding and ship-repairing	134	140	144	132	133	131	128	129	122	119
Chemical-manufacturing	114	114	111	110	109	107	108	106	104	105
Payment-by-results workers										
Engineering	146	148	152	151	149	148	143	138	132	131
Shipbuilding and ship-repairing	138	140	146	148	148	142	136	134	131	130
Chemical manufacturing	111	109	109	110	107	108	107	108	108	108

Source: Department of Employment Gazette (1977) p. 595.

ferential in building in London appears to have behaved in a broadly
similar manner over the period since 1914, and the findings of an early
study of the skill differential in a sample of industries by Knowles and
Robertson (1951) confirm that the reduction in skill differentials was
not uniform but was largely confined to the two war periods, while
evidence presented by Crossley (1966, p. 205) suggests that the wartime compressions in skill differentials in a number of other industries
continued until the mid-1950s. Analysis of data on collective agreements
in sectors other than building and engineering shows the pattern to be
broadly similar to that observed in these two sectors, with marked wartime compressions in skill differentials, followed by a slight upward
movement between about 1955 and 1969, which was then followed
by a further compression.[3]

The available evidence suggests that differentials for manual skill
in Britain remained remarkably stable over the long-run period up to
about 1914, after which date they contracted, with skill differentials
being compressed particularly rapidly during the two world wars. A
number of hypotheses have been put forward to explain this observed
behaviour, and it is convenient to consider these under two headings:
first, those seeking to explain the observed long-run behaviour of
skill differentials, and second, those seeking to explain their cyclical
fluctuations.

Skill Differentials Over The Long Run

Some writers (e.g. McCormick, 1969, p. 110; Perlman, 1969, p. 85)
have seen the observed long-run behaviour of occupational differentials
in general, and the differentials between skilled and unskilled occupations in particular, as reflecting the changes in the balance of the supply
of, and demand for, skilled and unskilled labour that occur as part of
the workings of the price mechanism during the development process.
According to this view, skill differentials widen during the early stages
of development as an increased demand for skilled labour comes up
against an inelastic short-run supply curve. As development proceeds,
skill differentials narrow as the supply of skilled labour is increased by
the extension of education and training and as the demand for skilled
labour of certain sorts perhaps decreases as technical progress of the
labour-saving sort occurs.

Cyclical Variations in Skill Differentials

Other investigators have analysed the observed cyclical rather than
secular (or long-run) changes in the skill differential. Various writers
have produced evidence to show that skill differentials tend to widen

during depressions and narrow during booms (i.e. that they fluctuate countercyclically, although see Phelps-Brown, 1977, p. 76), and Reder (1955) argued that this results from fluctuations that occur over the cycle in the hiring standards of employers. Reder's argument is that during boom periods, when skilled workers become difficult to recruit, employers respond by promoting existing but not fully qualified employees from lower to higher skill levels; they replace these workers (together with any additional vacancies created as a result of the boom conditions) by recruiting from outside by offering improved wages at lower skill levels, thus giving rise to a narrowing of the skill differential. As the demand for labour subsequently contracts and depression occurs, this process operates in reverse, with employers tightening their hiring and job qualification standards; this gives rise to a consequent downward pressure on wages at lower skill levels, as displaced workers now unable to meet the employers' more exacting skill standards move down the skill ladder, with the result that there is a widening of skill differentials during depressed periods. Thus, according to Reder, fluctuations in labour demand over the cycle will be concentrated upon the lower skill levels, whose rates of pay will consequently vary more widely than those of skilled workers, thereby generating the observed countercyclical variations in the skill differential. This effect is likely to be stronger if, as has often been the case, the pay of the higher skill level is more regulated by collective agreements, so that it increases more slowly when demand rises and is more resistant to cuts when demand falls.[4,5]

The rapid erosion of the differential for manual skill that occurred in Britain during the two world wars may in part be explained by the operation of the above forces during the boom conditions of wartime, but the failure of pre-war differentials to reassert themselves in the post-boom years seems to present something of a problem for Reder's dilution hypothesis. In the munitions industries the demand for increased numbers of skilled workers was, given their scarcity, in large part satisfied by the upgrading or training of persons formerly excluded or by breaking the work down, so that at least part of it could be done by the less skilled. In addition, there was also a general decline in resistance to the crossing of occupational boundaries, and women workers in particular were admitted in large numbers to jobs that they were previously excluded from or thought incapable of performing. Thus, as the brunt of the wartime increase in demand for labour of all kinds was concentrating upon the less skilled, the wages of this group tended to rise relative to those of the more skilled – a process that was made more marked because at the same time these were the workers being conscripted into the armed forces in greatest proportion. Further, when wartime scarcities manifested themselves in a rising price level, there was a marked tendency in both wars, particularly in employments under public control, for compensatory wage increases to be agreed in the interests of equity in equal absolute terms for both high- and low-paid workers, and this resulted in further compressions of the skill differential.

Unions and Skill Differentials

Turner (1952) argued that in Britain the observed narrowing of the differential for manual skill has been associated with periods charac-terised by the growth of mass trade unionism (as opposed to the craft unionism, with its emphasis on the maintenance of the skilled crafts-men's differential, that preceded it). As unskilled workers became organised during the new unionism era of the early twentieth century, and as previously closed (craft) unions subsequently began to open their doors to the unskilled, unions tended, in view of the numerical preponderance of less skilled workers and because of their desire to expand further by attracting additional unskilled workers to their membership, to seek equal cash (rather than percentage) across-the-board increases for their members, regardless of their skill level. Accord-ing to Turner, this was a major determinant of the historical narrowing of skill differentials.

WHITE COLLAR DIFFERENTIALS

The second dimension of the occupational wage structure that has attracted particular attention is the differential between white collar and manual (or blue collar) occupations. The British evidence here, like that relating to the skill differential, shows a compression of differen-tials over the long run. For example, in a study of pay in the British Civil Service, Routh (1954) examined the pay of white collar grades relative to that of manual grades and showed that between 1875 and 1950 the pay of higher civil servants (administrative class) fell from almost nine times that of a postman to only three times. The long-run contraction of white collar differentials in Britain can also be seen from Table 9.2, which shows that, while the average earnings of un-skilled male (and to a lesser extent) skilled male manual workers re-mained largely unchanged between 1913 and 1978 in relation to the average of all male employees, the corresponding earnings ratios of clerks, managers and higher professional employees fell markedly over the same period.

As in the case of skill differentials, the contraction of white collar differentials in Britain occurred particularly rapidly during the last war. The ratio of the average salary to the average wage is often taken as providing a measure of the differential between white collar and manual occupations, and the extent of the compression of white collar differentials that occurred during the Second World War period is illustrated by some estimates due to Seers (1951), which suggest that the average increase in salaries over this period was only about half of that of wages.

The main factor at work here seems to have been an increase in the conditions of labour supply to white collar occupations, brought about by the extension of education over the last 100 or so years. However, these supply side influences need to be seen alongside other changes, such as shifts in the conditions of labour demand, changes in non-pecuniary advantages and the role of custom. In Britain the fact that the pay of professional and clerical workers held up quite well relative to that of manual workers until about the Second World War (see Table 9.2) is usually attributed to the near matching of the increased conditions of supply of educated workers up to this time by increased conditions of demand (Phelps-Brown, 1977, p. 86). The current rapid pace of labour-saving technical progress in the form of automation and computerisation of many clerical functions, brought about by developments in the field of microelectronics, may well serve to depress further the relative earnings of clerical workers in the future. Notice, in addition, the important and general point that, in cases where employment in a particular occupation is increasing, the fact that the occupation will generally be taking in a larger proportion of young workers will of itself tend to depress the level of average earnings in the occupation, because such workers, being new entrants, tend, *ceteris paribus*, to earn less than older workers.

GOVERNMENT INTERVENTION AND DIFFERENTIALS

During the 1970s UK incomes policies (with the exception of the 1977–8 10 per cent limit) were to varying degrees marked by the introduction of flat rate elements to pay increase limits. For example, the Social Contract (stage 1) policy, which applied between July 1975 and July 1976, placed a limit on wage increases of £6 per week for all workers except those earning over £8,500 a year, who received nothing. The further compression of the UK occupational wage structure that appears to have been occurring since the late 1960s may perhaps be in some part attributable to the operation of these policies, since, if observed, controls that specify an absolute limit on wage increases will automatically narrow percentage differentials. However, on the basis of an analysis of the available data, Dean (1978) found little evidence to support the view that incomes policies have been responsible for a marked compression of differentials. It has often been argued that periods during which incomes policies are removed are characterised by the restoration of differentials, but this study found little evidence of this effect.

Another form of government intervention in the process of wage determination that may be expected to influence wage differentials is the implementation of minimum wage legislation. In Britain there are wages councils setting minimum wages in such industries as agriculture, catering and the retail trades, while in the USA a federal minimum wage of wide coverage was established under the Fair Labor Standards Act 1938. By raising the wages of the unskilled and lower-paid worker, minimum wage legislation may be expected to bring about a narrowing of skill differentials. (For discussion of the employment effects of such legislation, see above p. 67.) However, the available evidence (Phelps-Brown, 1977, p. 81), which is derived mainly from US studies, suggests that such effects are only temporary, with differentials tending (particularly in cases where the lower-paid represent the lowest grade within a common scale) to reassert themselves fairly rapidly.

HUMAN CAPITAL THEORY

As we have seen, Adam Smith (1776) drew attention in his discussion of occupational differentials to the importance of differences in net advantages between different employments. Although the most widely discussed dimension of the advantages and disadvantages of different employments is the agreeableness or otherwise of the job, other dimensions include the degree of constancy of employment, the probability of success in the job, the degree of responsibility, and the time spent and costs incurred in learning the trade. The human capital approach to differentials, which is especially popular among US economists, stresses one particular dimension of the net advantages of different employments, namely the costs incurred in learning the job.

This approach considers education as a process of investment, which leads to the accumulation of human capital, and it examines the nature and magnitude to both the individual and society of the costs incurred in, and benefits derived from, education. Investment in human capital takes a number of forms, ranging from full-time education and on-the-job training to expenditures on job search, migration and the consumption of medical services to improve worker health. In this section, however, we consider only the process of investment in full-time education, discussing its implications for the structure of occupational differentials.[6]

Investment in Education

The fundamental notion of human capital analysis is that of a choice between alternative income and consumption streams. To illustrate this, consider the case of an individual faced with the choice between the following two alternatives: first, leaving school at time t equals zero (at age 18, say) and entering the labour force immediately to receive income of y_0 per period over the course of his working life (i.e. time zero through to t_n), or secondly, undergoing further training at a university or college for the period from time zero to T, receiving income y_1 for that time and subsequently receiving an income of y_2 per period for the remainder of his working life (i.e. T through to t_n). If the individual in question is in receipt of only a grant for his period of university study, the income y_1 will equal the amount of the grant net of out-of-pocket expenses, such as expenditure on books and payment of tuition fees (where these are payable by the students) plus any other expenses specifically associated with the course of study. In practice, however, student income is often boosted above this level by earnings from vacation jobs and sometimes by earnings from part-time employment during term-time.

The private costs of education are those incurred by the student himself, and these are of two sorts: first, the out-of-pocket expenditure on books and so on referred to above, and second, the difference between what could be earned and what is earned while undergoing training. Costs of the former kind are sometimes termed *direct costs,* while those of the latter kind, being *foregone earnings*, are termed *indirect costs.*

The choices confronting this individual are illustrated in Figure 9.2, which shows the time profiles of earnings for each of the alternatives, where y_1 denotes earnings during university training net of direct or out-of-pocket costs. During university the individual incurs total costs of $(y_0 - y_1)$ per period, which is the sum of foregone earnings and out-of-pocket expenditure. However, on successful completion of university training, the individual's earnings rise to y_2 per period, a level in excess of the amount that he could have been earning had he entered the labour force at age 18, and the excess of y_2 over y_0 for the remainder of the individual's working life is the gross monetary return to university education. At age 18 the individual confronted with the choice between these two possible courses of action faces an investment decision that involves a comparison of the attractiveness of the two alternative income streams, one of which involves a sacrifice of consumption during the initial periods in order to achieve a higher level of consumption in the later ones.

There are two main methods of investment appraisal used in

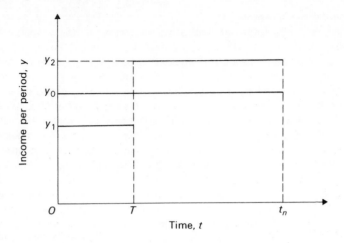

Figure 9.2 Investment in human capital

deciding from earnings profiles like those shown in Figure 9.2 whether investment in university education is worthwhile from the individual's viewpoint, the first being the *present value* approach and the second the *internal rate of return* approach.[7] In order to compare the different streams of income associated with the two alternatives, one calculates their present values by discounting back the relevant incomes to age 18 according to the following formulae:

$$PV(1) = \sum_{t=1}^{t_n} \frac{y_0}{(1 + i)^t}$$

$$PV(2) = \sum_{t=1}^{T} \frac{y_1}{(1 + i)^t} + \sum_{t=T+1}^{t_n} \frac{y_2}{(1 + i)^t}$$

where $PV(1)$ and $PV(2)$ denote, respectively, the present values of the income streams arising from the first and second alternatives and where i denotes a rate of interest or discount rate deemed to be appropriate in this context.

If the present values of these two income streams were equal, the individual would be indifferent between leaving school at age 18 and training for a job requiring T years of university education. According to the present value approach, investment in university education is worthwhile if the present value of income stream 2 exceeds that of stream 1, because in this case the individual is more than just compensated by increased earnings after completion of university education for the costs, both direct and indirect, incurred during the years spent at university.[8]

If one views university education as an investment opportunity, this criterion can be seen in a different but equivalent way. From this alternative viewpoint the *net present value* of the investment opportunity is calculated by discounting back to age 18 the difference in each time period between the income that will be derived if the investment in additional education is undertaken and that derived if it is not undertaken. Denoting the net present value of this investment opportunity by V, we have

$$V = \sum_{t=1}^{T} \frac{y_1 - y_0}{(1+i)^t} + \sum_{t=T+1}^{t_n} \frac{y_2 - y_0}{(1+i)^t}$$

and the appropriate criterion for undertaking university training is whether it yields a net benefit to the individual, as represented by a positive value of V. Notice that V is simply the difference between $PV(2)$ and $PV(1)$, so that this decision rule is equivalent to the previous one, namely, undertake the investment in university education if $PV(2)$ exceeds $PV(1)$.

The second method of evaluating investment in university education from the individual's viewpoint involves the derivation of an internal rate of return. This is a rate of interest at which the present values of the two alternative income streams are equal, and it is therefore a rate that will leave the individual in question indifferent between the two alternatives. To calculate this rate we set $V = 0$ in the above equation and solve for i. According to this method of appraisal, the criterion for undertaking the investment involves a comparison of the internal rate of return with the prevailing market rate of interest; the investment is undertaken if the internal rate of return exceeds the market rate of interest and not undertaken otherwise. Since the internal rate of return is such that the present value of the costs equals the present value of the returns, a prevailing market rate below this rate means that the investment opportunity is worthwhile, as it offers the individual a surplus of discounted benefits over discounted costs. There are, however, problems with this approach, because it involves solving an equation of high order whose properties are such that multiple roots may well be encountered.

Private versus Social Returns
The preceding analysis has been concerned with the private costs and benefits of investment in education (i.e. those borne by the student),

and this framework has been used to obtain estimates of the private (internal) rate of return on various alternative educational investments by comparing the costs borne by the individual in acquiring these educations with the resulting post-tax earnings streams. In one such study Ziderman (1973) estimated that in Britain during 1966–7 the average private rate of return on a first degree was 15 per cent for males, with corresponding rates for master's degrees and doctorates of 15.5 and 16 per cent respectively.

From the viewpoint of society as a whole, however, it is necessary when attempting to measure the economic benefits of additional education, to estimate a social rate of return. (See, for example, Morris, 1977.) This expresses the benefits derived by society as a whole (in the form of increased pretax earnings) as a return on the costs borne by society (i.e. total resource costs incurred in the provision of the educational facilities in question plus the private costs of education, where foregone earnings are taken as a measure of the production foregone by society while individuals are undergoing training). Morris and Ziderman (1971) estimated that the social rate of return on a first degree in 1966–7 was 10 per cent for males but that the rates for master's and doctoral degrees were only 8.6 and 7.6 per cent respectively.

Notice that in both these calculations education is treated solely as an investment good, with no attempt being made to allow for the benefits derived by either individuals or society from education as a consumption good in its own right.

Human Capital and Wage Differentials
The human capital approach has important implications for the structure of occupational wage differentials. Since some occupations require more training than others, human capital theory predicts that, once allowances have been made for differences between occupations in all non-pecuniary factors (other than training costs), the remaining wage differentials will reflect differences in training costs. To illustrate this, consider an economy in which there are only two occupations: 'unskilled' (which is entered immediately on leaving school) and 'skilled' (which requires three years of post school training). In the interests of simplicity, we assume that all workers possess identical tastes and equal natural abilities, that all jobs have identical non-monetary advantages, that each individual has the same length of working life and faces the same uncertainties of earnings and unemployment risks, and that each worker's income remains constant throughout his working life. In deciding whether to enter the skilled or the unskilled occupation, a rational school-leaver will compare the costs (i.e. foregone income plus out-of-pocket expenses) of undergoing the required training with the

benefits to be thus derived (in the form of an improved stream of future earnings), and under the above conditions he will opt for the skilled occupation only if the present value of the lifetime earnings stream from the skilled occupation, evaluated at school-leaving age, at least outweighs that of the unskilled one.

In the absence of any restrictions on either training places or entry into the skilled occupation, and with a general availability of grants or a perfect capital market when training is financed by borrowing (so that all individuals can borrow to finance their training at the prevailing rate of interest), we would expect competitive forces to operate so as to equalise the present values of the alternative income streams after allowance for repayment of loan and interest. Thus, in the above example, if the present value of lifetime earnings in the skilled occupation exceeds that of the unskilled one, the higher returns in the skilled occupation will attract an increased number of entrants, with the process continuing until these supply shifts bring about equality of the present values of lifetime earnings in both occupations. Supporters of human capital theory have argued that, if everyone can borrow money at the same rate of interest and if everyone has equal foresight, investments in human capital will be continued up to the point where the rate of return on all investments in human capital by people of equal ability equals the rate of interest.[9] Therefore in the long run (i.e. once present values have been equalised), the labour supply to each occupation in this example will be perfectly elastic, and there will exist a constant wage differential between the skilled and unskilled occupations, the magnitude of which will be just sufficient, when discounted back to school-leaving age, to cover the costs of training.

Although this explanation of occupational wage differentials is highly simplified, it is easily made more realistic by relaxation of the various simplifying assumptions made above. For example, if there exists a uniform retiring age, so that workers who have undergone training have a shorter working life, occupational differentials will have to be correspondingly higher in the long run to counteract this. If non-monetary advantages are not equal, with workers, say, preferring skilled to unskilled occupations, the monetary amount of the wage differential will in consequence be less than that necessary just to cover training costs. Similarly, differences in uncertainties regarding earnings and the stability of employment, and indeed death risks, between different occupations can be accounted for by introducing into the present value calculations estimates of the relevant probabilities. For instance, in occupations with a high risk of unemployment or fatal injuries and a high degree of uncertainty regarding earnings, long-run occupational differentials will need to be correspondingly increased, so as to bring about equality of the present value of expected lifetime earnings. If one allows for the existence of a range of skilled occupations, each requiring a different period of training, the human capital analysis predicts that, once net advantages have been equalised, the incomes of individuals will rise to higher levels the longer and the greater are the private costs of their training.[10]

Human capital theory has stimulated a large amount of empirical work, useful surveys of which can be found in Atkinson (1975, pp. 82–6) and Blaug (1976). The balance of this evidence seems to suggest that observed differentials are often greater than those required just to compensate for the training required to enter skilled occupations. More generally, US evidence suggests that only about 20 per cent of the inequality of earnings of full-time male employees can be explained by differences in education. However, recent evidence (Mincer, 1976) suggests that years of practical experience (taken as a measure of investment in on-the-job training and learning by doing) are of considerable importance as a determinant of earnings, and it shows that a human capital model including both years of education and years of practical experience can explain about half of the variation in the earnings of US males. (For British evidence, see Psacharopoulos and Layard, 1979.)

Summary

To summarise, the human capital approach to wage differentials (which is in essence a logical extension of Adam Smith's equalisation-of-net-advantages approach to allow for variations in the size and distribution over the worker's life cycle of the costs and benefits of the training required for different occupations) predicts that, in the long run, differentials between occupations will depend on the extent of training required and will be just sufficient to compensate for the costs of this training, after taking account of such factors as variations in non-monetary advantages, uncertainties in respect of earnings and unemployment, and variations in the length of working life.

INDUSTRIAL WAGE STRUCTURE

Another aspect of the wage structure that has attracted considerable attention is the structure of wages between different industries. Table 9.4 summarises results obtained from the New Earnings Survey of April 1979 concerning the average gross weekly and hourly earnings (the latter being exclusive of the effects of overtime) of full-time manual men aged 21 and over by their industry of employment. As can be seen from this table, average weekly (hourly) earnings varied widely

Table 9.4 *Industrial differentials in Great Britain: full-time manual men aged 21 and over, April 1979 (£).*

Industry	Average gross weekly earnings	Average hourly earnings exclusive of effects of overtime
Agriculture, forestry and fishing	68.7	1.457
Mining and quarrying	117.8	2.581
Food, drink and tobacco	97.7	1.924
Coal and petroleum products	114.9	2.422
Chemicals and allied industries	99.4	2.129
Metal manufacture	103.3	2.220
Mechanical engineering	97.7	2.072
Instrument engineering	94.4	1.986
Electrical engineering	92.8	2.015
Shipbuilding and marine engineering	106.4	2.106
Vehicles	102.8	2.246
Metal goods not elsewhere specified	95.6	2.044
Textiles	85.5	1.853
Clothing and footwear	79.3	1.832
Bricks, pottery, glass, cement, etc.	100.2	2.047
Textiles, furniture, etc.	88.1	1.940
Paper, printing and publishing	104.3	2.235
Other manufacturing	95.7	2.068
Construction	91.2	1.956
Gas, electricity and water	95.4	2.099
Transport and communication	95.8	1.887
Distribution trades	80.3	1.731
Insurance, banking and business services	84.7	1.856
Professional and scientific services	76.2	1.645
Miscellaneous services	76.0	1.682
Public administration	77.4	1.721
All industries and services	93.0	1.975

Note: These data refer to those whose pay for the survey pay period was not affected by absence.
Source: Department of Employment Gazette (1979), pp. 977–9.

between industries and ranged from £68.7 (£1.457) in agriculture, forestry and fishing to £117.8 (£2.581) in mining and quarrying.

Strictly speaking, industry differentials are differences in wages that exist between workers who differ solely in respect of the product that they make, and in measuring these one should ideally compare between different industries the wages of common occupations within a particular locality. However, the data available in practice (like those in Table 9.4) generally refer to averages across the various occupations and skill levels employed in the industries in question, with the consequence that the differentials in average earnings thus observed reflect not only industry differentials in the sense defined above, but also differences between industries in the distribution of their labour force by occupation, skill, region, size of firm and the like.

STABILITY OF THE INDUSTRIAL WAGE STRUCTURE

A notable feature of the industrial wage structure is the remarkable long-run stability of the rankings of industries by their average wage levels. One measure of the stability of the industrial wage structure that has frequently been used is the *rank correlation coefficient* (which provides a measure of the strength of association between two sets of rankings). In an analysis of data on hourly earnings in 132 separate industries in Britain, Crossley (1966, p. 200) obtained a value of + 0.87 for 1959 against 1948, and in a similar calculation based on data of average weekly earnings of male manual workers in twenty-nine industries in manufacturing, Norris (1979, p. 371) obtained a coefficient of + 0.69 for 1938 against 1906.[11]

The competitive model predicts that in the long run, when mobility between industries has wiped out any non-compensating wage differentials, the wage of a given occupation or grade of labour will, after due allowance for any differences in non-pecuniary factors, be equal in different industries. On the assumption that long-run labour-supply functions to industries are both perfectly elastic and fixed in their position, there will be no association in the long run between the wage that an industry pays to a given grade of labour and the amount of this labour that the industry employs. However, because different industries employ different mixes of occupations, it follows that in the long run the average wage that each industry pays will vary, other things being equal, with its skill mix, with industries that employ a high proportion of skilled workers paying higher average wages than those employing a low proportion.

In the short run, labour supply functions remain fixed but are likely to be less elastic than their long-run counterparts, so that, *ceteris paribus*, an increase in labour demand in one industry requires an increase in its relative wage in order to call forth the increase in labour supply required to re-establish equilibrium, and the greater the increase in employment over the recent past, the greater will be the change in the industry's wage. Thus, the competitive model predicts that the industrial wage structure will tend to vary more over the short period, being re-established as time passes. More precisely, the competitive analysis predicts the existence of a positive association in the short run between changes in employment and changes in wages by industry, but the absence of any such association in the long run.

A number of investigators have examined the relationship between wage and employment changes and found evidence consistent with the prediction of the competitive hypothesis. For example, Reddaway (1959) examined the relationship between employment changes and changes in hourly earnings in 111 British manufacturing industries between 1951 and 1956 and found the existence of a significant positive correlation between these two variables, with a simple correlation coefficient of + 0.43.[12] Phelps-Brown and Browne (1962) made a similar calculation from a sample of 132 UK industries (including non-manufacturing ones) between 1948 and 1958 and found a weaker, although still significant, positive correlation between changes in wages and employment, with the relevant correlation coefficient being + 0.24. The competitive model predicts that a positive correlation between wage and employment changes is only a short-run phenomenon, and the fact that the latter study, covering a longer time period, found a lower correlation is in conformity with expectations. Over the long run the competitive model predicts that the positive correlation between employment and wage change will disappear, and this is indeed the finding that emerged from a number of long-run studies of both the UK and US experiences.[13] For example, Crossley (1966, p. 219), using data relating to twenty-six UK industries over the period 1924–50, reported a correlation coefficient of − 0.22 between changes in earnings and employment, and since this value is not significantly different from zero at the 5 per cent level, this finding is consistent with the competitive hypothesis.

DETERMINANTS OF AVERAGE WAGES BY INDUSTRY

A number of recent studies have focused attention on the determinants of variations in the average level of wages in a cross-section of UK industries. (See, for example, Sawyer, 1973, Hood and Rees, 1974, and Wabe and Leech, 1978). Such studies have confirmed the influence of an industry's skill mix and rate of employment growth over the recent past on its average wage level, and they seem to confirm that, other things being equal, average wages are higher in industries characterised by a high degree of unionisation or collective agreement coverage (see Chapter 6). A number of other factors have emerged, with varying degrees of empirical support from these studies and their US predecessors, as determinants of inter-industry variations in average wages. These include measures of concentration (as proxies for the degree of product market monopoly), establishment size, the sex and age mix of the workforce, together with measures of its regional distribution and the incidence of shiftwork. Age and sex mix variables have been introduced into such studies on the grounds that average wages are expected to be lower in industries where there is a high proportion of women and workers at the beginning and end of their working lives, as such workers tend, other things being equal, to earn less than males and prime-aged workers (see above, p. 212). The proportion of workers employed in shiftworking schemes has been found to exert a significant positive influence on industry average earnings (reflecting the premiums commanded by such work to compensate for disruptions and inconveniences caused by working 'unsocial hours'), as has the proportion of employment that is in the South-East and Midlands regions (reflecting regional variations in pay).

Two hypotheses that have attracted particular attention in the recent literature concern the influence of monopoly power in the product market and of plant size on interindustry variations in average wages. A positive and significant relation between plant size and average earnings has been observed both in cross-sections of British and US industries (see respectively Sawyer, 1973; Masters, 1969) and within the British engineering industry (Mayhew, 1976). However, the precise reasons for this association are not clear, because plant size may well be correlated with a variety of other interindustry characteristics, which may themselves influence average earnings. For example, plant size may reflect some of the effects of unions on average earnings; to the extent that there are economies of scale in the unionisation and organisation of workers at the workplace level, plant size may be proxying the degree of unionisation and may also reflect the intensity and effectiveness of union activity. Alternatively, it has been suggested that the positive association between plant size and earnings reflects the fact that the average quality of labour within any given skill category is higher the larger is the size of plant. Finally, this association may simply reflect the fact that there are non-pecuniary disadvantages associated with working in large plants, so that any premium associated with plant size reflects, at least in part, a compensating differential for the disutility associated with such employments, consequential upon the high degree of dependibility and regimentation required by the greater interdependence and division of labour employed in large plant production.

The relation between an industry's average wage and its degree of monopoly power in the product market has been examined in a number of studies in order to test the hypothesis that, *ceteris paribus*, workers tend to receive higher wages in industries whose product markets are dominated by a small number of producers. There are several arguments underlying this hypothesis, but none has any easily recognisable counterpart in the conventional theory of the firm. A commonly advanced argument is that monopolistic firms will share any supernormal profits that they may earn with their employees in an attempt to purchase an amicable industrial-relations climate. Alternatively, it is sometimes suggested that existing firms will be more likely to agree to high wages the greater is their degree of monopoly power, as by so doing they can erect an additional barrier against new entrants in cases where these will have to face the same wage levels. On the strength of such arguments, a number of investigators have included among their explanatory variables concentration ratios (showing the proportion of the industry's sales accounted for by the largest four or five firms) to represent the degree of monopoly power, and the results of such studies provide some evidence to confirm that in both the UK and the USA the degree of product-market monopoly power is a significant determinant of inter-industry variations in the average level of wages (e.g. Weiss, 1966; Mulvey, 1976).

NOTES ON FURTHER READING

An extremely thorough and readable survey of the literature on the structure of pay is provided in Phelps-Brown (1977), and other useful references include Reynolds and Taft (1956), OECD (1965), Crossley (1966) and Atkinson (1975).

Although this chapter has concentrated on differentials in wages between different occupations and industries, the structure of wages can also be considered between different geographical regions, the sexes, different racial groups and most generally between different individuals. In Britain it is widely recognised that average earnings vary between regions. For example, results of the 1979 New Earnings Survey show that, in April of that year, the average gross weekly earnings of full-time men aged 21 and over in England were £101.6. On a regional basis the average earnings of these workers ranged from £92.4 in the South-West to £108.5 in the South-East, while further disaggregation shows that earnings were highest in the Greater London subregion at £115.5 per week. Because regions differ in respect of their industrial and skill mixes, at least part of the observed regional differentials in average earnings can be attributed to those factors. Once allowance has been made for such differences, evidence (Crossley, 1966, pp. 212–13) seems to suggest that some regional differentials remain. While it has sometimes been suggested that such differentials reflect in part regional variations in living costs and unemployment rates (as a proxy for excess demand in the labour market; see Chapter 7), the persistence of regional differentials for given types of labour seems to suggest that the equilibriating process by which workers move from high to low wage areas has occurred on a scale insufficient to remove regional wage differentials. The question of geographical differentials has attracted greater attention in the USA than in Britain, and for surveys of the literature relating to the US North–South differential, see Perlman (1969, pp. 124–40) and King (1972, pp. 40–2).

In Britain, as in most other countries, women's earnings are on average less than those of men, and there is also considerable evidence, derived mainly from US studies, to suggest that, even after allowing for differences in skill, blacks and some other minority groups earn less than whites. (For example, on an all industries basis, women's hourly earnings in Britain in 1960 were only 60.5 per cent of men's, while results from the 1979 New Earnings Survey show that on average the hourly earnings of full-time female manual workers were 70.2 per cent of those of male workers, with the corresponding figure for the earnings of all females relative to males being 71.3 per cent.) In Britain sex differentials narrowed sharply during the Second World War, and in the mid 1970s equal pay legislation, designed to achieve equal pay for equal work, came fully into force, but the precise effects of this legislation are not yet clear. Most investigations have concluded that sex differentials arise for the following two reasons rather than from any general tendency for women to be paid a lower rate for the same job: first, women are crowded into the low-paying industries and occupations, and second, within given occupations women tend to be disproportionately concentrated in the lowest-paying grades. It is usually argued that, because of family and particularly parental commitments, women have a lower degree of labour force attachment that men, with the consequence that, other things being equal, male and female labour may not be perfect substitutes from the employers' viewpoint. In recent years a number of writers (e.g. Becker, 1971) have considered this topic in more detail and have sought to explain sex (and race) differentials in terms of an economic theory of discrimination,[14] and these contributions have served to demonstrate that the issues and mechanisms involved here are complex and operate both prior to and after the individual's entry into the labour market. For survey of the literature on discrimination, see Marshall (1974), Chiplin and Sloane (1976), Phelps-Brown (1977, pp. 145–80) and Siebert and Addison (1977). For an analysis of sex differentials in professional employments in Britain see Chiplin and Sloane (1976a).

The distribution of earnings between individuals depends not only on the magnitude of occupational differentials but also on the number of workers in each occupational group and on the differentials that exist within occupational groups. On the basis of an examination of the earnings of US males in 1959, Lydall (1968) concluded that as little as 25 per cent of the variance in earnings could be attributed to variations between occupations, with the remainder being accounted for by intraoccupational variations. Size distributions of earnings were introduced in Chapter 1, and these have for a long time attracted considerable interest from economists. However, while the shape of such distributions has been well described algebraically,[15] there exists considerable controversy as to the precise nature of the underlying mechanisms and determinants that generate such distributions, and there is marked disagreement among economists on the exact roles of such factors as personal characteristics, environmental factors, education and chance. Useful surveys of the literature on the personal distribution of income are given in Lydall (1968), Mincer (1970) and Sahota (1978), and the human capital approach is discussed in Mincer (1958, 1976). See also Goldberger (1978). An important collection of papers illustrating the main alternative approaches to this topic may be found in Atkinson (1976), and the reports of the Diamond Commission, set up to examine the distribution of income (and wealth) in Britain, contain much of interest. See, in particular, Diamond (1975, 1979).

Notes

CHAPTER 2

1 Estimates of employees in employment include employees temporarily laid off and persons who are unable to work because of short-term illness but who are still on employers' payrolls. They also include part-time workers as full units.

2 For estimates of the numbers of so-called 'unregistered unemployed', see *Department of Employment Gazette* (1976), pp. 1331–6.

3 Bowen and Finegan (1969, p. 17) used the term 'earnings' to encompass not only monetary payments but also fringe benefits and working conditions.

4 It should be noted that Bowen and Finegan (1969, p. 18) dealt in terms of a set of imputed non-market earnings rates, rather than productivities.

5 For further discussion, see Hunter (1970, pp. 43–5) and Byers (1976, pp. 76–7).

6 The difficulties associated with defining full employment are well known. In US studies a figure of 4 per cent unemployment has frequently been taken as consistent with full employment. (See, for example, Dernburg and Strand, 1966.) In the UK's case Corry and Roberts (1974, p. 17) derived their potential labour-force estimates on the basis of a prevailing rate of unemployment equal to the average rate over their study period, 1951–70.

7 See Taylor (1974, pp. 37–9) for discussion of an alternative method of estimating hidden unemployment, referred to as the *trend through peaks* method.

8 The following analysis is, however, sometimes interpreted in terms of the supply of hours of households that consist of a single earner or potential worker (McClements, 1978, p. 69).

9 The equation of the budget line can be written as

$$Y = Y_0 + wH$$

But since $H = 24 - L$ and $Y_m = Y_0 + 24w$, we obtain by substitution,

$$Y = Y_0 + 24w - wL = Y_m - wL$$

which is the equation of a straight line with intercept Y_m and a slope of $-w$.

10 For a formal proof of this result together with a discussion of second-order conditions, the more mathematically inclined reader should consult Henderson and Quandt (1971, pp. 29–30).

11 The possibility of corner solutions is discussed in Fleisher (1970, pp. 42–3) and Rees (1973, p. 23). In cases where the indifference curves are steeper everywhere along the budget line than the line itself, the worker's utility is maximised at point Y_0'. In this case the worker chooses not to participate in the labour force and consumes 24 hours of leisure per day. At the other extreme is the case where the indifference curves are less steep than the budget line. In this case the utility-maximising worker's solution is at point Z, so that he works the maximum feasible number of hours per day.

12   Of particular interest is Robbin's (1930) paper, which is formulated in terms of the demand for income in terms of effort, rather than the supply of hours.

13   For a discussion of the identification problems involved here, see Feldstein (1968). See also Lewis (1957) for an intuitive interpretation of the observed behaviour of hours actually worked in terms of both supply and demand side forces.

14   *Department of Employment Gazette* (1978), p. 962. For further discussion of overtime working in British industry, see Whybrew (1968), Hughes and Leslie (1975) and Leslie (1976).

15   In practice, progressively higher rates of overtime premiums are sometimes paid for increasing amounts of overtime worked. For example, the first 2 hours of overtime may be paid at time and a quarter and the following 2 hours at time and a half, with subsequent hours at double time. In such a case the budget line contains several kinks, and the analysis of the text remains substantially unaltered.

16   It is interesting to notice that, if the segment of indifference curve I_1 to the left of point A were everywhere more steep than the section AE of the budget line, the worker would refuse to work overtime. If the worker were unable to choose the number of hours of overtime that he actually works (e.g. because the total available amount is rationed among the workforce according to seniority), he might not be able to reach his new equilibrium position at point B. For example, if only 1 hour of overtime were available to him, the worker would move from A to point C, and although the level of utility that he would achieve at C is less than that he would achieve if he were able to reach B, it is still in excess of that achieved at A in the absence of overtime payments. If each employee is in this position, the overtime premium is set higher than is necessary to call forth the total number of overtime hours that are demanded.

    Conversely, the worker, if he is to work any overtime at all, may be required to work more than his optimum amount. Such a situation may arise if the worker is offered the opportunity to work an additional complete shift or for a full rest, or weekend, day. In the example of Figure 2.4, the worker will decline the opportunity to work overtime in excess of 7 hours, as this will place him along segment DE and therefore on a lower indifference curve than could be achieved with no overtime working at A. However, the opportunity to work for an overtime stretch of between 2 and 7 hours will be accepted, because points between B and D are on indifference curves above I_1.

17   The determination of *actual* hours of work is, however, influenced by both demand and supply side forces. It is often argued that workers' preferences are likely to take effect in the long run through collective bargaining about the length of the standard working week (Hunter, 1970, p. 40) and that employers will, in any case, have an incentive to adjust offered hours to take account of workers' preferences, since by so doing an employer gains a competitive advantage in that he will be able to attract workers at a lower wage or to attract better workers, Friedman (1962, p. 205). For example, in cases where an employer finds difficulties in recruiting sufficient numbers to work his offered hours, he may choose to adjust these to workers' preferences, perhaps by introducing 'twilight' shifts or working schedules for married women consistent with school times, in preference to offering increased wage rates as a possible means of attracting sufficient labour hours.

18   *Social Trends 6* (London: HMSO, 1975), p. 88.

CHAPTER 3

1   For a useful survey of the historical origins of marginal productivity theory and a critique, see Cartter (1959, pp. 11–44).

2   A perfectly competitive labour market is one where a large number of buyers and sellers, each of whose volume of transactions is so small in relation to that of the market as a whole that its own actions have no perceptible influence on the ruling wage, negotiate the exchange of homogeneous labour. For further discussion, see Marshall *et al.* (1976, pp. 175–7).

3   The isoquants in Figure 3.1 are drawn as continuous curves on the assumption that the firm's production function is itself continuous. Their convexity to the origin follows from the usual assumption of a diminishing marginal rate of technical substitution as one factor is substituted for the other one. For further discussion, see Henderson and Quandt (1971, pp. 54–62) or Laidler (1974, pp. 99–111).

4   In geometric terms, average physical product at any point on the *TPP* curve is given by the slope of the straight line drawn from the origin to the point, while marginal physical product is given by the slope of the tangent to the *TPP* curve at the point in question.

5   In terms of the isoquant-mapping of Figure 3.1, total physical product achieves its maximum at the point where the horizontal line $K_0 K_0$ is tangential to an isoquant (i.e. at point A, where the firm's labour input is L_2 manhours). Since the slope of the isoquant at this point is zero, it must here be intersected by a *ridge line*.

6   For further discussion of this point, see Cartter (1959, pp. 15–18).

7   Since our analysis is confined in this section to the short-run period, it is not necessary to make a distinction between monopoly and monopolistic competition, because these two market structures essentially only differ in the long run. See, for example, Lipsey (1975, p. 279).

8   For further discussion of the relationship between competitive conditions in the product market and the labour demand of firms with given *MPP* curves, see Marshall *et al.* (1976, pp. 224–7). For discussion of the case of oligopolistic product markets, see Peel (1972).

9   More formally, if the firm sells its output in a perfectly competitive market at price P, its long-run profit function is

$$\pi = Pq - wL - rK$$

where $q = q(K, L)$ is its long-run production function and r denotes the price of capital services.

Long-run profits are a function of K and L and are maximised by setting the partial derivatives of π with respect to L and K equal to zero. Substituting and partially differentiating, we obtain

$$\frac{\partial \pi}{\partial L} = P \frac{\partial q}{\partial L} - w = 0$$

$$\frac{\partial \pi}{\partial K} = P \frac{\partial q}{\partial K} - r = 0$$

Noting that $\partial q / \partial L$ and $\partial q / \partial K$ equal the marginal physical products of labour (MPP_L) and capital (MPP_K) respectively, we obtain the first-order conditions

$$w = MPP_\text{L} \cdot P = MRP_\text{L}$$

$$r = MPP_\text{K} \cdot P = MRP_\text{K}$$

which require each input to be utilised up to the point where its marginal revenue product (which equals its value of marginal product in this case) equals its price. Second-order conditions require the marginal physical product of each input to be decreasing with respect to its own employment.

10   Letting c denote the level of total costs, we have

$$c = wL + rK$$

Rearranging, we obtain

$$K = \frac{c}{r} - \frac{wL}{r}$$

which is the equation of a straight line on the K–L plane with slope $-w/r$. By varying c, a family of isocost lines is obtained.

11   To show this, we totally differentiate the firm's long-run production function $q = q(L, K)$ to obtain

$$dq = \frac{\partial q}{\partial L} dL + \frac{\partial q}{\partial K} dK$$

Now, the partial derivatives of q with respect to L and K are the marginal physical products of labour (MPP_L) and capital (MPP_K) respectively, and therefore

$$dq = MPP_\text{L} \cdot dL + MPP_\text{K} \cdot dK$$

For movements along a given isoquant, $dq = 0$, so we obtain by rearrangement

$$\text{Marginal rate of technical substitution} = -\frac{dK}{dL} = \frac{MPP_\text{L}}{MPP_\text{K}}$$

12   For convenience the expansion path in Figure 3.6 is drawn as a straight line. Expansion paths are not necessarily linear, but it is interesting to notice that a sufficient condition for linearity is that the production function be homogeneous of any degree. For a proof, see Chiang (1974, pp. 415–6).

13   At each point on the expansion path

$$\frac{MPP_\text{L}}{MPP_\text{K}} = \frac{w}{r} \tag{1}$$

and for long-run profit maximisation, with perfect product markets, we have the conditions

$$w = MPP_\text{L} \cdot P$$
$$r = MPP_\text{K} \cdot P \tag{2}$$

Since (2) is a special case of (1), the firm's long-run equilibrium must lie on its expansion path.

14   Namely, that the marginal physical product of each factor increases as the employment of the other input is increased.

15   Note that point *C* must lie on the expansion path *OX* pertaining to the input prices w_1 and r.

16   It is worth noting that the scale effect, *Y* to *C*, can itself be subdivided into what Ferguson and Gould (1975, pp. 372–4) termed output and profit-maximising effects. The former is the movement along the expansion path from *Y* to the position where output is maximised for the initial expenditure on inputs. The latter effect is the movement along the expansion path from the output-maximising position to the new long-run equilibrium point *C*.

17   The *elasticity of substitution* is a measure of the extent to which one input can be substituted for another in the production of a given level of output. The elasticity of substitution of labour for capital is defined in a two-factor model as the proportionate rate of change of the labour–capital ratio divided by the proportionate rate of change of the ratio of input prices. For further discussion, see Laidler (1974, p. 184) or Ferguson and Gould (1975, pp. 387–8).

18   Hicks demonstrated that Marshall's third rule, 'the importance of being unimportant', only holds if the elasticity of demand for the final product exceeds the elasticity of substitution between labour and the other factor of production. If this condition does not hold (i.e. when the consumer can substitute less easily than the producer), Marshall's third rule is reversed.

The economic meaning of the Hicksian correction has generated considerable controversy over the years. See, in particular, Bronfenbrenner (1961, pp. 254–61; 1971, pp. 148–50), Hicks (1961, pp. 262–5) and, for a recent reconsideration, Maurice (1975, pp. 385–93). For more detailed discussion of Marshall's rules, see Layard and Walters (1978, pp. 259–76).

CHAPTER 4

1   For further discussion, see Cartter (1959, pp. 52–6).

2   This assumes the absence of unemployed workers, of the appropriate type, in the firm's local labour market. If, however, a pool of unemployed workers exists at the prevailing wage rate, it is possible for the firm to increase its employment by the extent of the unemployment, without increasing its wage rate. Thereafter, the monopsonistic firm faces a positively sloping labour-supply curve. In addition, it is sometimes argued that, if labour is not homogeneous, the employer may, in order to attract additional workers, lower his employment standards. In this case, even though the wage rate per worker may remain unchanged, the wage per *efficiency unit* of labour rises, with the consequence that the employer faces an upward-sloping supply curve of labour in efficiency units. For further discussion, see Cartter (1959, pp. 52–4).

3   There is an extensive literature concerning the nature and functioning of local labour markets. See, in particular, Robinson (1970) and MacKay *et al.* (1971).

4   Notice that employment in this case is measured in numbers of workers rather than hours on the basis of the simplifying assumption that at each wage rate all persons work a constant number of hours.

5   Notice from Figure 4.4 that, in equilibrium, the wage paid by the monop-
     sonist (w) is less than labour's marginal revenue product (i.e. w_A). The
     extent to which the wage rate diverges from labour's marginal revenue pro-
     duct is frequently seen as a measure of the *exploitation* of labour – a con-
     cept discussed in some detail by Cartter (1959, pp. 65–70). See also the
     early discussion by Bloom (1941).
6   The question of training is considered in more detail in Chapter 9 in our
     discussion of investment in human capital.
7   There is in existence an extensive literature covering the operation of the
     internal labour markets that exist within firms and organisations. See, in
     particular, Doeringer and Piore (1971).

CHAPTER 5

1   The origins of craft unions have been traced back to the medieval craft
     guilds. For a detailed historical analysis of the forerunners and origins of
     trade unionism in Britain, see Webb and Webb (1920, pp. 1–64). Notice, in
     particular, that the Combination Acts 1799 and 1800 (subsequently repealed
     in 1824) made combinations of workers illegal.
2   For further discussion, see Ulman (1955) and Reder (1960).
3   However, see Richardson (1977) for a critique. See also Ashenfelter and
     Pencavel's (1969) study of US union growth.
4   For an attempt to reconcile these two views by explicitly recognising the
     uncertainties associated with union–employer bargaining, see Mitchell
     (1972).
5   Marshall *et al.* (1976, p. 332) cited the behaviour of the US United Mine
     Workers union between 1930 and about 1950 as an example lending support
     to this wage-maximising model of union behaviour.
6   If one allows for the existence of union membership subscriptions, it is
     perhaps plausible to argue that workers will leave the union if their wage
     does not exceed that prevailing in the union's absence by an amount suf-
     ficient to outweigh membership subscriptions. In this case the maximum
     employment that the union can achieve will be below e members by the
     amount necessary to give a wage sufficiently in excess of w just to outweigh
     membership subscriptions.
7   For a generalisation of the wage-bill maximisation hypothesis to take
     account of the existence of unemployment compensation, see Cartter (1959,
     pp. 82–3).
8   In a closed shop only those workers who are already members of the union
     can be hired by the employer, but a union shop allows the employer to
     select workers according to his own criteria, provided that the new employees
     join the union within some specified time period.
9   Although it is usual to refer to the *MRP* curve in this diagram as the firm's
     labour demand curve (see, for example, Cartter, 1959, p. 84), it should be
     recalled that, strictly speaking, because the firm faces an upward-sloping
     labour-supply curve, it is a monopsonist and therefore does not possess a
     labour demand curve. (See Chapter 4, pp. 62–4).
10   For an n variable generalisation of this utility-maximising approach, see
     Wilkinson and Burkitt (1973), although watch out for some sloppy
     mathematics.
11   For a useful discussion, see Trevithick (1976).
12   As already noted, closed unions attach greatest weight in their policies to

wages, while open unions place particular emphasis on their members' employment. To the extent that closed unions place greater weight than open unions on increasing wages when labour demand increases and on resisting cuts in wages when labour demand decreases, one can expect the wage preference path in the case of a closed union to be more steeply sloped above the current equilibrium (*P*), and more shallowly sloped below it, than in the case of an open union.

CHAPTER 6

1 For an excellent concise summary of Fellner's own analysis, see Bronfenbrenner (1971, pp. 235–8).

2 For a more detailed treatment of union–employer preferences, which employs indifference curve analysis on the employer's side as well as on the union's, see Cartter (1959, pp. 95–115).

3 Ferguson, for example, argued that the 'precise result is determined by factors beyond the purview of economic analysis' (1972, p. 315). See Pen (1959, pp. 91–4) for a short history of economic thought on bilateral monopoly and the bargaining problem.

4 Others, however, have sought to achieve determinacy while remaining within the realms of orthodox microeconomic analysis, by making certain particular assumptions regarding such issues as the prevailing price-fixing arrangements. See, for example, the solutions put forward by Cournot (1897), Bowley (1928) and, more recently, Spindler (1974).

5 Hence, questions of the internal consensus of either organisation and intra-organisational bargaining are not considered. For a discussion of these issues, see Walton and McKersie (1965).

6 For further discussion of these and related issues, see de Menil (1971, p. 6). See also Bishop (1963, pp. 559–60) and Bacharach (1976, pp. 105–6).

7 This is defined in the usual manner as the locus of points such that, for any given attainable utility for one bargainer, the other's utility is maximised. See, for example, Laidler (1974, pp. 212–4) or George and Shorey (1978, pp. 26–8).

8 In cases where the frontier is, perhaps over a certain range, convex to the origin or discontinuous, these sections are usually eliminated by linear combinations representing expected utilities from probability deals. For further discussion, see de Menil (1971, p. 7).

9 As both Bishop (1963, p. 567) and Saraydar (1965, p. 804) pointed out, the alternative of a utility-based approach is explicit in Zeuthen's own exposition (Zeuthen, 1930, pp. 113, 115, 135), and as Harsanyi (1956, p. 148) noted, Zeuthen's money formulation is merely the special case in which the marginal utility of money is constant (although not necessarily equal) for both parties.

10 Bishop (1964, p. 411) termed this the bargainer's *subjective probability of conflict*.

11 Plus an implicit term of r_1. 0, since by definition the union, like the employer, receives zero utility in the event of disagreement (i.e. when threats are implemented).

12 The same result is obtained on differentiation with respect to u_2. Second-order conditions require

$$\frac{d^2(u_1 u_2)}{du_1^2} = u_1 \frac{d^2 u_2}{du_1^2} + 2\frac{du_2}{du_1} < 0$$

which is satisfied for all u_1 given the usually assumed concavity of the frontier to the origin. The conditions under which the bargaining process converges to settlement at point Q in Figure 6.4 are given in Sapsford (1979, p. 10), but it should be noted that a sufficient condition for convergence is that the utility increments frontier be everywhere concave to the origin or linear.

13 See, for example, Pen (1959, pp. 117–27) and Cross (1969, pp. 25–6). However, Harsanyi (1956, pp. 149–51) provided an explicit derivation of Zeuthen's assumption by considering five 'more general postulates'. See also Bishop (1964, p. 412) and Cross (1969, p. 25) for critiques of Harsanyi's approach.

14 See Saraydar (1965, pp. 806–13) and Cross (1969, p. 127) for two suggested modifications designed to overcome this feature of Zeuthen's own exposition.

15 For an attempt to improve on Zeuthen's theory by taking account of various psychological and subjective dimensions of bargaining and by explicitly considering the way in which the bargainers arrive at their subjective conflict probabilities, see Pen (1952, 1959).

16 For useful surveys, see Shubik (1959, pp. 38–56) and Bishop (1963, pp. 559–602). See also Coddington (1968, pp. 71–80) for a discussion of the limitations of this approach to the bargaining process.

17 Briefly, von Neumann–Morgenstern utility theory is concerned with situations characterised by uncertainty and assumes the maximisation of expected utility. The utility functions thus derived are unique up to an order preserving linear transformation. For further discussion, see Laidler (1974, pp. 74–85) or Layard and Walters (1978, pp. 369–73).

18 It is non-zero sum because there are gains from trade. However, as Coddington (1968, p. 72) pointed out, its treatment as co-operative is not inherent in the situation but depends on the way in which it is modelled.

19 Following Nash's (1950, p. 158) apparent intention, we interpret his theory as a positive description of the bargaining outcome. See Harsanyi (1956, p. 147) and de Menil (1971, p. 7) for a similar interpretation, but see Luce and Raiffa (1957, pp. 124–34) and Shubik (1959, pp. 48–50) for an alternative normative interpretation.

20 For a critical discussion of Nash's axioms, see Bishop (1963, pp. 574–82), but see also Cross's (1969, pp. 20–2) defence.

21 The following proof is a modification of that given by Cross (1969, pp. 38–9).

22 For example, Cross (1969, p. 33) argued that Hicks's theory is not determinate, Comay *et al.* (1974, p. 304) and Swidinsky (1976, p. 209) argued that it is, whereas Shackle abstained, noting that the 'whole meaning of Professor Hicks' construction is very elusive' (1957, p. 301).

Various criticisms of Hicks's theory have been put forward, a number of which stem from a determinate interpretation. Pen (1959, pp. 114–7), for example, argued that Hicks offered no explanation of disequilibrium behaviour or convergence, and Cartter (1959, pp. 127–8) argued that he failed to consider the interactive characteristics of bargaining and that, in cases where each bargainer holds different expectations about strike length, the analysis merely delineates a range of indeterminacy. Bishop (1964, p. 413) further criticised Hicks for his implicit asymmetrical treatment of union and employer, and Shackle (1957, p. 301) questioned the shape of Hicks's union resistance curve and replaced it with a *union inducement* curve, although the validity of this has further been questioned by Hicks (1963, pp. 353–4) and, more recently, Johnston (1972a, p. 844).

23 See Bishop (1964, p. 413) for a detailed discussion of this implicit asymmetry in Hicks's exposition.

24 In a number of recent studies, Hicks's theory has been reinterpreted, with the respective curves being specified as the actual paths of offers and counteroffers during strikes rather than as functions relating wage rates to expected strike length evaluated *ex ante* in advance of any strike (see Melnik and Comay, 1972; Comay *et al.*, 1974; Swidinsky 1976). However, it is clear from the above discussion that severe identification problems result from the shifts in the Hicksian curves that occur during the strike, with the consequence that the estimated curves presented in such studies bear in general little meaningful resemblance to those specified by Hicks.

25 Both Foldes (1964) and Bishop (1964) extended the Hicksian type of analysis by emphasising the time dependence of the bargaining process. Although their theoretical constructions differ, they both demonstrated that a static solution to the bargaining problem can be obtained by the formulation of a principle of compromise based on the time preferences of the bargainers. Notice also that Bishop presented his theory as a composite one, designed to incorporate the main characteristics of Zeuthen's and Hicks's.

26 These tactics are many and varied and are catalogued in depth in Cartter (1959, pp. 119–22). Tactics discussed include the adoption by bargainers of confident attitudes, which can be interpreted as attempts to convince the opponent of one's propensity to hold out in order to achieve one's own demand and thereby to increase his expected disagreement costs. At the same time a bargainer may try to raise his opponent's attitude ratio further by trying to convince the opponent that he has overestimated the costs of agreeing with the current offer. The union may, for example, present arguments to the employer to suggest that he has overestimated the effect of its current demand on profits, by failing to take full account of the improvements in productivity that will follow from the improved morale and living standards that will result from his conceding the claim, and so on. In addition, prenegotiation build-ups of inventories by employers and financial reserves by union can be interpreted as attempts by each to lower their own attitude ratios by decreasing their respective disagreement costs.

Especially important within this formulation is the compromise, the offer of which constitutes an attempt to increase the opponent's bargaining attitude through a lowering of his agreement costs, while also possibly decreasing one's own disagreement costs through a downward revision of expected length of stoppage necessary to achieve one's own demand. Notice, however, that the offered party may take the compromise offer as a sign of its opponent's weakness, with the consequence that its attitude ratio will tend to decrease, because its estimated disagreement costs fall as it revises downwards its assessment of the length of work stoppage necessary to obtain its own demand.

27 See Sapsford (1979a) for an application of modified version of the Zeuthen–Harsanyi model of the bargaining process to the study of UK strike activity.

28
$$\ln W_i = U_i \ln W_i^u + (1 - U_i) \ln W_i^n$$
$$= U_i (\ln W_i^u - \ln W_i^n) + \ln W_i^n$$

$$= U_i \ln \frac{W_i^u}{W_i^n} + \ln W_i^n$$

Denoting the proportionate union/non-union wage differential $(W_i^u - W_i^n)/W_i^n$ by r_i and substituting, we obtain

$$\ln W_i = U_i \ln (1 + r_i) + \ln W_i^n$$

24   For an alternative method of handling interindustry or occupational variations in the size of the union/non-union differential, see Pencavel (1974, pp. 200–1).

CHAPTER 7

1   In addition, Phillips observed a positive relation between changes in the cost of living and the rate of wage inflation and found the existence of anticlockwise loops around the estimated equation during the pre second World War period. These loops imply that, for any given level of unemployment, the rate of wage change is higher if unemployment is falling and lower if unemployment is rising.

2   The equation that Phillips fitted to the data was of the form

$$\dot{w} = a + bu^{-c}$$

which is non-linear in parameters as well as variables. To estimate the parameters of this equation, Phillips developed a novel iterative technique, and this is discussed in some depth in Desai (1975). Phillips's estimated equation was

$$\dot{w} + 0.9 = 9.638u^{-1.394}$$

implying an intercept on the unemployment axis of approximately $5\frac{1}{2}$ per cent. For further discussion of the original Phillips-curve estimates, see Gilbert (1976).

3   When excess demand is high, frictional unemployment is subject to two opposing forces. On the one hand, the duration of job search will decline as unfilled vacancies become plentiful and it becomes easier to find jobs. On the other hand, the voluntary quit rate rises as workers become optimistic, given the tight labour-market conditions, about finding more satisfactory alternative employment (Corry and Laidler, 1967). The downward-sloping excess demand–unemployment relation is therefore based on the assumption that the former tendency outweighs the latter.

4   The equation of the reaction function shown in Figure 7.4(a) is

$$\dot{w} = k\left(\frac{L_D - L_S}{L_S}\right)$$

Writing the equation of the excess demand–unemployment function as

$$\frac{L_D - L_S}{L_S} = g(u)$$

we obtain by substitution

$$\dot{w} = k[g(u)] = f(u)$$

which is the Phillips curve for the representative individual labour market.

5   For a useful discussion of the methodological problems involved in the analysis of wage inflation, see Burton (1972, pp. 15–30).

6   The alternative approach is to specify a simultaneous equation model of the wage–price system in which the rate of price inflation is a function of the rate of wage inflation and other variables, while the rate of wage inflation is itself a function of the rates of unemployment and price inflation and other variables. For discussion of this approach, see Lipsey and Parkin (1970).

7   Studies of the underlying trend rate of growth of labour productivity in the UK have typically given estimates to the order of 2.5 per cent per year.

8   For further discussion, see Lipsey (1965, pp. 210–18) and Hartley (1977, pp. 56–60).

9   It should, however, be noted that the dependent variable in the Bain and Elsheikh (1976) study was the proportional rate of change of the fraction of the labour force belonging to unions, i.e.

$$\frac{\Delta T_t}{T_t} = \frac{T_t - T_{t-1}}{T_t}$$

as opposed to Hines's (1964) proxy for union pushfulness, which was the absolute rate of change, i.e.

$$\Delta T_t = T_t - T_{t-1}$$

10   An interesting feature of Johnston and Timbrell's (1973) empirical work is their incorporation of the hypothesis that unions possess a target level, or rate of growth, of real wages. While this notion is not a new one (see, in particular, Sargan, 1964, 1971), this type of target real-wage model has recently received some encouraging empirical support (see Henry *et al.*, 1976; Henry and Ormerod, 1978).

11   Lipsey's (1960) findings, however, do seem to show that the relationship between $\dot{w}$ and u had not been quite as stable over time as Phillips suggested.

12   But see Dicks-Mireaux and Dow (1959) for the construction and use of a proxy for the excess demand for labour that utilises both vacancy and unemployment data.

13   Since the shift in the unemployment–vacancies relation in the UK meant that a given rate of unemployment became associated with a higher rate of unfilled vacancies, it follows that at each value of the unemployment rate (u) the excess demand for labour ($v - u$) had increased, and this is shown as an outward movement in the excess demand–unemployment relation (Figure 7.4(b)). With an unchanged reaction function the Phillips curve will, as a consequence of the unemployment–vacancies shift, move outwards, because, although a given value of $\dot{w}$ is associated with an unchanged level of excess demand for labour, the latter is now associated with a higher rate of unemployment. Alternatively, because a given rate of unemployment now represents a higher level of excess demand for labour, it gives rise to a higher rate of inflation.

14   If β denotes the expectations coefficient, the adaptive expectations hypothesis can be written as

$$\dot{p}_t^e - \dot{p}_{t-1}^e = \beta(\dot{p}_{t-1} - \dot{p}_{t-1}^e)$$

where $0 \leqslant \beta \leqslant 1$.

It is easy to show (by backward substitution into the above expression) that the adaptive expectations hypothesis is equivalent to the assumption that the expected rate of inflation in the current period ($\dot{p}_t^e$) is a weighted average of the previous actual rates of inflation ($\dot{p}_{t-1}, \dot{p}_{t-2}, \dot{p}_{t-3}$, and so on) with weights β, $\beta(1-\beta)$, $\beta(1-\beta)^2$, and so on, i.e. that

$$\dot{p}_t^e = \beta\dot{p}_{t-1} + \beta(1-\beta)\dot{p}_{t-2} + \beta(1-\beta)^2\dot{p}_{t-3} + \dots$$

As can be seen from this expression, the weights attached to past rates of inflation decay geometrically as one goes back in time, and it is easy to show that they sum to one. In the particular case where $\beta = 1$, we see that only the previous period's rate of inflation counts and that the above expression reduces to (7.3) of the text, i.e.

$$\dot{p}_t^e = \dot{p}_{t-1}$$

which says that the current expected rate of inflation is equal to last period's observed rate.

In the steady-state situation, where the actual rate of inflation becomes and remains constant, the adaptive expectations hypothesis implies that the expected inflation rate will move towards the constant actual rate, approaching it in the limit as time goes on.

15 In the second period in the example of the text, the expected rate of price inflation is equal to the first period's actual rate (i.e. 5 per cent), and from (7.1) and (7.2) we see that Friedman's model predicts that a government policy that succeeds in holding the rates of wage and price inflation at 5 per cent implies a rise in the unemployment rate sufficient to make $f(u)$ become zero. Since $f(u)$ is the original Phillips or zero price-expectations curve (A in Figure 7.7), we see that the unemployment rate in question is u_n, the intercept of curve A on the unemployment axis.

The process by which convergence to steady state equilibrium at u_n occurs in Friedman's model involves both employers and employees eventually becoming completely aware of the actual rate of inflation (i.e. the disappearance of money illusion in the long run). Once inflation becomes fully anticipated and adjusted to, both parties revert to their original positions on the labour demand and supply curves respectively, thus re-establishing the initial unemployment rate u_n. See Friedman (1976, pp. 223–6), and for a formal derivation of the steady-state equilibrium properties of the expectations-augmented Phillips curve, see Tobin (1968, pp. 49–55) or Johnson's (1971, pp. 162–3) restatement.

16 Friedman defined the natural rate of unemployment as that given by the solution of a system of general equilibrium equations that accurately describe the structure and imperfections of all labour and commodity markets (1968, p. 8). In terms of the labour market, the natural rate of unemployment is that present when labour demand and labour supply, both expressed as functions of the real wage, are in equilibrium (Friedman, 1975, pp. 13–20). Notice the close similarity between Friedman's natural rate concept and Lipsey's argument concerning the existence of frictional unemployment when the individual micro labour market is in equilibrium.

17 For further discussion, see Laidler (1975, pp. 44–6).
18 For the derivation of a similar sort of conclusion in the context of a short-run macro model, see Turnovsky (1974).
19 For detailed policy-oriented discussions of UK prices and incomes policies, see Hartley (1977, pp. 78–84) and Brooks and Evans (1978, pp. 68–91).
20 For a detailed calendar of the various incomes policies that operated in UK over the postwar period, see Lipsey and Parkin (1970, pp. 126–7) and Tarling and Wilkinson (1977, pp. 398–9).
21 As Johnson (1971, p. 160) pointed out, the fact that Smith's results show significant shift effects using weekly wage-rate data, but weaker effects when hourly wage-rate and earnings data are used, suggests a common resort to hidden wage increases during the operation of incomes policies, such as a shortening of normal hours of work and a rise in wage drift (i.e. the discrepancy between actual earnings and basic wage rates).
22 If inflationary expectations are formed, as is assumed in the adaptive expectations scheme, on the basis of only past actual rate of inflation, then at any time $\dot{p}^e$ will be predetermined. However, if other factors enter into the formation of expected rates of inflation, then during policy-on periods an *announcement effect* may lead to a reduction in the expected rate of inflation. If economic units believe that an incomes policy will succeed in moderating price inflation, the very fact that a policy is operating may reduce $\dot{p}^e$. Notice also that the operation of some form of prices policy (such as the existence of price controls on a range of goods and services, or the operation of a prices commission to vet proposed price increases) may, if economic units have faith in it, likewise succeed in dampening inflationary expectations.
23 In a recent paper Henry and Ormerod (1978) found evidence from a study of UK incomes policies over the period 1961–75 to suggest that, while some policies reduced the rate of wage inflation during the period in which they operated, this reduction was only temporary, as wage increases in the periods immediately following the ending of the policies were higher than they would otherwise have been. Moreover, their results suggest that these increases matched losses incurred during the operation of the incomes policies.

CHAPTER 8

1 For detailed discussion of the distinction between voluntary and involuntary unemployment as viewed from both classical and Keynesian viewpoints, see Perlman (1969, pp. 143–66) and Kahn (1976).
2 See also Thirlwall (1969) and Trevithick and Mulvey (1975, p. 44).
3 Holt (1971, p. 62).
4 For a more detailed discussion of the UK official unemployment statistics, see *Department of Employment Gazette* (1975, pp. 179–83) and Thatcher (1976).
5 *Department of Employment Gazette* (1976, pp. 1331–6).
6 The usual measures of UK unemployment in the interwar years are based on data derived from unemployment insurance records and therefore relate not to all workers but only to persons insured under the unemployment insurance scheme operating at the time. Estimates of the total number unemployed as a percentage of total employees over this period (Feinstein, 1976, table 58)

suggest that data relating to insured workers provide something of an over-statement of the actual extent of unemployment among all workers.

7   Department of Employment (1971, table 159, p. 305).

8   For a discussion of this view, see Moore *et al.* (1978, pp. 22–36).

9   See *Department of Employment Gazette* (1978, pp. 908–16) for further details and a review of possible explanations.

10 An alternative approach in the analysis of unemployment is to study the characteristics of the unemployed themselves. In June 1964, 1973 and 1976 the Department of Employment carried out sample surveys of the characteristics of the registered unemployed. (For summaries of the major findings, see *Department of Employment Gazette*, 1977, pp. 559–74, 965–75). Several findings are of particular interest. In both the 1973 and 1976 surveys over 70 per cent of the registered unemployed were assessed by their local offices as being 'keen' to find work – a result close to the findings of an independent survey by Daniel (1974). In addition, results of these surveys show that the prospects of obtaining work decrease with age (being particularly poor for ages 55 and over) and that a considerable proportion of unemployed men have had recent previous spells of unemployment. For example, in the 1976 survey 45 per cent of men aged 18–24 with a current unemployment duration of less than three months were found to have had at least one spell of unemployment in the year prior to the survey date, while for men aged 25–54 and 55 and over the percentages were 38 and 23 respectively. For an analysis of recurrent spells and the concentration of unemployment in Britain, see Disney (1979).

11 *Department of Employment Gazette* (1978, pp. 1048–58), where a useful detailed analysis of duration data is presented. For an analysis of the duration of male unemployment in Britain between 1923 and 1973, see Cripps and Tarling (1974), and for an analysis of duration and re-employment probability, see McGregor (1978).

12 In a similar way Benjamin and Kochin (1979) came to the surprising conclusion that the generosity of the system of unemployment insurance that operated in Britain during the interwar years was the chief cause for the chronic unemployment of the period!

13 Earnings-related supplement is calculated on the basis of the claimant's income in a previous tax year and is payable on top of the flat rate of unemployment benefit for twenty-six weeks after the first two weeks of unemployment. The Redundancy Payments Act provides for a lump sum payment at the beginning of a spell of unemployment following redundancy, with payments calculated according to a sliding scale, which takes into account years of service, weekly pay and the age of the individual.

14 Notice the distinction between these definitions of unemployment and those given by Lipsey in his analysis of the Phillips curve. As we saw in Chapter 7, the unemployment rate given by the intercept of the Phillips curve for an individual micro labour market on the horizontal axis represents frictional unemployment as that which corresponds to equilibrium in the individual micro labour market. As the individual micro labour market is in this context assumed to be composed of labour that is homogeneous in type and location, only frictional and not structural unemployment can exist, as unemployed workers and job vacancies are of the same sort, with unemployment and unfilled job vacancies coexisting because of the time lags involved in job-changing.

    If we drop the assumption of homogeneous labour, the level of unemployment corresponding to equilibrium in the labour market is the sum of frictional and structural unemployment. In this case frictional plus structural unemployment is given by the intercept of the Phillips curve on the horizontal axis (a in Figure 8.1), and this rate differs from that given by Lipsey's alternative definition, namely, that which corresponds to the acceptable rate of inflation (u_0 in Figure 8.1). Notice that, in the case where the acceptable rate of inflation is equal to zero, both definitions are equivalent.

15 It is often assumed that the U–V relationship can be adequately represented by a *rectangular hyperbola*, i.e. by the equation

$$UV = K$$

where U and V denote the numbers of unemployed workers and unfilled vacancies respectively and K is some positive constant (see Hansen, 1970). However, in cases where the observations on U and V are confined within a narrow range, a linear relation may provide an adequate approximation (see Thirlwall, 1969).

16 According to this legislation, the cost of the redundancy payment scheme introduced under the Act was to be the responsibility of employers alone and to be financed in two ways. Each employer was to pay increased National Insurance contributions, which would then be placed in a central redundancy fund out of which any employer making workers redundant would claim approximately 60 per cent of the severance payments, while meeting the remaining cost himself. These contributions, like training levies, represented an addition to the overhead or fixed element of labour costs, and as we saw in Chapter 4, any increase in these can be expected to induce employers during an upswing (particularly if recovery is expected to be only short lived) to increase the average hours worked per week rather than the number of workers on their books.

CHAPTER 9

1 It is important to recognise that the structure of wage differentials is only one aspect of the wider topic of economic inequality. Other aspects of this topic include the distribution of wealth, as distinct from income, and the distribution of national income between the various factors of production. For a useful survey of the economics of inequality, see Atkinson (1975), and for a concise survey of the distribution of income between the different factors of production, see King and Regan (1976).

2 See, in particular, Routh (1965, 1974), Crossley (1966, pp. 201–7) and Phelps-Brown (1977, pp. 1–144).

3 For further discussion, see *Department of Employment Gazette* (1977), pp. 593–9).

4 In the case where the skilled sector is unionised and unskilled one nonunionised, this effect is closely related to the Rees–Friedman effect discussed above (see pp. 124–127).

5 For an investigation of cyclical fluctuations in the skill differential in the UK engineering industry, see Hawkesworth (1978). In this study the close similarity between the predictions of Reder's analysis and those of Oi's (1962) analysis of labour as a quasi-fixed factor are considered. As we have seen, the latter approach predicts that over the cycle there will be a greater

instability in labour demand (and hence, *ceteris paribus*, wages) at lower skill levels because of the lower level of employer investment embodied in such workers.

6   For a detailed discussion of the human capital approach and its implications for a variety of issues, including on-the-job training, see Becker (1964).

7   For those unfamiliar with techniques of investment appraisal, a useful survey is given in Hawkins and Pearce (1971).

8   The example of the text assumes that the relevant earnings profiles are horizontal and that immediately upon graduation the earnings of students rise to a level in excess of the level they would otherwise be. The analysis is easily generalised by simply replacing the constant incomes y_0, y_1 and y_2 by suitable series of variables to allow for non-linear profiles and for the fact that graduate earnings may not immediately exceed those which would be earned had the individual entered the labour force at 18 and received on-the-job training.

9   For a summary of the evidence on this point, see Phelps-Brown (1977, p. 238).

10   The human capital analysis is equally applicable to cases where the training required for the skilled occupation takes the form of on-the-job training rather than full-time education, examples being apprenticeships or graduates articled to accountants or solicitors. In some cases the worker bears the full cost of his own on-the-job training (in the sense of being paid only his marginal revenue product during training), receiving a lower wage during training and subsequently receiving the full amount of his increased marginal revenue product once training has been completed. In such cases earnings during training are not zero or equal to a student grant but are simply lower than in jobs where no such training is required.

For further discussion of the human capital approach to occupational differentials, see Fisher (1974).

11   A similar degree of stability has also been observed in the US industrial wage structure. For example, Cullen (1956, p. 359), considering average annual earnings in seventy-six US manufacturing industries, found a rank correlation coefficient of + 0.66 for 1950 relative to 1899, and Slichter (1950, p. 88) obtained a coefficient of rank correlation equal to + 0.7289 when considering movements in the average hourly earnings of unskilled male workers in twenty US manufacturing industries between 1923 and 1946.

12   One interesting feature of Reddaway's analysis is the large increase in the correlation coefficient from + 0.43 to + 0.92 that occurs when the 111 manufacturing industries of his sample are grouped into the fourteen orders of the relevant Standard Industrial Classification. As Crossley (1966, p. 219) pointed out, this may be explained by the fact that labour supply curves to industries within orders are more elastic than those for orders as a whole, reflecting the greater degree of homogeneity of industries classified by product within orders.

13   For a review of the US evidence, see Reder (1962).

14   Becker (1971) defined an employer as a discriminator if, being able to hire, say, a female or minority group worker for wage w, he behaves as though this wage is $w(1 + d)$, where $d > 0$ denotes the employer's *discrimination coefficient*.

15   Size distributions of earnings are typically found to have a single peak, or mode, and a long right hand tail (i.e. to be *positively skewed*). After a

detailed comparison of the earnings distributions of a standard group of workers in a large number of countries, Lydall (1968) concluded that the central part of the distribution is approximately *lognormal* and that the upper tail of the distribution, covering about the top 20 per cent of earners, is well fitted by the Pareto distribution, except perhaps in some communist countries. The Pareto distribution (which was itself derived from Pareto's analysis of income distribution in a sample of places) is described by the formula

$$Y = AX^{-\alpha}$$

where Y denotes the number of persons with earnings greater than, or equal to, a given value X and where A and α are constants. Notice that Pareto himself estimated the parameter α to be typically of the order of 1.5.

References

Alden, J. D., (1977) 'The extent and nature of double jobholding in Great Britain', *Industrial Relations Journal*, vol. 8, no. 3, pp. 14–30.

Ashenfelter, O. and Heckman, J. (1974), 'The estimation of income and substitution effects in a model of family labour supply', *Econometrica*, vol. 42, no. 1, pp. 73–85.

Ashenfelter, O. and Johnson, G. E. (1972), 'Unionism, relative wages and labour quality in US manufacturing industries', *International Economic Review*, vol. 13, pp. 488–508.

Ashenfelter, O., Johnson, G. E. and Pencavel, J. H. (1972), 'Trade unions and the rate of change of money wage rates in United States manufacturing industry', *Review of Economic Studies*, vol. 39, no. 117, pp. 27–54.

Ashenfelter, O. and Pencavel, J. H. (1969), 'American trade union growth, 1900–1960', *Quarterly Journal of Economics*, vol. 83, no. 3, pp. 434–48.

Atkinson, A. B. (1975), *The Economics of Inequality* (London: Oxford University Press).

Atkinson, A. B. (ed.) (1976), *The Personal Distribution of Incomes* (London: Allen & Unwin).

Bacharach, M. (1976), *Economics and the Theory of Games* (London: Macmillan).

Bain, G. S. and Elsheikh, F. (1976), *Union Growth and the Business Cycle: An Econometric Analysis* (Oxford: Blackwell).

Bain, G. S. and Elsheikh, F. (1979), 'An inter-industry analysis of unionisation in Britain', *British Journal of Industrial Relations*, vol. 17, no. 2, pp. 137–57.

Ball, R. J. and St Cyr, E. B. A. (1966), 'Short term employment functions in British manufacturing industry', *Review of Economic Studies*, vol. 33, no. 3, pp. 179–207.

Becker, G. S. (1964), *Human Capital: A Theoretical and Empirical Analysis* (New York: National Bureau of Economic Research).

Becker, G. S. (1965), 'A theory of the allocation of time', *Economic Journal*, vol. 75, no. 299, pp. 493–517.

Becker, G. S. (1971), *The Economics of Discrimination*, 2nd edn (Chicago: University of Chicago Press).

Benjamin, D. K. and Kochin, L. A. (1979), 'Searching for an explanation of unemployment in inter-war Britain', *Journal of Political Economy*, vol. 89, no. 3, pp. 441–78.

Berg, S. V. and Dalton, T. R. (1977), 'United Kingdom labour force activity rates: unemployment and real wages', *Applied Economics*, vol. 9, no. 3, pp. 265–70.

Beveridge, W. H. (1944), *Full Employment in a Free Society* (London: Allen & Unwin).

Bhatia, R. J. (1961), 'Unemployment and the rate of change of money earnings in the US, 1900–1958', *Economica*, new series, vol. 28, no. 111, pp. 286–96.

Bishop, R. L. (1963), 'Game theoretic analyses of bargaining', *Quarterly Journal of Economics*, vol. 77, no. 4, pp. 559–602.

Bishop, R. L. (1964), 'A Zeuthen–Hicks theory of bargaining', *Econometrica*, vol. 32, no. 3, pp. 410–17.

Blaug, M. (1976), 'Human capital theory: a slightly jaundiced survey', *Journal of Economic Literature*, vol. 14, no. 3, pp. 827–55.

Bloom, G. F. (1941), 'A reconsideration of the theory of exploitation', *Quarterly Journal of Economics*, vol. 55, no. 2, pp. 413–42.

Bodkin, R. G., Bond, E. P., Reuber, G. L. and Robinson, T. R. (1967), *Price Stability and High Employment: The Options for Canadian Economic Policy* (Ottawa: Queen's Printer).

Bowen, W. A. and Finegan, T. A. (1969), *The Economics of Labor Force Participation* (Princeton, NJ: Princeton University Press).

Bowers, J. K. (1975), 'British activity rates: a survey of research', *Scottish Journal of Political Economy*, vol. 22, no. 1, pp. 57–90.

Bowers, J. K., Cheshire, P. C. and Webb, A. E. (1970), 'The change in the relationship between unemployment and earnings increases: a review of some possible explanations', *National Institute Economic Review*, no. 54, pp. 44–63.

Bowers, J. K., Cheshire, P. C., Webb, A. E. and Weeden, R. (1972), 'Some aspects of unemployment and the labour market, 1966–71', *National Institute Economic Review*, no. 62, pp. 75–88.

Bowers, J. K. and Harkess, D. (1979), 'Duration of unemployment by age and sex', *Economica*, new series, vol. 46, no. 183, pp. 239–60.

Bowley, A. L. (1928), 'On bilateral monopoly', *Economic Journal*, vol. 38, no. 152, pp. 651–9.

Brechling, F. (1965), 'The relationship between output and employment in British manufacturing industries', *Review of Economic Studies*, vol. 32, no. 3, pp. 187–216.

Bronfenbrenner, M. (1961), 'Notes on the elasticity of derived demand', *Oxford Economic Papers*, vol. 13, no. 3, pp. 254–61.

Bronfenbrenner, M. (1971), *Income Distribution Theory* (Chicago: Aldine).

Brooks, J. and Evans, R. W. (1978), *Macroeconomic Policy in Theory and Practice* (London: Allen & Unwin).

Brown, A. J. (1976), '*UV* analysis', in *The Concept and Measurement of Involuntary Unemployment*, ed. G. D. N. Worswick (London: Allen & Unwin), pp. 134–45.

Brown, C. V., Levin, E. and Ulph, D. T. (1976), 'Estimates of labour hours supplied by married male workers in Great Britain', *Scottish Journal of Political Economy*, vol. 23, no. 3, pp. 261–77.

Burkitt, B. (1975), *Trade Unions and Wages* (London: Bradford University Press in association with Crosby Lockwood Staples).

Burkitt, B. and Bowers, D. (1978), 'The determination of the rate of change of unionisation in the United Kingdom, 1924–1966', *Applied Economics*, vol. 10, no. 2, pp. 161–72.

Burkitt, B. and Bowers, D. (1979), *Trade Unions and the Economy* (London: Macmillan).

Burrows, P. and Hitiris, T. (1972), 'Estimating the impact of incomes policy', *Bulletin of Economic Research*, vol. 24, no. 2, pp. 42–51.

Burton, J. (1972), *Wage Inflation* (London: Macmillan).

Burton, J. (1977), 'Employment subsidies: the cases for and against', *National Westminster Bank Quarterly Review* (February), pp. 33–43.

Burton, J. (1977a), 'Depression, unemployment, union wage rigidity and employment subsidies', *International Journal of Social Economics*, vol. 4, no. 1, pp. 25–31.

Byers, J. D. (1976), 'The supply of labour', in *Topics in Applied Macroeconomics*, ed. D. F. Heathfield (London: Macmillan), pp. 69–90.

Cain, G. (1966), *Married Women in the Labor Force: An Economic Analysis* (Chicago: University of Chicago Press).

Cairnes, J. E. (1874), *Some Leading Principles of Political Economy Newly Expounded* (London: Macmillan; reprinted New York: Kelley, 1967).

Cartter, A. M. (1959), *Theory of Wages and Employment* (Homewood, Ill.: Irwin).

Chamberlain, N. W. (1951), *Collective Bargaining* (New York: McGraw-Hill).

Chiang, A. C. (1974), *Fundamental Methods of Mathematical Economics*, 2nd edn (London: McGraw-Hill).

Chiplin, B. and Sloane, P. J. (1976), *Sex Discrimination in the Labour Market* (London: Macmillan).

Chiplin, B. and Sloane, P. J. (1976a), 'Personal characteristics and sex differentials in professional employment', *Economic Journal*, vol. 86, no. 344, pp. 729–45.

Clegg, H. A. (1972), *The System of Industrial Relations in Great Britain*, 2nd edn (Oxford: Blackwell).

Coddington, A. (1968), *Theories of the Bargaining Process* (London: Allen & Unwin).

Comay, Y., Melnik, A. and Subotnik, A. (1974), 'Bargaining yield curves and wage settlements: an empirical analysis', *Journal of Political Economy*, vol. 82, no. 2, pp. 303–13.

Corry, B. A. and Laidler, D. E. W. (1967), 'The Phillips relation: a theoretical explanation', *Economica*, new series, vol. 34, no. 134, pp. 189–97.

Corry, B. A. and Roberts, J. A. (1970), 'Activity rules and unemployment: the experience of the United Kingdom, 1951–1966', *Applied Economics*, vol. 2, no. 3, pp. 179–201.

Corry, B. A. and Roberts, J. A. (1974), 'Activity rates and unemployment: the UK experience: some further results', *Applied Economics*, vol. 6, no. 1, pp. 1–21.

Cournot, A. (1897), *Researches into the Mathematical Principles of the Theory of Wealth*, trans. by N. T. Bacon (New York: Macmillan).

Cripps, T. F. and Tarling, R. J. (1974), 'An analysis of the duration of male unemployment in Great Britain, 1932–73', *Economic Journal*, vol. 84, no. 334, pp. 289–316.

Cross, J. G. (1969), *The Economics of Bargaining* (London: Basic Books).

Crossley, J. R. (1966), 'Collective bargaining, wage structure and the labour market in the United Kingdom', in *Wage-Structure in Theory and Practice*, ed. E. M. Hugh-Jones (Amsterdam: North-Holland), pp. 157–235.

Crossley, J. R. (1973), 'A mixed strategy for labour economists', *Scottish Journal of Political Economy*, vol. 20, no. 3, pp. 211–38.

Cubbin, J. S. and Foley, K. (1977), 'The extent of benefit-induced unemployment in Great Britain: some new evidence', *Oxford Economic Papers*, new series, vol. 29, no. 1, pp. 128–40.

Cullen, D. E. (1956), 'The inter-industry wage structure, 1899–1950', *American Economic Review*, vol. 46, no. 3, pp. 353–69.

Daniel, W. W. (1974), *A National Survey of the Unemployed* (London: Political and Economic Planning, Broadsheet No. 546).

Davis, H. B. (1941), 'The theory of union growth', *Quarterly Journal of Economics*, vol. 55, no. 3, pp. 611–37.

Dean, A. J. H. (1976), 'Unemployment among school leavers: an analysis of the problem', *National Institute Economic Review*, no. 78, pp. 63–8.

Dean, A. J. H. (1978), 'Incomes policies and differentials', *National Institute Economic Review*, no. 85, pp. 40–8.

de Menil, G. (1971), *Bargaining: Monopoly Power versus Union Power* (Cambridge, Mass.: MIT Press).

Demery, D. and McNabb, R. (1978), 'The effects of demand on the union relative wage effect in the United Kingdom', *British Journal of Industrial Relations*, vol. 16, no. 3, pp. 303–8.

Department of Employment (1971), *British Labour Statistics: Historical Abstract, 1886–1968* (London: HMSO).

Department of Employment (1976), *Final Report of the Working Party on the Changed Relation Between Unemployment and Vacancies* (London: HMSO).

Dernburg, T. and Strand, K., 'Hidden unemployment, 1953–62: a quantitative analysis by age and sex', *American Economic Review*, vol. 56, no. 1, pp. 71–95.

Desai, M. (1975), 'The Phillips curve: a revisionist interpretation', *Economica*, new series, vol. 42, no. 165, pp. 1–19.

Diamond, Lord (1975), *Report No. 1 of the Royal Commission on the Distribution of Income and Wealth,* chaired by Lord Diamond, Cmnd 6171 (London: HMSO).

Diamond, Lord (1979), *Report No. 8 of the Royal Commission on the Distribution of Income and Wealth,* chaired by Lord Diamond, Cmnd 7679 (London: HMSO).

Dicks-Mireaux, L. A. and Dow, J. C. R. (1959), 'The determinants of wage inflation in the United Kingdom, 1946–1956', *Journal of the Royal Statistical Society*, series A (general), vol. 122, no. 2, pp. 145–84.

Disney, R. (1979), 'Recurrent spells and the concentration of unemployment in Great Britain', *Economic Journal*, vol. 89, no. 353, pp. 109–19.

Doeringer, P. B. and Piore, M. (1971), *Internal Labor Markets and Manpower Analysis* (Lexington, Mass.: Heath).

Dogas, D. and Hines, A. G. (1975), 'Trade unions and wage inflation in the UK: a critique of Purdy and Zis', *Applied Economics*, vol. 7, no. 3, pp. 195–211.

Donovan, Lord (1968), *Report of the Royal Commission on Trade Unions and Employers' Associations, 1965–1968,* chaired by Lord Donovan, Cmnd 3623 (London: HMSO).

Douglas, P. H. (1939), *The Theory of Wages* (New York: Macmillan).

Dunlop, J. T. (1944), *Wage Determination under Trade Unions* (New York; Macmillan).

Durcan, J. W. and McCarthy, W. E. J. (1974), 'The state subsidy theory of strikes: an examination of the statistical data for the period 1956–1970', *British Journal of Industrial Relations*, vol. 12, no. 1, pp. 26–47.

Eckstein, O. and Wilson, T. A. (1962), 'The determination of money wages in American industry', *Quarterly Journal of Economics*, vol. 76, no. 3, pp. 379–414.

Edgeworth, F. Y. (1881), *Mathematical Psychics* (London: Kegan Paul).

Evans, A. (1977), 'Notes on the changing relationship between registered unemployment and notified vacancies, 1961–1966 and 1966–1971', *Economica*, new series, vol. 44, no. 174, pp. 179–96.

Fair, R. C. (1969), *The Short-Run Demand for Workers and Hours* (Amsterdam: North-Holland).

Feinstein, C. H. (1976), *Statistical Tables of National Income, Expenditure and Output of the UK, 1855–1965* (Cambridge: Cambridge University Press).

Feldstein, M. S. (1968), 'Estimating the supply curve of working hours', *Oxford Economic Papers*, new series, vol. 20, no. 1, pp. 74–80.

Fellner, W. J. (1951), *Competition Among the Few* (New York: Knopf).

Ferguson, C. E. (1972), *Microeconomic Theory*, 3rd edn (Homewood, Ill.: Irwin).

Ferguson, C. E. and Gould, J. P. (1975), *Microeconomic Theory*, 4th edn (Homewood, Ill.: Irwin).

Finegan, T. A. (1962), 'Hours of work in the United States: a cross sectional analysis', *Journal of Political Economy*, vol. 70, no. 5, pp. 452–70.

Fisher, I. (1926), 'A statistical relation between unemployment and price changes', *International Labour Review*, vol. 13, no. 6, pp. 785–92; reprinted as 'I discovered the Phillips curve', *Journal of Political Economy*, vol. 81, no. 2 (1972), pp. 496–502.

Fisher, M. R. (1971), *The Economic Analysis of Labour* (London: Weidenfeld & Nicolson).

Fisher, M. R. (1974), 'The human capital approach to occupational differentials', *International Journal of Social Economics*, vol. 1, no. 1, pp. 41–62.

Fleisher, B. M. (1970), *Labor Economics: Theory and Evidence* (Englewood Cliffs, NH: Prentice Hall).

Foldes, L. (1964), 'A determinate model of bilateral monopoly', *Economica*, new series, vol. 31, no. 1, pp. 117–31.

Foster, J. L. (1974), 'The relationship between unemployment and vacancies in Great Britain (1958–72): some further evidence', in *Inflation and Labour Markets*, ed. D. Laidler and D. R. Purdy (Manchester: Manchester University Press), pp. 164–96.

Fowler, R. F. (1968), *Duration of Unemployment on the Register of Wholly Unemployed*, Studies in Official Statistics, Research Paper No. 1 (London: HMSO).

Friedman, M. (1951), 'Some comments on the significance of labor unions for economic policy', in *The Impact of the Union*, ed. D. McCord Wright (New York: Harcourt Brace), pp. 204–34.

Friedman, M. (1957), *A Theory of the Consumption Function* (Princeton, NJ: National Bureau of Economic Research).

Friedman, M. (1962), *Price Theory: A Provisional Text*, revised edn (Chicago: Aldine).

Friedman, M. (1968), 'The role of monetary policy', *American Economic Review*, vol. 58, no. 1, pp. 1–17.

Friedman, M. (1975), *Unemployment versus Inflation*, with a British commentary by D. E. W. Laidler (London: Institute of Economic Affairs, Occasional Paper, No. 44).

Friedman, M. (1976), *Price Theory* (Chicago: Aldine).

Friedman, M. and Kuznets, S. (1945), *Income from Independent Professional Practice* (New York: National Bureau of Economic Research).

Frisch, H. (1977), 'Inflation theory, 1963–75: a 'second generation' survey', *Journal of Economic Literature*, vol. 15, no. 4, pp. 1289–1317.

Gennard, J. (1977), *Financing Strikers* (London: Macmillan).

George, K. D. and Shorey, J. (1978), *The Allocation of Resources: Theory and Policy* (London: Allen & Unwin).

Gilbert, C. L. (1976), 'The original Phillips curve estimates', *Economica*, new series, vol. 43, no. 169, pp. 51–7.

Gitlow, A. L. (1971), *Labor and Manpower Economics*, 3rd edn (Homewood, Ill.: Irwin).

Godfrey, L. (1971), 'The Phillips curve: incomes policy and trade union effects', in *The Current Inflation*, ed. H. G. Johnson and A. R. Nobay (London: Macmillan), pp. 99–124.

Godfrey, L. (1975), *Theoretical and Empirical Aspects of the Effects of Taxation on the Supply of Labour* (Paris: Organisation for Economic Co-operation and Development).

Godfrey, L. and Taylor, J. (1973), 'Earnings changes in the UK, 1954–1970: excess labour supply, expected inflation and union influence', *Bulletin of the Oxford University Institute of Economics and Statistics*, vol. 35, no. 3, pp. 197–216.

Goldberger, A. S. (1978), 'The genetic determination of income: comment', *American Economic Review*, vol. 68, no. 5, pp. 960–9.

Goldstein, M. (1972), 'The trade-off between inflation and unemployment: a survey of the econometric evidence for selected countries', *International Monetary Fund Staff Papers*, vol. 19, no. 3, pp. 647–95.

Gordon, R. A. (1975), 'Wages, prices and unemployment, 1900–1970', *Industrial Relations*, vol. 14, no. 3, pp. 273–301.

Greenhalgh, C. (1977), 'A labour supply function for married women in Great Britain', *Economica*, new series, vol. 44, no. 175, pp. 249–65.

Gronau, R. (1973), 'The intrafamily allocation of time: the value of housewives' time', *American Economic Review*, vol. 63, no. 4, pp. 634–51.

Gujarati, D. (1972), 'The behaviour of unemployment and unfilled vacancies: Great Britain, 1958–71', *Economic Journal*, vol. 82, no. 325, pp. 195–204.

Haines, B. (1978), *Introduction to Quantitative Economics* (London: Allen & Unwin).

Hansen, B. (1970), 'Excess demand, unemployment, vacancies and wages', *Quarterly Journal of Economics*, vol. 84, no. 334, pp. 1–23.

Harbury, C. D. (1980), *Economic Behaviour: An Introduction* (London: Allen & Unwin).

Harsanyi, J. C. (1956), 'Approaches to the bargaining problem before and after the theory of games: a critical discussion of Zeuthen's, Hicks' and Nash's theories', *Econometrica*, vol. 24, no. 2, pp. 144–57.

Hart, R. A. and MacKay, D. I. (1975), 'Engineering earnings in Britain, 1914–68', *Journal of the Royal Statistical Society*, series A (general), vol. 138, no. 1, pp. 32–50.

Hart, R. A. and Sharot, T. (1978), 'The short-run demand for workers and hours: a recursive model', *Review of Economic Studies*, vol. 45, no. 140, pp. 299–309.

Hartley, K. (1977), *Problems of Economic Policy* (London: Allen & Unwin).

Hawkesworth, R. I. (1978), 'The movement of skill differentials in the UK engineering industry', *British Journal of Industrial Relations*, vol. 16, no. 3, pp. 277–286.

Hawkins, C. J. and Pearce, D. W. (1971), *Capital Investment Appraisal* (London: Macmillan).

Hazledine, T. (1978), 'New specifications for employment and hours functions', *Economica*, new series, vol. 45, no. 178, pp. 179–93.

Henderson, J. M. and Quandt, R. E. (1971), *Micro-Economic Theory: A Mathematical Approach*, 2nd edn (London: McGraw-Hill).

Henry, S. G. B. and Ormerod, P. A. (1978), 'Incomes policy and wage inflation: empirical evidence for the UK, 1961–1977', *National Institute Economic Review*, no. 85, pp. 31–9.

Henry, S. G. B., Sawyer, M. C. and Smith, P. (1976), 'Models of inflation in the United Kingdom: an evaluation', *National Institute Economic Review*, no. 77, pp. 60–71.

Hicks, J. R. (1976), 'Marshall's third rule: a further comment', *Oxford Economic Papers*, vol. 13, no. 3, pp. 262–5.

Hicks, J. R. (1963), *The Theory of Wages,* 2nd edn (London: Macmillan).

Hieser, R. O. (1970), 'Wage determination with bilateral monopoly in the labour market: a theoretical treatment', *Economic Record,* vol. 46, no. 113, pp. 55–72.

Hines, A. G. (1964), 'Trade unions and wage inflation in the United Kingdom, 1893–1961', *Review of Economic Studies,* vol. 31, no. 88, pp. 221–52.

Hines, A. G. (1968), 'Unemployment and the rate of change of money wage rates in the United Kingdom, 1862–1963: a reappraisal', *Review of Economics and Statistics,* vol. 50, no. 1, pp. 60–7.

Hines, A. G. (1969), 'Wage inflation in the United Kingdom, 1948–1962: a disaggregated study', *Economic Journal,* vol. 79, no. 313, pp. 66–89.

Hines, A. G., 'The determinants of the rate of change of money wage rates and the effectiveness of incomes policy', in *The Current Inflation,* ed. H. G. Johnson and A. R. Nobay (London: Macmillan), pp. 143–75.

Holt, C. C. (1971), 'Job search, Phillips' wage relation and union influence: theory and evidence', in E. S. Phelps *et al., Microeconomic Foundations of Employment and Inflation Theory* (London: Macmillan), pp. 53–123.

Hood, W. and Rees, R. D. (1974), 'Inter-industry wage levels in United Kingdom manufacturing', *Manchester School,* vol. 42, no. 2, pp. 171–85.

Hughes, B. and Leslie, D. (1975), 'Hours of work in British manufacturing industry', *Scottish Journal of Political Economy,* vol. 22, no. 3, pp. 293–304.

Hunter, L. C. (1970), 'Some problems in the theory of labour supply', *Scottish Journal of Political Economy,* vol. 17, no. 1, pp. 39–59.

Hunter, L. C. (1974), 'The state subsidy theory of strikes: a reconsideration', *British Journal of Industrial Relations,* vol. 12, no. 3, pp. 438–44.

Johnson, G. E. (1975), 'Economic analysis of trade unionism', *American Economic Review (Papers and Proceedings),* vol. 65, no. 2, pp. 23–8.

Johnson, H. G. (1971), *Macroeconomics and Monetary Theory* (London: GrayMills).

Johnson, H. G. and Mieszkowski, P. (1970), 'The effects of unionisation on the distribution of income: a general equilibrium approach', *Quarterly Journal of Economics,* vol. 84, no. 4, pp. 539–61.

Johnson, H. G. and Nobay, A. R. (eds) (1971), *The Current Inflation* (London: Macmillan).

Johnston, J. (1971), 'Wage determination with bilateral monopoly in the labour market', in *Uses of Economics,* ed. G. D. N. Worswick (Oxford: Blackwell), pp. 88–113.

Johnston, J. (1972), *Econometric Methods,* 2nd edn (London: McGraw-Hill).

Johnston, J. (1972a), 'A model of wage determination under bilateral monopoly', *Economic Journal,* vol. 82, no. 327, pp. 837–52.

Johnston, J. and Timbrell, M. (1973), 'Empirical tests of a bargaining theory of wage rate determination', *Manchester School,* vol. 41, no. 2, pp. 141–67.

Kahn, R. (1976), 'Unemployment as seen by the Keynesians', in *The Concept and Measurement of Involuntary Unemployment,* ed. G. D. N. Worswick (London: Allen & Unwin), pp. 19–34.

Kaldor, N. (1959), 'Economic growth and the problem of inflation, part 2', *Economica,* new series, vol. 26, no. 104, pp. 287–98.

Keynes, J. M. (1936), *The General Theory of Employment, Interest and Money* (London: Macmillan).

King, J. (1972), *Labour Economics* (London: Macmillan).

King, J. and Regan, P. (1976), *Relative Income Shares* (London: Macmillan).

Knight, K. G. (1972), 'Strikes and wage inflation in British manufacturing industry, 1950–1968', *Bulletin of the Oxford University Institute of Economics and Statistics,* vol. 34, no. 3, pp. 281–94.

Knowles, K. G. J. C. and Robertson, D. J. (1951), 'Differences between the wages of skilled and unskilled workers, 1880–1950', *Bulletin of the Oxford Institute of Statistics,* vol. 13, no. 4, pp. 109–27.

Laidler, D. E. W. (1974), *Introduction to Microeconomics* (Oxford: Philip Allan).

Laidler, D. E. W. (1975), 'The end of "demand management": how to reduce unemployment in the late 1970s: a British commentary', in M. Friedman, *Unemployment versus Inflation* (London: Institute of Economic Affairs, Occasional Paper No. 44), pp. 36–48.

Laidler, D. E. W. and Parkin, J. M. (1975), 'Inflation: a survey', *Economic Journal,* vol. 85, no. 340, pp. 741–809.

Laidler, D. E. W. and Purdy, D. (eds) (1974), *Labour Markets and Inflation* (Manchester: Manchester University Press).

Lancaster, T. (1979), 'Econometric methods for the duration of unemployment', *Econometrica,* vol. 47, no. 4, pp. 939–56.

Layard, P. R. G. and Walters, A. A. (1978), *Micro-Economic Theory* (London: McGraw-Hill).

Leslie, D. (1976), 'Hours of overtime in British and United States manufacturing industries: a comparison', *British Journal of Industrial Relations,* vol. 14, no. 2, pp. 194–201.

Lester, R. A. (1946), 'Shortcomings of marginal analysis for wage–employment problems', *American Economic Review,* vol. 36, no. 1, pp. 63–82.

Lewis, H. G. (1957), 'Hours of work and hours of leisure', in *Proceedings of the Ninth Annual Meeting of the Industrial Relations Research Association,* ed. L. Reed Trip (Madison, Wisc.: Industrial Relations Research Association), pp. 196–206; reprinted in J. F. Burton *et al.* (eds), *Readings in Labor Market Analysis* (London: Holt, Rinehart & Winston, 1971).

Lewis, H. G. (1963), *Unionism and Relative Wages in the United States* (Chicago: Chicago University Press).

Lewis, H. G. (1963a), 'Relative employment effects of unionism', in *Proceedings of the Sixteenth Annual Meeting of the Industrial Relations Research Association* (Madison, Wisc.: Industrial Relations Research Association), pp. 104–15.

Lipsey, R. G., 'The relationship between unemployment and the rate of change of money wage rates in the UK, 1862–1957: a further analysis', *Economica,* new series, vol. 27, no. 105, pp. 1–31.

Lipsey, R. G. (1965), 'Structural and deficient-demand unemployment reconsidered', in *Employment Policy and the Labour Market,* ed. A. M. Ross (Berkeley, Cal.: University of California Press), pp. 210–55.

Lipsey, R. G. (1975), *An Introduction to Positive Economics,* 4th edn (London: Weidenfeld & Nicolson).

Lipsey, R. G. and Parkin, J. M. (1970), 'Incomes policy: a reappraisal', *Economica,* new series, vol. 37, no. 146, pp. 115–38.

Lipsey, R. G. and Steuer, M. D. (1961), 'The relation between profits and wage rates', *Economica,* new series, vol. 28, no. 110, pp. 137–55.

Luce, R. D. and Raiffa, H. (1957), *Games and Decisions* (New York: Wiley).

Lydall, H. F. (1968), *The Structure of Earnings* (London: Oxford University Press).

Machlup, F. (1946), 'Marginal analysis and empirical research', *American Economic Review,* vol. 36, no. 3, pp. 519–54.

MacKay, D. I., Boddy, D., Brack, J., Diack, J. A. and Jones, N. (1971), *Labour Markets under Different Employment Conditions* (London: Allen & Unwin).

MacKay, D. I. and Reid, G. G. (1972), 'Redundancy, unemployment and man-power policy', *Economic Journal*, vol. 82, no. 328, pp. 1256–72.

Maki, D. and Spindler, Z. A. (1975), 'The effect of unemployment compensation on the rate of unemployment in Great Britain', *Oxford Economic Papers*, new series, vol. 27, no. 3, pp. 440–54.

Mansfield, E. (1975), *Micro-Economics: Theory and Applications*, 2nd edn (New York: Norton).

Marin, A. (1972), 'The Phillips curve (born 1958 – died ?)', *Three Banks Review*, no. 96, pp. 28–42.

Marshall, A. (1890), *Principles of Economics*, 8th edn (London: Macmillan).

Marshall, F. R., Cartter, A. M. and King, A. G. (1976), *Labor Economics: Wages, Employment, and Trade Unionism*, 3rd edn (Homewood, Ill.: Irwin).

Marshall, R. (1974), 'The economics of racial discrimination: a survey', *Journal of Economic Literature*, vol. 12, no. 3, pp. 849–71.

Masters, S. H. (1969), 'Wages and plant size: an inter-industry analysis', *Review of Economics and Statistics*, vol. 51, no. 3, pp. 341–5.

Maurice, S. C. (1975), 'On the importance of being unimportant: an analysis of the paradox in Marshall's third rule of derived demand', *Economica*, new series, vol. 42, no. 168, pp. 385–93.

Mayhew, K. (1976), 'Plant size and the earnings of manual workers in engineering', *Oxford Bulletin of Economics and Statistics*, vol. 38, no. 3, pp. 149–60.

McClements, L. (1978), *The Economics of Social Security* (London: Heinemann).

McCormick, B. J. (1969), *Wages* (Harmondsworth: Penguin).

McGregor, A. (1978), 'Unemployment duration and re-employment probability', *Economic Journal*, vol. 88, no. 352, pp. 693–706; McNabb (1977).

Melnik, A. and Comay, Y. (1972), 'The effect of bargaining strategies in strike situations', *Western Economic Journal*, vol. 10, no. 4, pp. 370–5.

Metcalf, D. (19770, 'Unions, incomes policy and relative earnings in Great Britain', *British Journal of Industrial Relations*, vol. 15, no. 2, pp. 157–75.

Mincer, J. (1958), 'Investment in human capital and personal income distribution', *Journal of Political Economy*, vol. 66, no. 4, pp. 281–302.

Mincer, J. (1962), 'Labor force participation of married women: a study of labor supply', in *Aspects of Labor Economics*, ed. H. G. Lewis (Princeton, NJ: Princeton University Press), pp. 63–97.

Mincer, J. (1966), 'Labor-force participation and unemployment: a review of recent evidence', in *Prosperity and Unemployment*, ed. R. A. Gordon and M. S. Gordon (New York: Wiley), pp. 73–112.

Mincer, J. (1970), 'The distribution of labor incomes: a survey with special reference to the human capital approach', *Journal of Economic Literature*, vol. 8, no. 1, pp. 1–26.

Mincer, J. (1976), 'Progress in human capital analyses of the distribution of earnings', in *The Personal Distribution of Incomes*, ed. A. B. Atkinson (London: Allen & Unwin), pp. 136–76.

Mitchell, D. J. B. (1972), 'Union wage policies: the Ross–Dunlop debate reopened', *Industrial Relations*, vol. 11, no. 1, pp. 46–61.

Moore, B., Rhodes, J., Tarling, R. and Wilkinson, F. (1978), 'A return to full employment', *Economic Policy Review*, no. 4 (Cambridge: University of Cambridge Department of Applied Economics), pp. 22–30.

Morris, V. (1977), 'Investment in higher education in England and Wales: a subject analysis', in *Economics and Education Policy*, ed. C. Baxter, P. J. O'Leary and A. Westoby (London: Longman), pp. 72–91.

Morris, V. and Ziderman, A. (1971), 'The economic rreturn on investment in higher education in England and Wales', *Economic Trends,* no. 211, pp. xx–xxxi.

Mulvey, C. (1976), 'Collective agreements and relative earnings in UK manufacturing in 1973', *Economica,* new series, vol. 43, no. 172, pp. 419–27.

Mulvey, C. (1978), *The Economic Analysis of Trade Unions* (Oxford: Martin Robertson).

Muth, J. F. (1961), 'Rational expectations and the theory of price movements', *Econometrica,* vol. 29, no. 3, pp. 315–35.

Nash, J. F. (1950), 'The bargaining problem', *Econometrica,* vol. 18, no. 2, pp. 155–62.

Nash, J. F. (1953), 'Two-person co-operative games', *Econometrica,* vol. 21, no. 1, pp. 128–40.

Nickell, S. J. (1977), 'Trade unions and the position of women in the industrial wage structure', *British Journal of Industrial Relations,* vol. 15, no. 2, pp. 192–210.

Nickell, S. J. (1978), 'Fixed costs, employment and labour demand over the cycle', *Economica,* new series, vol. 45, no. 180, pp. 329–45.

Nickell, S. J. (1979), 'Estimating the probability of leaving unemployment', *Econometrica,* vol. 47, no. 5, pp. 1249–66.

Nickell, S. J. (1979a), 'The effect of unemployment and related benefits on the duration of unemployment', *Economic Journal,* vol. 89, no. 353, pp. 34–49.

Norris, K. (1979), 'The industrial wage structure in Britain, 1906–38', *Economic Journal,* vol. 89, no. 354, pp. 370–6.

Oi, W. (1962), 'Labor as a quasi-fixed factor', *Journal of Political Economy,* vol. 70, no. 6, pp. 538–55.

Organisation for Economic Co-operation and Development (OECD) (1965), *Wages and Labour Mobility* (Paris).

Parkin, J. M. and Sumner, M. T. (eds) (1972), *Incomes Policy and Inflation* (Manchester: Manchester University Press).

Parkin, J. M. and Sumner, M. T. (eds) (1978), *Inflation in the United Kingdom* (Manchester: Manchester University Press).

Parkin, J. M., Sumner, M. T. and Jones, R. A. (1972), 'A survey of the econometric evidence of the effects of incomes policy on the rate of inflation', in *Incomes Policy and Inflation,* ed. J. M. Parkin and M. T. Sumner (Manchester: Manchester University Press), pp. 1–29.

Parr, M. (1978), 'Review article: unemployment: its measurement, causes and remedies', *Economics,* vol. 14, pt 2, pp. 33–49.

Peel, D. A. (1972), 'The kinked demand curve: the demand for labour', *Recherches économiques de Louvain,* no. 3, pp. 267–74.

Peel, D. A. and Walker, I. (1978), 'Short-run employment functions, excess supply and the speed of adjustment: a note', *Economica,* new series, vol. 45, no. 178, pp. 195–202.

Pelling, H. (1971), *A History of British Trade Unionism,* 2nd edn (Harmondsworth: Penguin).

Pen, J. (1952), 'A general theory of bargaining', *American Economic Review,* vol. 42, no. 1, pp. 24–42.

Pen, J. (1959), *The Wage Rate under Collective Bargaining,* trans. by T. S. Preston (Cambridge, Mass: Harvard University Press).

Pen, J. (1974), *Income Distribution* (Harmondsworth: Penguin).

Pencavel, J. H. (1970), 'An investigation into industrial strike activity in Britain', *Economica,* new series, vol. 37, no. 147, pp. 239–56.

Pencavel, J. H. (1974), 'Relative wages and trade unions in the United Kingdom', *Economica*, new series, vol. 41, no. 162, pp. 194–210.

Perlman, R. (1969), *Labor Theory* (London: Wiley).

Perry, G. L. (1964), 'The determinants of wage rate changes and the inflation–unemployment trade-off for the United States', *Review of Economic Studies*, vol. 31, no. 88, pp. 287–308.

Peston, M. (1971), 'The micro-economics of the Phillips curve', in *The Current Inflation*, ed. H. G. Johnson and A. R. Nobay (London: Macmillan), pp. 125–42.

Phelps, E. S. (1968), 'Money wage dynamics and labor market equilibrium', *Journal of Political Economy*, vol. 74, no. 4, pp. 678–711.

Phelps, E. S. *et al.* (1971), *Microeconomic Foundations of Employment and Inflation Theory* (London: Macmillan).

Phelps-Brown, E. H. (1977), *The Inequality of Pay* (London: Oxford University Press).

Phelps-Brown, E. H. and Browne, M. H. (1962), 'Earnings in industries of the United Kingdom, 1948–59', *Economic Journal*, vol. 72, no. 287, pp. 517–49.

Phelps-Brown, E. H. and Hopkins, S. V. (1955), 'Seven centuries of building wages', *Economica*, new series, vol. 22, no. 87, pp. 195–206.

Phillips, A. W. (1958), 'The relationship between unemployment and the rate of change of money wage rates in the UK, 1861–1957', *Economica*, new series, vol. 25, no. 100, pp. 283–99.

Psacharopoulos, G. and Layard, R. (1979), 'Human capital and earnings: British evidence and a critique', *Review of Economic Studies*, vol. 46, no. 144, pp. 485–503.

Purdy, D. L. and Zis, G. (1974), 'Trade unions and wage inflation in the UK: a reappraisal' in *Labour Markets and Inflation*, ed. D. E. W. Laidler and D. L. Purdy (Manchester: Manchester University Press), pp. 1–37.

Rabinovitch, R. and Swary, I. (1976), 'On the theory of bargaining, strikes and wage determination under uncertainty', *Canadian Journal of Economics*, vol. 9, no. 4, pp. 668–84.

Reddaway, W. B. (1959), 'Wage flexibility and the distribution of labour', *Lloyds Bank Review*, no. 54, pp. 32–48.

Reder, M. (1952), 'The theory of union wage policy', *Review of Economics and Statistics*, vol. 34, no. 1, pp. 34–55.

Reder, M. W. (1955), 'The theory of occupational wage differentials', *American Economic Review*, vol. 45, no. 4, pp. 833–52.

Reder, M. W. (1960), 'Job scarcity and the nature of union power', *Industrial and Labor Relations Review*, vol. 13, no. 3, pp. 349–62.

Reder, M. W. (1962), 'Wage differentials: theory and measurement', in *Aspects of Labor Economics*, ed. H. G. Lewis (Princeton, NJ: Princeton University Press), pp. 257–99.

Reder, M. W. (1965), 'Unions and wages: the problems of measurement', *Journal of Political Economy*, vol. 63, no. 2, pp. 188–96.

Rees, A. (1963), 'The effects of unions on resource allocation', *Journal of Law and Economics*, vol. 6, pp. 69–78.

Rees, A. (1970), 'The Phillips curve as a menu for policy choice', *Economica*, new series, vol. 37, no. 147, pp. 227–38.

Rees, A. (1973), *The Economics of Work and Pay* (New York: Harper & Row).

Rees, A. (1977), *The Economics of Trade Unions*, 2nd edn (London: University of Chicago Press).

Reynolds, L. G. (1978), *Labor Economics and Labor Relations*, 7th edn (Englewood Cliffs, NJ: Prentice Hall).

Reynolds, L. G. and Taft, C. (1956), *The Evolution of Wage Structure* (New Haven, Conn.: Yale University Press).

Richardson, R. (1977), 'Review article, 'Trade union growth', *British Journal of Industrial Relations,* vol. 15, no. 2, pp. 279–82.

Robbins, L. (1930), 'On the elasticity of demand for income in terms of effort', *Economica,* vol. 10, no. 29, pp. 123–9.

Robinson, D. (ed.) (1970), *Local Labour Markets and Wage Structures* (London: Gower).

Rosen, S. (1969), 'Trade union power, threat effects and the extent of organisation', *Review of Economic Studies,* vol. 36, no. 106, pp. 185–96.

Rosen, S. (1977), 'Human capital: a survey of empirical research', *Research in Labor Economics,* vol. 1, pp. 3–39.

Ross, A. M. (1948), *Trade Union Wage Policy* (Berkeley, Cal.: University of California Press).

Routh, G. G. C. (1954), 'Civil service pay, 1875 to 1950', *Economica,* new series, vol. 21, no. 83, pp. 201–23.

Routh, G. G. C. (1965), *Occupation and Pay in Great Britain, 1906–60* (London: Cambridge University Press).

Routh, G. G. C. (1974), 'Interpretations of pay structure', *International Journal of Social Economics,* vol. 1, no. 1, pp. 13–39.

Sahota, G. S. (1978), 'Theories of personal income distribution: a survey', *Journal of Economic Literature,* vol. 16, no. 1, pp. 1–55.

Santomero, A. and Seater, J. J. (1978), 'The inflation–unemployment trade-off: a critique of the literature', *Journal of Economic Literature,* vol. 16, no. 2, pp. 499–544.

Sapsford, D. R. (1975), 'A time series analysis of UK industrial disputes', *Industrial Relations,* vol. 14, no. 2, pp. 242–9.

Sapsford, D. R. (1978), 'Employer resistance and strikes: a contradition resolved', *Scottish Journal of Political Economy,* vol. 25, no. 3, pp. 311–15.

Sapsford, D. R. (1979), 'The theory of bargaining: a selective survey with particular reference to union–employer negotiations and the occurrence of strikes', *Economic and Social Research Institute, Memorandum Series,* no. 132.

Sapsford, D. R. (1979a), 'An econometric study of strike activity', paper presented to the Irish Association of University Teachers of Economics Conference, Renvyle, Co. Galway.

Sapsford, D. R. and Ladd, J. D. (1978), *Essential Economics* (London: Hart-Davis Educational).

Saraydar, E. (1965), 'Zeuthen's theory of bargaining: a note', *Econometrica,* vol. 33, no. 4, pp. 802–13.

Sargan, J. D. (1964), 'Wages and prices in the United Kingdom: a study in econometric methodology', in *Econometric Analysis for National Economic Planning,* ed. P. E. Hart, G. Mills and J. K. Whitaker (London: Butterworth), pp. 25–54.

Sargan, J. D. (1971), 'A study of wages and prices in the UK, 1949–1968', in *The Current Inflation,* ed. H. G. Johnson and A. R. Nobay (London: Macmillan, pp. 52–71).

Sawyer, M. C. (1973), 'The earnings of manual workers: a cross-section analysis', *Scottish Journal of Political Economy,* vol. 20, no. 2, pp. 141–57.

Schmidt, P. and Strauss, R. P. (1976), 'The effects of unions on earnings and earnings on unions: a mixed logit approach', *International Economic Review,* vol. 17, no. 1, pp. 204–12.

Seers, D. (1951), *The Levelling of Incomes since 1938* (Oxford: Oxford University Institute of Statistics).

Shackle, G. L. S. (1957), 'The nature of the bargaining process', in *The Theory of Wage Determination,* ed. J. T. Dunlop (London: Macmillan), pp. 292–314.

Shubik, M. (1959), *Strategy and Market Structure* (New York: Wiley).

Siebert, W. S. and Addison, J. T. (1977), 'Discrimination within the labour market: theory with evidence from Britain and the United States', *International Journal of Social Economics,* vol. 4, no. 3, pp. 159–91.

Slichter, S. H. (1950), 'Notes on the structure of wages', *Review of Economics and Statistics,* vol. 32, no. 1, pp. 80–91.

Smith, A. (1776), *The Wealth of Nations* (London: Strahan & Cadell, 1776; reprinted London: Everyman's Library, 1977),

Smith, D. C. (1968), 'Incomes policy', in *Britain's Economic Prospects,* ed. R. E. Caves (London: Allen & Unwin), pp. 104–44.

Solow, R. M. (1969), *Price Expectations and the Behavior of the Price Level* (Manchester: Manchester University Press).

Spindler, Z. A. (1974), 'A simple determinate solution for bilateral monopoly', *Journal of Economic Studies,* new series, vol. 1, no. 1, pp. 53–64.

Stafford, F. P. (1968), 'Concentration, and labor earnings: comment', *American Economic Review,* vol. 58, no. 1, pp. 174–81.

Strand, K. and Dernburg, T. (1964), 'Cyclical variation in civilian labour force participation', *Review of Economics and Statistics,* vol. 46, no. 4, pp. 378–91.

Swidinsky, R. (1976), 'Strike settlement and economic activity: an empirical analysis', *Relations Industrielles,* vol. 31, no. 2, pp. 209–23.

Tarling, R. (1978), 'A return to full employment: appendix, evidence and estimates of the voluntary increase in unemployment', *Economic Policy Review,* no. 4 (Cambridge: University of Cambridge Department of Applied Economics), pp. 30–6.

Taylor, J. (1972), 'Incomes policy, the structure of unemployment and the Phillips curve: the United Kingdom experience, 1953–1970', in *Incomes Policy and Inflation,* ed. J. M. Parkin and M. T. Sumner (Manchester: Manchester University Press), pp. 182–200.

Taylor, J. (1972a), 'The behaviour of unemployment and unfilled vacancies: Great Britain, 1958–71: an alternative view', *Economic Journal,* vol. 82, no. 328, pp. 1352–65.

Taylor, J. (1974), *Unemployment and Wage Inflation with Special Reference to Britain and the USA* (London: Longman).

Tella, A. (1964), 'The relation of labor force to employment', *Industrial and Labor Relations Review,* vol. 17, no. 3, pp. 454–69.

Tella, A. (1965), 'Labor force sensitivity to employment by age, sex', *Industrial Relations,* vol. 4, no. 2, pp. 69–83.

Thatcher, A. R. (1976), 'Statistics of unemployment in the United Kingdom', in *The Concept and Measurement of Involuntary Unemployment,* ed. G. D. N. Worswick (London: Allen & Unwin), pp. 83–94.

Thatcher, A. R. (1979), 'Labour supply and employment trends', in *De-Industrialisation,* ed. F. Blackaby (London: Heinemann, National Institute for Economic and Social Research, Economic Policy Paper No. 2), pp. 26–48.

Thirlwall, A. P. (1969), 'Types of unemployment: with special reference to "non-demand-deficient" unemployment in Great Britain', *Scottish Journal of Political Economy,* vol. 16, no. 1, pp. 20–49.

Throop, A. W. (1968), 'The union–non-union wage differential and cost-push inflation', *American Economic Review,* vol. 58, no. 1, pp. 79–99.

Tobin, J. (1968), Comment on 'Theories of mild continuing inflation: a critique and extension' by P. Cagan, in *Inflation: Its Causes, Consequences and Con-*

trol, ed. S. W. Rousseau (Wilton, Conn.: Calvin K. Kazanjian Economics Foundation), pp. 49–54.

Trevithick, J. A. (1976), 'Money wage inflexibility and the Keynesian labour supply functions', *Economic Journal,* vol. 86, no. 342, pp. 327–32.

Trevithick, J. A. and Mulvey, C. (1975), *The Economics of Inflation* (London: Martin Robertson).

Turner, H. A. (1952), 'Trade unions, differentials and the levelling of wages', *Manchester School,* vol. 2, no. 3, pp. 227–82.

Turner, H. A. (1962), *Trade Union Growth, Structure and Policy* (London: Allen & Unwin).

Turnovsky, S. J. (1974), 'On the role of inflationary expectations in a short-run macro economic model', *Economic Journal,* vol. 84, no. 334, pp. 317–37.

Ulman, L. (1955), 'Marshall and Friedman on union strength', *Review of Economics and Statistics,* vol. 37, no. 4, pp. 384–401.

Wabe, S. and Leech, D. (1978), 'Relative earnings in UK manufacturing: a reconsideration of the evidence', *Economic Journal,* vol. 88, no. 350, pp. 296–313.

Wachter, M. L. (1972), 'A labor supply model for secondary workers', *Review of Economics and Statistics,* vol. 54, no. 2, pp. 141–51.

Wachter, M. L. (1974), 'A new approach to equilibrium labor force', *Economica,* new series, vol. 41, no. 161, pp. 35–51.

Wallis, K. F. (1971), 'Wages, prices and incomes policies: some comments', *Economica,* new series, vol. 38, no. 151, pp. 304–10.

Walton, R. E. and McKersie, R. B. (1965), *A Behavioral Theory of Labor Negotiations* (New York: McGraw-Hill).

Ward, R. and Zis, G. (1974), 'Trade union militancy as an explanation of inflation: an international comparison', *Manchester School,* vol. 42, no. 1, pp. 44–65.

Webb, A. E. (1974), *Unemployment, Vacancies and the Rate of Change of Earnings: A Regional Analysis* (London: Cambridge University Press for The National Institute of Economic and Social Research, Regional Papers No. 3).

Webb, S. and Webb, B. (1920), *The History of Trade Unionism,* revised edn (London: Longmans Green).

Weiss, L. W. (1966), 'Concentration and labor earnings', *American Economic Review,* vol. 56, no. 1, pp. 96–117.

Whybrew, E. (1968), *Overtime Working in Britain,* Royal Commission on Trade Unions and Employers' Associations, Research Paper No. 9 (London: HMSO).

Wickens, M. R. (1974), 'Towards a theory of the labour market', *Economica,* new series, vol. 41, no. 163, pp. 278–94.

Wickens, M. R. (1978), 'An econometric model of labour turnover in UK manufacturing industries, 1956–73', *Review of Economic Studies,* vol. 45, no. 141, pp. 469–77.

Wilkinson, R. K. and Burkitt, B. (1973), 'Wage determination and trade unions', *Scottish Journal of Political Economy,* vol. 20, no. 2, pp. 107–22.

Wood, J. B. (1972), *How Much Unemployment?* (London: Institute of Economic Affairs, Research Monograph No. 28).

Wood, J. B. (1975), *How Little Unemployment?* (London: Institute of Economic Affairs, Hobart Paper No. 65).

Worswick, G. D. N. (ed.) (1976), *The Concept and Measurement of Involuntary Unemployment* (London: Allen & Unwin).

Zeuthen, F. (1930), *Problems of Monopoly and Economic Warfare* (London: Routledge).

Ziderman, A. (1973), 'Does it pay to take a degree?', *Oxford Economic Papers,* new series, vol. 25, no. 2, pp. 262–74.

Zis, G. (1979), 'On the role of strikes variables in UK wage equations', *Scottish Journal of Political Economy,* vol. 24, no. 1, pp. 43–53.

Index